COLLAPSED

COLLAPSED

A SURVIVOR'S CLIMB

FROM THE WRECKAGE

OF THE  BRIDGE

GARRETT EBLING

TWO HARBORS PRESS

Two Harbors Press
212 3rd Avenue North, Suite 290
Minneapolis, MN 55401
612.455.2293
www.TwoHarborsPress.com

ISBN-13: 978-1-937293-75-8
LCCN: 2011942228

Distributed by Itasca Books

Book Design by Kristeen Ott

Printed in the United States of America

DEDICATION

To the members of "Team Garrett" for rallying around me, for their strength when I had none, and for their unwavering support in putting Humpty Dumpty back together again.

FOREWORD

VERY FEW IN THE TWIN CITIES—or all of Minnesota, for that matter—had heard of the Interstate 35W Bridge prior to its collapse on August 1, 2007. To the average Minnesotan, it didn't have a name; it was simply a stretch of elevated asphalt that shuttled commuters in and out of downtown Minneapolis. In Minnesota Department of Transportation (MnDOT) nomenclature, it was known as Bridge 9340.

When hundreds of 911 emergency calls flooded the seven dispatchers on duty inside Minneapolis City Hall shortly after 6:05 p.m. on that Wednesday evening, callers had difficulty explaining not only what had just happened, but *where* it happened. Some tried to describe the location using landmarks, such as the Gold Medal Flour sign atop the Mill City Museum. According to a *Minneapolis Star Tribune* article, when confused dispatchers asked for a location—even a cross street—the answers were all over the map. Downtown. In the river. By the University of Minnesota. Near the Metrodome. East Bank. West Bank. Where does a dispatcher send an ambulance, let alone fifty of them?

Without warning, smack-dab in the middle of rush hour, the bridge snapped, tumbling cars into the river and onto embankments. In about ten seconds, it scattered steel, concrete, and chaos. A place of ambiguity suddenly became the tragic epicenter of the world, hissing smoke and flames.

National and international media swept in to describe the carnage and dispense blame. Politicians from both liberal and conservative persuasions, including President George W. Bush, walked alongside the rubble, offering condolences, promising to find the cause, and shaking hands in front of cameras.

Not quite forgotten in the whirlwind were the survivors and the families of the deceased. Members of the media, pumped with the adrenaline of covering the biggest infrastructure tragedy in Minnesota history, fought to scoop the competition. The headlines were along the lines of

Extra! Extra! Read All about It!
Children Escape School Bus near Flames
Doctors Induce Pregnant Woman Plucked from Debris

Most likely, editors in newsrooms across the nation were shouting, "Get me that story!" In Minnesota, the bridge collapse wasn't just the top story of the day, it was the biggest story in several years.

After a few days, the national media dispersed to sink its talons into the next big crisis. Search-and-rescue missions became recovery missions. The hundreds of spectators on the neighboring Tenth Avenue Bridge, who had gazed avidly at the aftermath of the collapse, dissipated into handfuls of curiosity seekers armed with digital cameras. The bodies were recovered, the wreckage hauled away.

When the concrete dust had settled, thirteen people had lost their lives and roughly 145 were forced to begin second ones. Survivors and family members of those who had perished found themselves faced with new, life-altering realities: permanent injuries, the loss of wage earners, the emotional and psychological traumas of witnessing horror. While others could walk away from it, they were walking with it.

In the months and years following the collapse, the public discussion turned largely political, focusing on too-thin gusset plates and the possible negligence of MnDOT, the bridge-inspection firm, and the construction company. But there is another side to the story that deserves to be told: the human element. Of all that fell that day in August, only one segment, the survivors, were expected ever to stand again. This book chronicles how they're doing it.

The site of the 35W Bridge collapse is a scar on a metropolitan landscape. Each August 1, the state government orders flags flown at half-staff, and Minnesotans are asked to pause for a moment to reflect on the significance of that day. Most ponder, then move on. But some don't. Some can't. And some are trying.

1

PREDICTING THE WEATHER IN AUGUST on the North Shore of Lake Superior can be a crapshoot, and as 6 p.m. approached, friends and family who had arrived for the outdoor barbecue found themselves winners as they basked under sunny skies and in a pleasant breeze. Nieces and nephews chased each other around the cabin in rural Little Marais, Minnesota, raising Cain and skinning knees in the process. Last rites were given to the pig now spinning on a spit. A celebratory din rustled the forest leaves, as relatives reunited and future in-laws met for the first time. It was two days before my wedding, August 1, 2008.

Down on the shore, I stared into the tide, wondering when the submerged stones had last touched air. Time had washed them smooth. I peered further, and for a brief second saw pale, ghostly faces superimposed on the igneous rocks of the lake bottom. Their countenances were restless and sad. These lost souls didn't belong in that body of chilled water. I bent over to scoop them out, but my hands drew from the lake only their tears. I clenched my eyelids and reopened them. The thirteen faces were gone, replaced with a slab of gabbro, and the crash of the waves awoke me from my momentary trance.

I looked over my left shoulder and stared at the palisade behind me. It poked into the clean blue sky, carrying on its shoulder a phalanx of evergreen and birch that waved to the ships carrying freight from Thunder Bay to Duluth. It had stood for thousands, maybe millions, of years. Just beyond that, my joyful family and my soon-to-be family celebrated as my fiancée, Sonja, and I prepared to merge our lives.

Everyone was going forward, putting in motion the months and months of planning for this very weekend. I, however, was standing in the pit, buffeted and imprisoned by the waves of a trauma that returned like the tide. I, too, wanted to move forward. I *had* to move forward. Two families expected it. My fiancée depended on it. Yet there I stood, frozen like the January rivers that flowed into Lake Gitchi-Gumi.

I pawed at the chunk of concrete that sat in the front pocket of my khaki shorts. Unlike the stones piled on the shore, it was jagged and grainy, its edges sharp. Cement and pebbles, it was a fragment of what had been tasked with carrying traffic along Interstate 35W into downtown Minneapolis. Now it was rubble, and as I held it, I felt it burning my palm. Nobody had expected the concrete and steel of the bridge to rival the lifespan of a coastal cliff, but all were caught off guard when it tumbled, like a pinecone from the stand of conifers above me.

It had been exactly one year since the 35W Bridge ripped itself from its perch over the Mississippi River. Thirteen individuals didn't survive. I did—barely. Now I was picking up the pieces of my life, like a child plucking shells from the sandy shore with a plastic shovel and bucket, only to carry them home and ask, "Now what do I do with them?"

In a hushed whisper, I prayed as I looked out at the blurred, gray horizon. I didn't close my eyes or bow my head, as the parochial teachers or my mother had instructed. I was searching for God at the other end of Superior, hoping my words didn't simply drop into the glassy lake.

Heavenly Father, I thank you for your unending love. I thank you for allowing me to stand here today. I don't know why this has happened. I cannot understand why some of us had to go away. Why did you spare me, yet deny me the ability to step into tomorrow? I'm breathing, but feel dead like my thirteen brothers and sisters. I firmly believe you have a plan, but it feels elusive. Bring me peace. Bring comfort to those like me who are still here. Bring resolution to

those whose lives crumbled when they lost someone they loved on that bridge.
Help me see the bigger picture. Let there be a bigger picture, for without it, I
feel this was nothing but a senseless tragedy. Amen.

I trusted that God would provide the answers in time but, nonetheless, felt I could speed the process along. Like Christ to the swine, I decided it was time to transfer the demons from the bridge out of me, a thirty-three-year-old southpaw, and into this shard of debris. I withdrew it from my pocket and gripped it tightly. I was never going to be an Olympic shot-putter—certainly not with five-inch-long scars on either side of my left forearm and stainless-steel rods and screws holding the bones together—so this sedimentary Satan wasn't going to land in the middle of the world's largest freshwater lake. I launched the missile into the air, and with a plop it found its watery grave a few yards in front of me.

I turned to retrace the steps that had brought me down to the shore. The path ahead of me crossed a spring that flowed into the lake. More than a year earlier, I had grabbed several large rocks to create a footbridge, providing dry access to Superior from the cabin. It had become known as Garrett's Love Bridge, as I had dedicated it to Sonja. At one point, that name was even posted on a sign next to it. On this day, however, the rocks only jutted from a dry spring bed. It was a bridge no more.

While my physical disabilities had taken their toll, they paled in comparison to the emotional gorilla that now sat on my shoulders. I had cast off the bridge collapse in a literal sense. That was the easy part. But I had a nauseating feeling that what I had just done was nothing more than showmanship. The bridge had done more than crush bone. It had crushed spirit.

I got married two days later, in a quaint Lutheran chapel. To an outsider, the wedding appeared to go with nary a hitch. The temperature hung comfortably in the low seventies. My closest family and friends were there, as well as my father, even though we rarely spoke; to my surprise, he made the six-hour trip.

Sonja was anxious, a customary trait of all brides. I, on the other hand, was calm. I wanted to get married, but disappointingly, I couldn't feel joy. This holiest of ceremonies felt little different than getting my hair cut. And while Sonja's bridesmaids painted on her makeup, I painted on a smile and signed the documents in the church basement that made our marriage official.

I felt guilty. I was handing my life over to Sonja, and what was she getting? This was supposed to be the happiest day of my life. Instead, it felt like every other day, and after the accident, every other day was void of emotion. A wedding day is a bridge from singleness to a life of two souls melded. I wasn't so sure this bridge was going to hold up either.

****

Four days before the 35W Bridge collapsed, I'd proposed to Sonja. It was my second attempt. The first had come at the North Shore cabin and was interrupted by illness. On the day I had planned to propose, I started getting bad stomach cramps. It wasn't the jitters, but severe constipation, and rather than tears of joy over a proposal, I cried tears of pain as Sonja drove me thirty miles down the winding shore to the hospital in Two Harbors, which housed the nearest emergency room. I stayed there for roughly six hours while nurses pumped me with fluids. A successful proposal would have to wait.

The actual event, a few weeks later, was hardly spectacular: I asked for Sonja's hand as we sat on the couch in my apartment during a TV commercial break. But that's all we needed. Swans and violins weren't necessary. Only a simple question was. When she accepted, we felt closer than we ever had been. I placed the ring on her finger, and we met up with friends for a night of celebration and betting at the Canterbury Downs racetrack in Shakopee. As the public address announcer cried, "And they're off!" I smiled and looked into Sonja's sparkling eyes. It was Saturday, July 28, 2007. We were off and running.

Because Sonja has a penchant for conversation, word of the engagement spread quickly. The next couple of days were filled with congratulatory phone calls, e-mails, and Facebook entries. And while I had devoted a mere handful of my life's hours to planning my wedding, Sonja now had the go-ahead to put decades of little-girl scribbles and daydreams into action. When Monday rolled around, I headed to work. Sonja had other plans: it was time to prepare for a Minnesota North Shore wedding.

Sonja's family had owned Lake Superior shoreline property since before Sonja wore diapers. Dad, Mom, and the three siblings made regular visits there, inhaling the four seasons in their purest form, away from the bustle of the Twin

Cities. It was her cradle, and there was no other place she wanted to be on her most special day. I, on the other hand, had had a nomadic childhood. My parents had divorced when I was five, and my mother, sister, and I moved from city to city as Mom first went to school to get her education degree and then across the state to land her first teaching job. Attached to no particular place, I had no qualms about Sonja deciding our wedding location.

"Would you mind if I went up to the cabin on Wednesday?" Sonja asked me during our nightly phone call to each other. "I want to check out some churches and a reception idea. Oh, and there's a neat shop along the highway that sells cool stuff. I'd like them to be on the wedding registry."

"Fine," I said. I wasn't a big phone conversationalist. I still am not.

"It would help if you were a little more into this," she replied. "This is *our* wedding, you know."

"I'm sorry. It's just I have no opinion, really. You do what makes you happy," I said.

And so she did.

****

At the time of the 35W Bridge collapse, I was the senior communications specialist for Edina-based Great Clips, in its human resources department. I spent most days inside a cubicle pecking on my laptop, alternating my gaze between the computer screen and the beige walls decked with schedules, policies, important numbers, and other less-than-exciting data. So when something came along to break the monotony, I usually jumped at it. When I caught wind of our department needing somebody to plan our summer picnic, I eagerly volunteered.

The day of the picnic, Wednesday, August 1, arrived, and I was excited. Having been employed in this position for only five months, this was my first opportunity to coordinate an event for the entire department. If the day was successful, it would reflect well on me, I thought. By vote, we decided to hold our picnic at the Como Park Zoo in neighboring St. Paul. Our normal world of off-white would soon be replaced with flamingo pink, peacock blue, and baboon-butt red.

The afternoon at the zoo went really well. The dozen of us participated in a scavenger hunt and took in the dazzling Sparky the Seal Show. Though its entertainment value dwindled with each bead of sweat running down my back, I would have gladly traded places with Sparky as he dove in and out of the pool's cool waters, chasing rings and beach balls—all for a little applause and a fish or two. When the show ended, we agreed to meet up at the Buffalo Wild Wings down the road in nearby Roseville for more refreshments. At the restaurant, my work team surprised me with an engagement card. I opened it, and up popped a paper bride and groom on a swing. I thanked them all and set the card down next to my first and only frosty bottle of Miller Chill.

The conversation petered out when the food arrived. We feasted on poultry and nachos, and time crept up on us like a Sunday evening. It was 5:30 p.m., and my coworkers, many of them moms, were jolted back to reality as cell phones began ringing. Husbands and kids needed dinners and rides to practice. As quickly as they had congregated, they evacuated the bar and grill. "See you!" I called after my cubicle neighbors, a bit saddened that tomorrow wouldn't also include bears and beers.

I hopped into my maroon, three-door Ford Focus hatchback, pulled out my cell phone, and called Sonja. She was probably halfway to the cabin.

"Hey, honey," I said. "How's the drive?"

"Long as always," replied Sonja with a sigh. "How was the picnic?"

"The heat was a scorcher, but everybody had fun. At least they said they did. What's your agenda while you're up on the shore?"

"Well, there are two churches I want to check out, one in Lutsen and one in Tofte. And I was thinking about checking out the Lutsen resort for the reception and groom's dinner," she said, with a strain in her voice that I couldn't place as excitement or exhaustion.

"Don't jump on anything right away," I advised. "There's plenty of time to negotiate. We haven't even set a date yet."

It was right about then that I noticed the sign for Snelling Avenue, the street I wanted to take. I wasn't in the correct lane and was about to miss my turn. "Honey, can I call you back? I'm getting mixed up talking and driving, and it's rush hour."

"Okay," said Sonja. "I'll call you when I get up to the cabin."

"All right. Love you. Bye." And I hung up the phone.

Now, there are several ways to get from Roseville to the Minnetonka apartment I lived in. My preferred route was to take Snelling down to Interstate 94, cut through downtown Minneapolis to I-394, and then turn south onto Highway 169. But I had missed my turn. I was about to make a U-turn when I saw another traffic sign: "35W Ahead." *Well*, I thought, *I suppose I can take I-35W south to I-94 rather than Snelling. What's the difference?*

I turned onto I-35W. Facing the horde of rush-hour vehicles, I resigned myself to a slow crawl. I rolled down my window and turned up my iPod, which was connected to my car stereo speakers. If I was going to spend dinnertime in the car, I might as well enjoy it with a summer breeze in my face and some good tunes.

As I approached the Mississippi River heading south, traffic all but stopped. I looked ahead and saw orange signs that could only mean one thing: road construction. "Why are they doing road work during rush hour?" I wondered aloud, drumming my steering wheel to the beat of the music. As my car inched forward, I realized that traffic was merging. Frustrated, I fought to get into the far-right lane. *This isn't going to work for me*, I thought, and planned my escape. I decided to take my chances with the next exit and wind through the side streets of downtown Minneapolis. Hopefully, I'd emerge from the other side onto I-394. I just had to cross the Mississippi River to get to the next exit.

Although I had general knowledge of the area, this was a part of the Twin Cities that I didn't know well. I was a west-metro guy, so anything north and east of the Hubert H. Humphrey Metrodome was likely something I had heard of but rarely visited. I could have counted my trips to Como Zoo on one hand. My commute that evening was being guided only by green road signs and a general sense of the cardinal directions.

My car trundled onto the 35W Bridge with dozens of others as the left lane of traffic merged. Because of my unfamiliarity with the area, I didn't know I was moving onto a bridge. It seemed as if it were merely an extension of the roadway. The concrete shoulders of the span were so high that I couldn't see over and down; the only notification that the Mississippi River was below was a small sign along the side of the road, which I paid no attention to. I thought I was on terra firma.

I felt a sudden jolt. *What was that?* Perhaps it was some pile driving by the construction crew? Or maybe I had imagined it? After all, I had spent a long day in the sun. Maybe the heat was getting to me. The crawling cars ahead braked, blanketing me in red light. I stopped.

And then they disappeared.

In an instant, my windshield turned into a cinema screen. An abyss emerged in front of me and swallowed all of the vehicles like a dinosaur with an appetite for metal and flesh. My jaw dropped, and *What the f——?* raced through my mind. I hadn't realized that the piece of roadway my car sat on had been connected to what was now at the bottom of—of what?

I sat flabbergasted in my movie seat, and it took about one second for me to understand the gravity of my situation. The concrete below me disappeared, unhinged from my tires, and for an instant I was weightless. I felt as if I were at the apex of a roller coaster hill, and my stomach was in my throat. My car started to tip forward and down in what felt like slow motion. I braced for what was about to happen, and my foot slammed against the brake as if to halt the car in midair. I didn't know what I was falling into, or how far this plummet would go. With no time to pray, I coached myself out loud, repeating, "Ride it down."

And then I stopped remembering, as if the filmstrip of my life had suddenly torn and now flapped wildly on the projector reel of my mind. I didn't know what had happened. Was I alive? Was I dead?

****

The 35W Bridge crossed a bend in the river, connecting the suburbs beyond its north bank with the skyscrapers of downtown Minneapolis on the south bank. The main span contained deck trusses, and multigirder construction was used on much of the rest. Its style was popular when it was completed in 1967, but was nonredundant, which meant that if one part of the bridge ever failed it could collapse. Its eight lanes carried some 140,000 commuter vehicles daily, which made it the fifth-busiest in the entire Gopher State.

When the 35W Bridge collapsed, it did so in a sequence, like the toppling of dominoes, and I was in the middle of the chain. Think of the bridge as four main sections, with two of them over the nearly four-hundred-foot-wide Mississippi River and the other two attached to land on either side. The collapse started with the failure of a single steel beam, one of many holding the southern section of the bridge over the river in place. It was the section I first noticed through my windshield disappearing from the landscape. The first domino had fallen.

The bridge now started collapsing in two directions. To the south of the initial failure, away from me, the span buckled and twisted as it fell apart above the embankment. This is where TV cameras recorded a fallen school bus packed with kids and a Taystee truck in flames. The collapse ripped up the asphalt and concrete of the interstate leading up to the bridge.

Meanwhile, the bridge was also tumbling to the north, coming right for me and my vehicle, which sat on the northern section of the bridge over the river. This section of bridge was now only connected at one end. While the first section fell as a whole piece and landed parallel to the river, the chunk that I was on fell at a severe slope. My car was at the high end, so as the section dropped, my vehicle fell nose first, from a height equal to that of an eleven-story building.

The section behind my vehicle dropped in the opposite direction; vehicles on that patch of concrete and asphalt rolled backward. Beyond that, the bridge surface crushed train cars parked on railroad tracks. It dropped vehicles sixty feet or more before breaking up on the roadway at the far northern end.

The collapse littered the river's waters with islands of debris. In some cases, survivors heard others' voices around them, but weren't able to see them over the fragments of concrete and jutting metal. Though victims were mere feet apart in several instances, debris made physical contact impossible. The islands of debris were safer than the river, but were unstable, dangerous places to be nonetheless.

A security camera at the lock and dam caught images of the bridge's instant dismantling. It fell in nothing more than a handful of seconds. There was a giant splash. Dust rose into the air. Then silence.

When it was over, thirteen people were dead:
- *Julia Blackhawk*
- *Richard Chit*
- *Paul Eickstadt*
- *Sherry Engebretsen*
- *Peter Hausmann*
- *Patrick Holmes*

- *Greg Jolstad*
- *Vera Peck*
- *Christina Sacorafas*
- *Scott Sathers*
- *Sadiyah Sahal*
- *Hanah Sahal*
- *Artemio Trinidad-Mena*

The survivors' injuries ran the gamut from bruises to permanent disabilities. People's injuries were as varied as their falls. Some fell a few feet. Others fell more than a hundred feet, while others didn't fall at all. Some were carried away on stretchers. Others walked from the scene. Some landed in the water, some on debris. Some landed in open areas; others were trapped. Everyone's story is different. Surprisingly, nobody was left paralyzed, even though many people suffered back injuries. Fractured and compressed vertebrae were common. Internal injuries were also numerous, as were broken bones, especially foot and ankle injuries.

The cleanup was exhaustive and meticulous. It took several weeks for workers to clear the debris; the last victim was located nearly three weeks after the collapse. About one hundred vehicles needed to be removed. Each piece of steel had to be examined as possible evidence for impending investigations.

A replacement bridge was designed almost immediately, with a price tag of approximately $234 million. Construction crews worked around the clock as commuters found alternative, more time-consuming routes to work. The new bridge, built with the latest technology and safety features, opened in September 2008—one day short of a year after it was announced.

The cause of the collapse is a matter of debate. The National Transportation Safety Board determined that the reason the bridge fell was two-fold: the bridge was constructed with gusset plates that were only half the thickness that architectural plans had called for, and they couldn't bear the increase of weight on the bridge. This weight increase was due to thickening of the bridge's surface from years of repaving projects, as well as the construction equipment on the bridge the day it tumbled (this weight was estimated at nearly 290 tons). Photos from four years earlier showed bends in some gusset plates. Another investigation, conducted by a renowned architectural engineering firm working with my attorneys, uncovered evidence that bridge inspections included remarks about "frozen" roller bearings. Roller bearings relieve pressure by allowing a bridge to expand and contract. When bearings are not working properly, years of expansion in the hot summers and contraction in the harsh winters put severe stress on the bridge's components. The inspectors said they informed the State of Minnesota about the condition of the bearings, but nothing was done.

As a result, hundreds of lives—including mine—had become *undone*.

2

IT'S NOT EASY DOING ANYTHING on land while wearing a tight-fitting scuba suit that rides up every nook and cranny God blessed you with. Add a pair of flippers, a mask, a snorkel, and a fifty-pound air tank, and it's quite apparent that being a man-fish has more cons than pros.

I was thinking this as I stood in the bottom of an empty pool, decked out in such attire and holding a long-handled scrub brush. I wasn't sure how long I had been doing this, but I did know that I was a victim of forced labor. The armed guards peering down from the towering captain's deck made sure I was continuing with my duties. I was exhausted, worn down by the summer sun and the countless hours I had spent scraping grime and algae from the sides of the pool, which was one of several aboard a ship whose sole purpose was to entertain cruise patrons with various animal acts. Apparently, hiring workers was too difficult a chore. Why else would I be here against my will?

In my dream, I cleaned those pools dawn till dusk, day after day. It was rhythmic and tedious. It was seemingly never ending. At the conclusion of each fourteen-hour day, I would be told to shed my bodysuit and head to the top level of the ship, where my sleeping quarters were. While my days were spent like those of an inmate in a labor camp, my nights were quite different. The sleeping area was decorated like a child's nursery: mobiles hung above the beds, which were covered in pink-and-blue blankets. The curtains were decorated with drawings of palm branches and cartoon jungle animals. The beds were very small, circular, and arranged in pods. While there were many beds, I was the only person there, and I routinely jumped from bed to bed throughout the course of the night. It calmed me to revert to the mental and emotional state of a small child. It was a sort of escapism from the harsh reality of my capture.

Days turned into weeks, then months. Each day, I was forced at gunpoint to put on the black, rubbery skin and its various accoutrements and return to the pools. I was always alone, and one day I had had enough. At the end of my daylong shift, I pulled myself out of the crater. Still in my scuba gear, I lumbered like the Swamp Thing toward the ship's railing, hell-bent on jumping overboard to freedom. Failure was not an option; the guards were hot on my tail. But just a few yards from the side of the boat, I heard a thwack as my head hit the shiny, wooden deck.

When I regained consciousness, I found myself tied down to a gurney in what seemed like a dark, narrow closet. Men—different from the armed guards—entered the room with irregularity. They would press buttons and scribble on clipboards, then walk away. I didn't know who they were or what they were doing, but I pleaded with them. "Please untie me. I need to go, I don't belong here." But they did nothing, either out of bewilderment or fear. Both possibilities were equally frustrating to me.

As morning broke, I was slowly able to make out my location. Surrounded by pails of sliced pickles and canisters of various sauces, I soon realized that I had been stowed in the dry-storage area of a restaurant. And not just any restaurant, but my favorite: Buffalo Wild Wings. *There must be a wings joint somewhere on this ship*, I surmised. *There must be outsiders here.*

Two hours passed, and a young waitress popped her head into the storeroom.

"Can you help me?" I asked.

"Why do you need help?" responded the woman, who appeared to be college-aged, petite, with thin, blond hair. She, too, seemed not to know why she was there, even though it was her place of work.

"I—I don't know," I stammered, unsure if she was friend or foe. "I feel stuck, and it's been a long time."

"Hold on. As a patient, you have to be *patient*," the twenty-something replied, and she turned and disappeared.

****

A rapid transition of environments can be startling, confusing, and frightening. When a newborn sees light for the first time, it is blinded. It is suddenly ripped from the only home it has known, a warm, dark womb that supplied all its wants. Now the infant senses cold, light, pain. This uncomfortable new reality is permanent.

It was sensations such as these that accompanied my return to permanent consciousness following the bridge collapse. Unbeknownst to me, I had been transported to the intensive care unit at Hennepin County Medical Center (HCMC) in downtown Minneapolis, barely a mile from the site of the accident, on the other side of the river from which I had been pulled. Initially, none of my coworkers, friends, or relatives knew that I was on the bridge when it collapsed. However, several people did attempt to reach me by cell phone when they heard about the tragedy, hoping to make sure I wasn't involved. They reached only my voice mail, until my phone's mailbox reached its limit. Because I never allowed that to happen, it gave them a hint that something was amiss. (I had placed my cell phone in my car's console; my best guess is that it was at the bottom of the Mississippi River as people were calling it.) Darin, my best friend from grade school and my apartment roommate, came down to the site of the bridge collapse to search for me that night, but he was met only with barricades and instructions by police officers to turn around. The hospitals were of equally little help. For some reason, my name wasn't on HCMC's patient roster, even though they had my driver's license along with the rest of the contents of my wallet. Darin returned to our apartment. Around 4 a.m., while watching the round-the-clock news coverage, he noticed a man on a gurney being pulled out of an ambulance and into HCMC's emergency room entrance. He called my boss to verify what I had been wearing the day before. The description matched.

He rushed down to HCMC—about ten miles from our apartment—and the rest was history. It took about ten hours, but I had been found.

****

I opened my left eye and quickly shut it again as my pupil fought with the fluorescent lighting. I attempted the task again, this time much more slowly. I tried to do the same with my right eye, but my eyelids were stuck shut. Some type of tube was attached to my nose, pumping air into me as if my lungs were gas tanks. My throat burned with dryness, and my jaw was wired shut. I couldn't move. Both feet were in casts, as was my left arm. In fact, the only thing that seemed fine was my right arm, which would have given me a glint of satisfaction, except that I'm left-handed. My first thought following my self-examination? *This isn't good, but at least I'm off that stupid ship.*

"Garrett? Garrett, this is the nurse. Can you hear me?"

I tried to say yes, but nothing came out due to the tracheotomy. I turned my head, and even that movement was a small gift. Now at least I knew I wouldn't be spending the rest of my days only staring forward. I nodded slightly, unaware that I had a hole in my neck.

"Garrett, do you know what today's date is?" she asked.

It was a tricky question. I remembered being on the road and then falling, and that was Wednesday, August 1. I guessed a few days must have passed. I mean, they'd placed me in casts and wired my jaw shut. I threw out my best guess. I raised three fingers.

"It's August nineteenth," she replied.

Somewhere, somehow, nearly three weeks had gone MIA. How was that possible? Sure, I remembered a long dream about being held captive on a ship—but dreams don't last three weeks! Foggy images began to emerge in my mind: visits by relatives I hadn't seen in years, the gift of a team-autographed Minnesota Twins jersey. Did these things really happen, or was I imagining them? What was real and what wasn't? Was this nurse even real? And if she was, was she telling the truth? When you can't trust your own mind, who or what can you trust?

As a former newspaper journalist, I needed answers. I craved them. What had happened? Why was I in the hospital?

My mom, Joyce, approached the bed. As always, she was calm and reassuring, but I knew better. I knew her better than I knew anybody else.

"The bridge you were on collapsed, honey, but you're going to be okay," she said in a soft voice, which, in her twenty-odd years as a teacher, had reassured countless elementary school kids who hadn't done as well as they'd hoped on their exams. "The doctors said you have no permanent brain or spinal damage, and soon, you'll be up and running like you used to be. *Everything is fixable.*"

Her reassuring words seemed crudely oversimplified. I knew how she could run on autopilot when she needed to, stuffing her emotions deep down in order to cope. I knew because I could do the same thing. Still, I held fast to what she was saying as truth.

"It's going to be all right. You broke some bones in your feet and one arm. And they wired your jaw shut because you broke it, too. But soon, sweetie, you'll be coming to New Ulm to visit me, your sister, and your nieces and nephews, and eating Happy Joe's pizza just like before. I love you. I love you so much."

Spoken like that, my list of injuries didn't seem very daunting at all. Broken bones heal in six weeks. *I should be back to normal by October*, I naively thought. I could deal with that.

Mom had told the truth, but not the whole truth. Lying motionless in that hospital bed didn't allow for a comprehensive self-evaluation. It took weeks, even months, before I was able to patch together a complete list of injuries.

The damage inflicted to my body was consistent with how my vehicle landed: nose first. My car was one of the few to land in this manner, and my injuries ended up being among the more severe of the survivors. I had suffered a traumatic brain injury, as it was my skull that took the brunt of the force when my vehicle crashed. The airbag had inflated, but when you're already kissing the steering wheel and the dashboard, a pop-up head pillow isn't going to be fast enough to cushion the crunch. That I not only survived such a collision but am, in most aspects, functioning normally isn't just surprising, it's miraculous.

As far as bones went, I had broken the talus in each of my ankles, and the left one had been crushed as I braced for impact. I also broke the ulna and radius, the two bones in my left forearm. The fractures were so bad that much of the bone between my wrist and elbow was gone. I also fractured one of the bones in my back. My seatbelt, while it ultimately saved me by keeping me inside my car, had severed my colon. I ruptured my diaphragm and had a collapsed lung. The impact also pinched the optic nerve in my right eye, causing short-term double vision.

Maybe the most obvious catastrophic injuries were to my face. My surgeon later told me the damage was similar to that of a person whose face had hit a brick wall at a hundred miles per hour. Every facial bone plate was shattered; one physician later told me those bones were slivered "like potato flakes." Under my left eye, I had broken the orbital bone (the floor of my eye socket), which supports the eye. My jaw was broken in three places. The impact was so forceful that it severed my olfactory nerves, causing a permanent loss of smell. Structurally, my face—like the bridge—had collapsed.

While I was under heavy sedation during those lost two and a half weeks, surgeons had performed more than a half-dozen surgeries in an attempt to reassemble me. My severed colon caused heavy internal bleeding, and within one hour of the bridge collapse, I was on the operating table. The surgery did not go smoothly. My vital signs would not stabilize. The doctors had to pause the surgery until my body proved it could handle the invasive procedure. In a newspaper interview months later, the head surgeon said that, at one point, he didn't think I was going to make it.

Other surgeries followed:

- Arm surgery in which two stainless steel rods were inserted (August 7)
- The first of two facial reconstruction surgeries, during which surgeons used titanium to rebuild the front of my face. Sonja supplied the surgeons with three photos of me, so they would have a point of reference. (August 7)
- Surgery on my left ankle, in which three screws were inserted to hold it together (August 10)
- A second facial reconstruction surgery to create better symmetry (August 16)
- Surgery to reset my jaw (August 16)

Per my mother's orders, nobody was allowed to take photos of me while I was in the ICU. She said she didn't want me to see what I looked like then. Reflecting on this, I understand her thinking, but am disappointed that photos weren't taken. It would have helped me understand the full scope of my recovery, and see just how far I've come. According to Sonja, when she first saw my face, it looked like one of those stress dolls you squeeze. My swollen eyes were black and purple, closed but for tiny slits. My body was a giant bag of fluid, my bones floating in flesh covered in yellow skin. My stomach was covered in plastic wrap because the surgery on my abdomen had been interrupted. "It was like I could see right into you," Sonja said. "It was like you were dead." A tube protruded from the top of my skull, draining any excess fluid.

The time between surgeries was filled with crescendos of hope and plunges into despair. Some days I'd barely move; other days, nurses would have to restrain my arms as I pulled at the tubes and wires that aided and monitored my recovery. I'd spike high fevers, sparking fears of infection. My health would seem to stabilize, then slide. My then-fiancée wrote in one of her journal entries on www.caringbridge.org, "It seems some spinal fluid was collecting somewhere on Garrett's brain and had begun to seep out through his face. A catheter was placed into his spinal cord to collect the fluid."

Though there were times during those two and a half weeks after the collapse that I was awake and responsive, the heavy cocktail of pain medications and sedatives produced amnesia and delusions. I don't remember what the ICU looked like, even though I was there for eighteen days. I had many visitors, but I don't recall most of them. I do, however, recall the feeling of ants crawling all over my body as I lay in my hospital bed. I'd try to reassure myself that it was crazy to think that a hospital would allow bugs to march all over patients, so I'd try to ignore them, but it seemed almost impossible. I would swat at insects that weren't there. And when I slept, I'd have wild dreams. One time, I awoke and swore to my mom that I had seen a buffalo in the hospital room. (The memory of the autographed Minnesota Twins jersey turned out to be true.)

Even worse, I couldn't hold my bowels, and the sheets needed to be changed regularly.

As I retell this story, I struggle with my ignorance of those first two weeks. I wish I could go back in time and be that journalist I had once been, standing off to the side and recording what happened during those days, so I could have a complete, first-person account of this entire journey. Instead, I was an infant with an adult mind, rattled by a 110-foot fall and now marinated in pain medication. I couldn't see clearly. I couldn't talk. I couldn't smell. For now, thinking would have to do, whether or not what I was thinking was legitimate.

****

When the bridge collapsed, my mom was at her parents' house in Eyota, a small farm town turned bedroom community twelve miles east of Rochester. She had traveled from her home in New Ulm to help clean up their flooded house. A thunderstorm had soaked the attic while it was being reshingled, and water had run down the interior of the walls and into the basement. Forty years of valuables had been ruined.

I had gone there about a month before the collapse to help out my grandparents, who were both in their eighties. To say that cleaning the house was a daunting task was an understatement. We filled countless trash bags with memorabilia, salvaging what we could. It hurt me deeply to see my grandparents suffer. I had no idea I would be next in line.

A year after the bridge collapse, my mother handed me a thick binder. Inside were printouts of all of the CaringBridge website journal entries written over the course of that year. As a preface, she added her reflections on those first two days:

While clearing the table after supper, the Rochester news station had a breaking news bulletin. The 35W Bridge in Minneapolis had fallen into the river during rush-hour traffic. I remember standing in the kitchen with plates in my hand as I heard the words. Immediately, I felt it—a feeling of deadness in my entire body. Without saying a word, I set the dishes down and went into the living room to get my cell phone. Frantically, I dialed your phone number. "You have reached Garrett. Leave a message." I left the message I had left so many times before when you lived out East and I had heard that the Pentagon had been hit by an airplane or the Washington, D.C., snipers had struck again.

"Garrett, call me when you get this. I'm worried about you. The 35W Bridge collapsed and I need to know that you're okay." This time was different. I felt different inside. I felt disconnected from you. I felt hollow. I felt numb. I told your grandparents that you were gone.

I waited for you to call, but you didn't. [I was also unable to find anyone else who'd been in contact with you.]

Pictures started appearing on the television. Why were the firemen just standing by the side of the river? Why weren't they doing more? There was a red car in the water. Your grandpa and I looked at each other painfully, but we did not speak. We couldn't speak. A female search-and-rescue member kept checking the backseat of that car. I didn't want to look. I didn't want to see what she had found. I walked away from the television and sat at the kitchen table with the phone in front of me…

[I remembered] that you had gone to Como Park Zoo that day and possibly could have gone to the Twins game and crossed the bridge at that time. How would I know that? I didn't know where anything was located in the Cities. But in my heart I knew…

At 10 p.m. I spoke with Darin. He was home at your apartment. You were not there. I began calling the hospitals that were taking victims. I talked to nurses, Red Cross volunteers, and chaplains. No one had your name on file. I called police stations in the Cities and Rochester for help. No one could assist me. The Red Cross told me they were setting up a command center but advised that I not come up until morning. [I stayed on the phone all night, arranging with friends to drive up to the cities in the morning.]

I sat at the table and I wanted to ask God, "Why?" I knew that I wouldn't have that answer here on Earth, so I didn't ask. I wanted so badly to bargain with God. I wanted it to be me that was on the bridge. I wanted to trade places. I didn't ask or bargain. I knew that God could see what was in my heart. I knew that I had to have faith in his plan. My one comfort was in knowing that you would be in God's arms. You would be safe. I told him that I did not understand why he would take you away from me, but I would accept his decision. I also told him that I would need his help to live without you, because I could not imagine a day in my life on this planet without you in it.

I had never felt so drained of life. I had never felt so defeated. I thought of your body remaining trapped in your car in the cold, dirty Mississippi River and

I couldn't breathe. I was sickened because I am your mother and I shouldn't be allowing this to happen and yet I couldn't stop it. I had let you down.

At 4 a.m., Darin called. He thought he had seen someone resembling you being loaded into an HCMC ambulance. He had called your boss and verified that you had been wearing a striped shirt like the one he had seen on the victim on TV. He had tried to go to the command center earlier and was turned back; now he would go to HCMC.

My heart began racing. I had hope. I didn't tell anyone about this one ray of hope. I quickly packed my suitcase and waited for Darin to call again. The phone rang, and Darin said the words I needed to hear. "Garrett is alive. He's in ICU, but alive."

I literally danced down the hallway to where your grandparents were. All I could say over and over was "Garrett's alive!" I quickly called Rhonda [Garrett's sister] and then Diane [Joyce's cousin and best friend]. Diane and Nick [Diane's husband], would leave immediately from their home in Mankato and meet me in Owatonna. Grandma cautioned me to drive safely, because she knew I'd had no sleep and was very anxious.

As I was driving to Owatonna, I imagined seeing you in bed propped up on a pillow. You would look at me and say, "Hey, Ma." I played that scene in my head over and over…I don't recall much except just wanting to reach you. Now I needed to see you. I needed to touch you. I needed to make you real to me again. You were Jesus. I was Thomas.

We found the hospital to be a confusing mass of corridors. People were helpful and a nurse from another station walked us the final steps to ICU. I finally stood before the door that separated me from you…We walked past a row of beds cradling people barely clothed and covered, lying helplessly. You were in the last bed. I recognized you by your feet. You were propped up on pillows, but you did not say, "Hey, Ma." I was in a new kind of hell.

Your nurse kindly explained your injuries, but I felt like I was in a fog and her words were not sinking in. She said that your injuries were severe but there wasn't any permanent brain injury. She said that was very positive. Darin appeared. He had been sleeping in his car in the ramp while the nurses had changed shifts. We all stood by your bed. We prayed. We wondered. We rarely spoke.

The nurse brought your clothes. They were dirty and wet. She explained that you were wet up to your neck when they brought you in. I was given your billfold; everything in it was soaked. The phone on the wall by your bed rang and rang. I was amazed how suddenly people were finding out that you were injured on the bridge and taken to HCMC, when just a few hours earlier I couldn't obtain any information. I didn't realize that Diane had been making phone calls. She located Sonja's parents. Soon they arrived, and their concern was evident. They had contacted Sonja. A friend of hers was driving her back from Duluth.

All I wanted to do was take you home. I knew that that would not happen for a long time.

Love,
Your mother

****

LINDSAY PETTERSON

Unless you're working with farm machinery, there doesn't seem to be much danger in rural Minnesota. Farms and small towns are tucked along river or creek beds, or snuggled within groves of trees. These are places where everybody knows everybody, where you look out for your neighbor, where you live out the clichés of a Garrison Keillor tale.

Lindsay Petterson grew up in one of these towns. Lake Lillian—roughly twenty miles southeast of Willmar—boasts roughly 250 inhabitants, a kitschy Milkiway Avenue, a post office, a bank, and not much else.

But like residents of the urban jungle of Minneapolis, small-town Minnesotans aren't immune to tragedy. Lindsay's uncle, aunt, and cousin from Texas perished in a traffic accident while returning home from New Mexico. "It was the first time I was directly affected by trauma," Lindsay recalled. As a result, Lindsay's parents became the legal guardians of three of her cousins, though they stayed with Lindsay's seventy-five-year-old grandmother a block from her parents' home. She learned early on that life can change dramatically in an instant, and that helping others regroup and move forward was something she wanted to do when she got older.

When August 1, 2007, rolled around, Lindsay was employed by Karibu House, a Shoreview group home for adolescent boys and girls experiencing difficulties at home. They were removed from their homes for a variety of reasons: everything from drug addiction to parents who simply couldn't care for them. Lindsay, a 2005 University of Minnesota graduate with a major in family social science, worked as an independent-living skills coordinator for sixteen- to eighteen-year-olds, teaching them basic life skills. Activities included learning how to balance a checkbook and hunt for an apartment. This was Lindsay's first full-time job out of college, and on that particular day, the job fueled her.

"It was a really good day," she remembered. "The groups can be challenging, and we were starting an exercise on budgeting...I was looking forward to the next two months working with them on it, but then I didn't come back."

Lindsay left work in the northern suburb of Shoreview that evening and headed for her apartment in Minneapolis a little later than normal. Sometimes, when the traffic was bad, she would take Highway 100 south from Interstate 694. She had planned to use this route on August 1, but got distracted and missed the exit.

"I was debating that day which way to go. I was coming down I-35W, and I thought, *Oh, I'll just take 694*. I was thinking about work, what I had done and what needed to be done the next day. I totally lost track of things and drove right past the exit."

Lindsay continued southbound on I-35W in her Volkswagen Passat. A couple of miles north of downtown Minneapolis, traffic came to a standstill. "Usually at this time of day, going into downtown wasn't a problem," she said. To avoid the stop-and-go traffic, Lindsay planned to get off at the University Avenue exit. "But I was in the left lane, and nobody seemed to want to let anyone over, and I couldn't get over because traffic was so heavy."

She called her boyfriend Dave to tell him she would likely be home late, as they had planned to go out for dinner. Dave's voice mail picked up, which wasn't surprising, as he had just worked an overnight shift at the group home, where they had met.

"He didn't get the call, which is probably good, or he might have been on the phone with me when the bridge collapsed," said Lindsay.

Her vehicle crawled forward, and then…

"I don't remember anything specific until hearing the beam snap. It was like a clank, a loud snap," she recounted. "It's like if you're at a construction site and somebody's hammering metal. Kind of like that, but really distinct and didn't have the 'tang' at the end of it."

Lindsay's Passat fell straight down, a motion, she said, that others recalled differently. "Some have described it as seeing a wave or feeling like you're on a roller coaster or seeing things move—there was none of that for me. I heard the sound, I knew it was collapsing, and basically within seconds I was under the water."

Lindsay's past fears of falling now became reality. She recalled on several occasions driving over the 35W Bridge while repairs were being made, noticing cracks in the road and along the framework, and wondering about the span's stability. She described being able to see through inch-wide gaps in the bridge, as construction workers had peeled off layers of the roadway. Yet when she fell, she didn't comprehend that she was more than a hundred feet over the Mississippi River.

"I didn't even think about being over the water," Lindsay noted. "It didn't occur to me as I was falling, *Oh, I should open my window.* All I could imagine was being smashed like a pancake onto cement. I figured I was driving on cement, so I would land on cement and end up a pile of blood and guts."

She braced as she expected the worst. In midair, the Volkswagen's airbags activated (Lindsay doesn't know why), and the car hit the river nose down, with the front passenger side making contact with the surface first. Immediately, the brown, murky water filled the car.

"My car was like a swimmer, diving into the water. It wasn't a gradual rise of water flowing into my car," she said. Everything was pitch black, and Lindsay had no idea how deep her car had sunk. Quickly underwater, she began to panic.

"It didn't occur to me to try opening the window or door," she mentioned. (At the time, the auto locks were enabled and all of the electronic windows were rolled up.) "The only clear thought I had was, *I need to unlock my seatbelt.*"

Freeing herself from her seatbelt, Lindsay began pushing on the windows and the ceiling. "I just pushed on everything, thinking that's what's keeping me in and I have to find a way out. It's a desperation to find a way out. I thought that maybe a window had broken, but nothing I was pushing on was giving way. It was all black; I just had to feel."

It was at this point that buoyancy added to the problem. Lindsay floated out of her driver's seat, leaving her shoes behind. In a moment void of clarity, she became irritated—by her footwear. "They weren't special shoes by any means—they were from Target. But they were my favorite shoes, and I wore them every day. I was like, *Oh God, my shoes!* And while it seems stupid now, it was the first tangible loss for me."

Her desperation compounded as seconds turned into minutes underwater.

> I knew that nobody was going to get to my car in time. When I was thinking about people not finding me, I was still holding my breath, but it was getting painful, and I knew that soon I would have to gulp. I started to gulp in water, and once that started to happen I began to give up. I had pushed on everything I felt and nothing gave way.
>
> So, I basically resigned myself to the fact that I was going to die. I started thinking about my family and Dave and my cats, and what I had done in life and what I'd never get to do, like be a mom. [She stopped pushing and had taken in five or six gulps of dirty, brown water.]
>
> I saw a flash of white light and thought, *Oh, I'm dead now,* and then I started to float. But I felt like I was in my body and that I was still alive. I realized that I had floated far enough that I must have been out of my car.

She started kicking furiously, and in a moment she broke through the river's surface. How did she get out of the car? She doesn't know.

"I've got scars on my right fist, and it looks like it got eaten up by glass," Lindsay said. "It's quite possible that I punched a window, but I have no recollection of such a forceful impact. But adrenaline could protect me from that. I didn't try kicking windows or using my feet at all in the car, as I was floating so much."

Her lungs full of water, she popped up in the middle of the river facing upstream, so she turned around to orient herself and got an up-close-and-personal look at the destruction that had just taken place. Lindsay gasped for breath and wondered if anyone had seen her. *I think I'm alive—but am I?* she asked herself. She screamed and flailed amid the debris covering the surface of the water.

> I ended up finding a piece of the bridge and swam to it. Jeff Ringate, one of the construction workers, saw me and waved me over to the island of concrete. I was probably about ten to fifteen feet away from it when I surfaced. There was a part that was really angled, and then there was a part that was climbable. He had a broom and tried to pull me up with it. My foot slipped and I feared getting sucked down by the current. I heard voices crying for help that seemed to come from under the concrete. It was such a helpless feeling, that nobody could get to them, but I later found out they were rescued too.

Time spent on the island of bridge debris was a surreal experience, according to Lindsay. There was an eerie chatter coming from above: sirens, helicopters, and general commotion. Down on the river, it was quiet. Most survivors reacted with stunned silence. Lindsay went and stood by the median and took a good look around. She could see people standing next to their cars on the northbound side of the bridge, crying and distressed.

"It looked like their tires had been glued to the cement and they had just ridden it down. I couldn't comprehend how they could just be standing there, seemingly okay, after what had just happened," she remembered. "People were calling loved ones. I thought everybody would be dead."

It was at this point that pain replaced the adrenaline in her body. "Eventually, I had to sit down. I remember the cement from the median was really warm and it felt really good, but everything else felt really cold. Everybody

27

talks about how warm it was that day, but I just remember being cold…I sat down and eventually Amy Lindholm met me." Amy, a medical assistant, was wearing her navy-and-tan scrubs, as she'd been heading north to her home in Minneapolis, according to the *Star Tribune*.

> At first, I thought she was help, but she had fallen too—she was a victim. She asked me how I was doing, to wiggle my fingers and toes. There were some scrapes that I didn't even realize I had, and I had cuts and I was bleeding. Amy called over to the northbound side of the median and asked if anybody had a bottle of water and a towel. Within ten seconds, there was a bottle of water flying over and a towel flying over. It was one of those moments where people come together; whatever they've got is theirs to give.

There were probably at least twenty people on the island, Lindsay recalled. Everyone whose vehicle was near hers at the time of the collapse had ended up in the water and had found their way onto the exposed chunk of debris—or had died. She recalled a man next to her complaining on the phone about his car being wrecked. Two teenage boys were just milling about. One woman just stood there in a daze, soaked to the bone. "I asked her how she got out of her car, hoping her answer might help me figure out how I had done it, and in a distant voice she said, 'I just opened the window.'"

Once rescued by boat from the island, she and the others were placed beneath the adjacent Tenth Avenue Bridge, in a makeshift triage.

> I had to wait on the shore for a long time between getting off the island and leaving for the hospital. I felt really alone during that time— people kept walking past me but no one seemed to see me—which was really hard because I had been so alone under the water. There was one nurse who stopped at one point because my skirt

kept flying up as the wind was picking up, and it looked like a storm was approaching from the north (that was my next thought—that there would be severe weather and I would surely die then). She said she'd watch to make sure it stayed down.

A phalanx of gawkers peered down from the Tenth Avenue Bridge above. "One guy was a sports photographer headed to the Minnesota Twins game, and he had a big zoom lens." Lindsay admitted feeling as though her privacy was being somewhat violated. "In one of the pictures, I'm looking directly at the camera."

It took about two hours after the collapse for Lindsay to reach the emergency-room doors of University of Minnesota–Fairview Hospital, and she got there in the bed of a pickup alongside another bridge victim. At one point, the other victim asked her to hold hands, and she accepted. The wait didn't bother her, as "there were others who needed help more immediately than I did."

Once at the hospital, Lindsay underwent a slew of tests to determine her injuries: a broken L1 vertebrae and multiple scrapes and bruises. She would spend the next five days there.

****

While she was on the island, Lindsay used Amy's cell phone and left a message for her boyfriend Dave. She said that she had been in a major accident and that a bridge had collapsed. "Turn on the TV," she said. "They're probably taking me to a hospital." She then called Karibu House to let them know. Her coworkers called her parents, who lived ninety miles away but just happened to be attending a concert at the Minnesota Zoo in Apple Valley. While in the southern suburb, they had heard a rumor about a bridge falling. When they got the message, they rushed out of the zoo. Dave got the message and headed for Hennepin County Medical Center, but Lindsay was not there, so he just kept on driving. At one point, Lindsay called his number again—this time getting Dave and not his voice mail. She told him that she was at Fairview. "I have to pull over," he told her, as his emotions took over.

Receiving her diagnosis, Lindsay was informed that her injuries would not require back surgery. Rather, she would have to endure a hard, plastic brace for five months. It was like wearing a turtle shell. "The first three days, I didn't move in the hospital bed. I slept all the time. Pretty sure I fell asleep during my interview with the NTSB [National Transportation Safety Board]," she said with a laugh. "I have a vague memory of talking with them."

How is she feeling physically, two and a half years after the bridge collapse?

> Today, my back is okay—not one hundred percent, but that's something I've grown accustomed to. Anytime there's repetitive movement or balance, my back tends to act up. I tried ice skating once, and after two laps my back felt like it was on fire. I want to try to snowboard again, but I have anxiety about it. I don't want to be in pain the first time I try it, because I don't want to be turned off by something I was passionate about.

Today, there is nothing that Lindsay feels she physically cannot do. However, there are things, like riding a bicycle, that have become more difficult and uncomfortable. "I used to go on long rides, but now I go half that distance and I'm really, really sore. That creates anger, and I don't want to feel that. So I'm apt to not do something in order to avoid the frustration."

****

Working with teenagers in a group home, Lindsay was accustomed to the emotional side of trauma. Anger, frustration, hopelessness—the feelings that accompany post-traumatic stress disorder weren't foreign words that needed deciphering on Google. And Lindsay knew to prepare for the emotional issues she was sure would follow her.

"There was no question that I would go to therapy, and I started therapy probably two months after the collapse. It took a little bit of time to find a therapist who specialized in PTSD," she said.

She became acutely aware of everything. "The first time I was in a car riding home from the hospital, I was hypervigilant, totally aware of all the cars around me and their slightest movements. Initially, I couldn't ride in the car for more than five miles because of my back, but it was scary to be in a car and think about all the things that could happen," she noted.

> Initially, my emotions were more about my physical pain. That first month, I was in a lot of constant pain despite the medications. Once I was able to move around without physical pain, more of the emotional pain came out. I was able to do certain things but still had this brace on that restrained me from doing things I wanted to do. I had to rely on others, and that produced anger. When I started to be out in the world a little more, I found that I didn't like being in elevators, and I began questioning every bridge I went under or over. Anything that had some human element to its construction or maintenance became unsafe. Everything in my world became a risk: loud noises like thunderstorms would freak me out.
>
> I started going to therapy and talking about all those different things and trying to reconcile the fact that, although the world feels completely unsafe, the probability of a bridge falling again was astronomical—but it was astronomical to begin with, and it happened when I was on it! I'm still thinking about it when I cross a bridge, but I can get myself through it.

Lindsay recalled a couple of incidents in which such thoughts passed through her mind.

Last summer, I took a class where I had to walk across the Washington Avenue Bridge in Minneapolis, and with every step I thought about the bridge falling. I knew exactly what I was over: *Okay, if I fell right now I'd plummet onto rocks, and that would suck, so let's move faster so that I'll be over water because I know I can survive that*. Or when I'm on a balcony at a concert, I'll wonder what would happen if it collapsed.

In the past, these thoughts might have seemed macabre to her, but now it's normal for her to be very aware of her surroundings and to reject many of the routine assumptions she once had.

"I don't think I had lost ultimate trust in anything before the bridge collapse," she said. "It takes twenty-four years of no bridges falling and roads being safe for me to trust that would not happen and then—in a split second—the entire world is completely unsafe and everything has a what-if."

Lindsay said that the bridge collapse gave her a new appreciation for what some of those teens she worked with had gone through. "They lost trust in a parent, somebody who was supposed to love them unconditionally, and yet they lost that trust. I understand why they can't trust."

For Lindsay, the anger produced by PTSD flared regularly for a period of time. "I do have to have a trigger, but it doesn't have to be about the bridge," she said. "It's commonly called 'flooding.'" Her boyfriend may say something in what she perceives to be a certain tone. In the past, she could have just let it go. Now it stays with her. "I'm just gone for the whole day. I hide away. It doesn't necessarily make me feel better, because I *want* to be interacting with other people. I'm a social person naturally, so it feels like torture. I can't even have a conversation about what I'm feeling at that moment."

She admits that, in a way, there are before-and-after Lindsays.

"Pre-bridge, one of my top three traits was my optimism. Now, I still feel optimistic in some ways, especially at work, but overall, I feel more pessimistic. It's unpleasant being me. I think, *Why does my boyfriend even want to be here with me? I wouldn't.* And I don't have the control to just turn it around. The flooding just takes over and I'm lost to it."

The PTSD, she said, causes her to question her own emotions.

"What am I allowed to be mad about? What's a normal thing to be upset with?" she asks herself. "I don't know if what's in my head is what normal people would be upset about. Do I sound like a crazy person, or do I have a valid point? What would I have done before [the collapse], and will I ever get back to that place where I can recognize these things?"

PTSD also has changed how she interacts with others, Lindsay said. In a way, her relationships seem to be not as strong or as deep. She can feel herself being more withdrawn now. "I don't talk as much, because part of me feels I should be over it, and life around me has moved on."

The diminished optimism has been replaced with caution.

> I'm more fearful. I wasn't a fearful person before. I feel like if I had kids right now, I'd be the hovering, protective mother. I would never have been that way before. My hope is those fears will dissipate. I feel like I had a strong conception of who I was before the bridge, so there are times where I question myself more, where I don't have the confidence I had, but I hope it comes back.
>
> I think because the emotional aspect of recovery is so hard to gauge, it makes it the hardest to grasp. You don't know where you're going to be on any given day. With physical pain, you can take Tylenol and know you'll feel better.

Lindsay wasn't about to give in to her PTSD, however.

> Being in the social services field, I get acquainted with people who have had things happen in their lives and they have not dealt with them, and I see the repercussions of it years later and how angry they are, and they don't necessarily equate it to what happened originally. From the get-go, I was very much like, *I'm not*

going to do that. I'm not going to pretend I'm just
okay and then become this angry monster person
I don't want to be.

She began very actively searching for relief. She started going to therapy every week, then every other week. She participated in soul painting and writing retreats, Reiki (a Japanese technique for stress reduction) and acupuncture. "I'm like a little sponge for healing methods," she quipped.

Months after the collapse, she left her job. "I went back, but I couldn't handle it physically and emotionally. It took about six months to find a new job," she said. "In between, I worked a lot on the lobbying efforts at the legislature, and was doing all the alternative therapies. Looking back on all that, I feel like they helped me become a more balanced person." After she stopped working full time at Karibu House, she returned to volunteer and work with kids on art projects.

"It was like walking into a world that I had been a part of and wasn't anymore," she said. "This is what it would have looked like had I died on the bridge. Life was still going on, though I wasn't there. It was a gut-wrenching moment. Life would have gone on had I died. It was really hard for me."

Now she has moved on, to a degree. "I'm at this point where life feels normal again in a lot of ways. I go to a job where I'm not 'Lindsay from the Bridge,' and that feels normal. But I also have 'monster days' that happen too frequently for my taste."

Sometimes "normal" can be trying, though; Lindsay can get disturbed by the monotony of everyday life, a common reaction among trauma survivors who feel the need to live their second chance to the fullest. "Life can also feel too routine—go to work, come home, play with the dog, go to sleep, over and over," she said.

Looking back on the preceding two and a half years, Lindsay called recovery "the best thing you never wanted to happen."

> All the crap that's gone along with it,
> and it still feels like there must be some greater
> good to come from within it. I feel really strongly
> about helping people understand trauma because
> now that I have experienced it and understand

it more, I can see that trauma is so prevalent in our society, whether it's a soldier or a kid whose parent hits him on a weekly basis. It takes on so many forms, but it's so lasting on the psyche and who they are and what they become.

Pre-bridge, my ultimate goal was to open a youth center or have a youth organization of my own that focused on something. When I was sitting on the bridge and heard a voice shout, 'Somebody's gonna pay!' my next few thoughts were, *I suppose in the potential, foreseeable future somebody might have to pay, and what would I do with that money?* My thought was to open a youth organization.

Now, with all of my healing and all the things I've done for myself, maybe I can incorporate all those things I've learned into something that can help the kids that I work with that have had trauma and experienced mistrust in their lives. My path hasn't necessarily changed, but has been strengthened and fortified by my experience.

I've been depressed and been on medication. There were weeks when I felt there was no light at the end of the tunnel. But I've also been in the light, and I know it exists, and I know it will come back. And that makes me hopeful.

3

I'VE ALWAYS BEEN A GOOD BULLSHITTER. I'm pretty sure that comes from my Ebling side, where, if bullshitting were an Olympic event, my father and all my uncles would be rich and famous gold medalists endorsing lawn fertilizer on TV commercials. Bullshitting is a grand trait, in that it preys on the gullible and naive for one's own gain. So I was always gleeful when I found out that a teacher could be categorized as either. I was naturally likeable to them, because I got good grades and was courteous. But once out of their sight, I really liked to tease girls and use them as experiments for practical jokes. "Notebook covers smeared with a glue stick? Don't know who could have perpetrated that, ma'am." The teacher would let me return to my desk, grinning all the way.

The chicanery continued into high school. It was the dawn of the age of student computers. When we finished our in-class home economics assignment, we were allowed to play with the Kid Art program on our primitive Apple desktop computers. I decided to get creative with the stamp application. There was a stamp of a dog, so I stamped two dogs—one strategically on top of the other—and then a bunch of little dogs all around them. It was my special way of visually demonstrating the miracle of life. I thought I was being hilarious, as did my classmates. However, my teacher, who also happened to be the wife of the mayor of my hometown of New Ulm, did not see it that way. She sent me to the principal.

"Well, Garrett, what brings you here today? I've never seen you in my office before," said the principal, who looked about fifteen years older than his real age. I think that only happens to educators and U.S. presidents.

"It's a big mix-up, sir," I said calmly. "I was using a computer program to stamp images on the screen. I was stamping dogs, and the teacher thought the positioning of two of the pooches was obscene. Personally, I think it's hard to reach the status of obscene when using a program called Kid Art. But I guess we've all heard that phrase, 'I know obscenity when I see it.'"

The principal cut me off. "She sent you down here for that?"

"Yes, sir." I could tell he felt this was a waste of his time, so I shook my head and shrugged my shoulders as if to say, "Yeah, man. Like you don't have anything else to do, like *run a school*!"

"You can go now. Just try to be extra careful in Home Ec, okay?"

"All right, sir. You have a great weekend," I remarked, almost shocked by my powers.

He grumbled something, and I sprinted past the school secretary's desk. It almost seemed too easy.

These sorts of events continued through college and even into my career in the newspaper industry. Yes, I was a hard worker, creative and motivated. But I was also not above a little workplace mischief. Regardless, I achieved golden-boy status, impervious to criticism and blame and soaked in praise. My colleagues knew it, and would regularly joke about it. "Oh, Garrett. Yeah, he can do no wrong. Gotta be rough," they'd say. I'd blush and deny it, but I knew it was true.

So here I was, the Harry Houdini of trouble, lying in a hospital bed. I was so injured that I couldn't even roll onto my side without assistance. I could not feed myself. I could not sit up by myself. I could not stand by myself. I could not talk. I could not even wipe my own bum. I was in a straight jacket, locked in chains in a glass tank underwater, and I had just dropped the key that was clenched between my teeth. There was no escape for this artist, it seemed. Pull my goose from the oven, because it was cooked.

The last thing I remember from the day of the 35W Bridge collapse is falling. In an instant, the strict control I had over my life vanished into the dust, smoke, and water. I had always been my own man. At the age of twenty-one, I left family behind in New Ulm to attend the University of Wisconsin at Madison. At twenty-four, I left my friends behind in Madison and ventured east to West Virginia to give newspaper journalism a shot. I made subsequent decisions to move my career forward by taking new jobs in Virginia and Washington, D.C. Then, at thirty, I returned to Minnesota to advance my career again and to be closer to my family, including six nieces and nephews I'd never really gotten to know. Every step was done on my own terms.

The bridge collapse was the first time I couldn't pull myself out of the fire unscathed. In fact, I couldn't even pull myself out of the fire. Well, make that the Ford Focus.

****

When the bridge fell, my car landed upright in the river, tilted so that the driver's side was higher than the passenger's. A white, four-door vehicle lay a few feet from mine, and from how it rested, it appeared to have collided with mine as the two cars fell. My car's roof remained above water, I believe, partly because of its positioning atop some debris. If it hadn't, I would probably be dead.

When the nose of my car struck the river after its 110-foot free fall, I took a monstrous blow to my head. Somehow I clung to semiconsciousness. But since I do not recall the events immediately following the collapse, I've pieced together the following from the accounts of others.

A young man named Rick was finishing up his day as a service technician for Comcast Cable and sitting at a traffic light when he heard the bridge tumble into the river. While some might have thought to flee for safety, he drove down to the riverbank. A surreal scene lay before his eyes: dust and debris, smoke and shrieks, dazed survivors sitting and crying along the shoreline. Vehicles were sinking into the muddy water, and from within them came cries for help. With dozens of cars and trucks sinking, whom do you help first? Rick had grown up along the Mississippi River in Wisconsin, and knew danger lurked below the surface. Currents can suck a person down and away in a second. Debris can trap a foot or a leg. Going into that river would be like sticking your hand into a jar of razor blades while blindfolded.

The twenty-something rushed to the river's edge. Rick helped two women get safely to shore before he reached me. According to a *Reader's Digest* article titled "Split-Second Heroes" by Christopher Davis,

> About 30 feet from the shore, Rick noticed a car in the river—the water was up to the driver's window. Behind the wheel, he saw a man, bleeding profusely from his mouth, trying to open the door...His boots and shirt off, Rick started into the water, going to the aid of the man in the half-submerged car. The driver was hurt. Another volunteer appeared and he and Rick waded over to the car and cut the man free. "Okay," Rick told the driver, "we're going to do this slowly." He and the volunteer grasped the injured man under his armpits and inched him out. His leg banged against something and he screamed. Once he was free, Rick wrapped an arm round the man's chest and pulled him through the murky water to shore. Rick was exhausted when they finally made it. He looked around for help, for someone with a backboard. When he turned away, the man slipped back into the river. Rick grabbed him and held his head out of the water. The man's mouth was bloody. It looked like all his teeth had been knocked out. Then his eyes began to close. "Hey! Hey," Rick shouted at him, snapping his fingers. "Hey, what's your name?" Rick kept him talking until paramedics arrived.

Not surprisingly, my mother desperately wanted to find out who had helped pull me from my would-be tomb. She needed Rick to fill in the blanks for her, to understand what was happening to me when her stomach gnawed at her heart as she stood in the kitchen. When she connected with Rick several weeks after the collapse, she asked him to stop by the hospital. My first glimpse of Rick after the bridge collapse was of his shoulders and upper back. He was wearing a Minnesota Vikings jersey that spelled out his last name across the back. I had just come out of one of my many deep slumbers in my hospital bed.

I was overwhelmed. I became very upset by his appearance and began to bawl with my face buried in my hospital blanket, not because I was unhappy that he was there, but because I simply didn't know how to react. What do you say to somebody who risks his life to save yours? I had no answer for him. I had no gold to give him. I was a wreck inside and out. While my mother got her answers from Rick that day, I couldn't connect.

Over the next few months, I had other opportunities to catch up with Rick. I was now ready and eager for these encounters. We spoke on the phone a few times and did eventually meet and have a conversation. Rick even came to the capitol in St. Paul the following spring, as I and other bridge survivors fought for a victims' compensation bill. And while I did not keep in regular contact with Rick, I did worry about him. He witnessed so much horror and devastation firsthand. My memory of those moments had been erased, and I had doctors for my body and mind to help me cope. Who was helping him and others like him who now had to fight the demons and nightmares of what they had witnessed? They undoubtedly took with them some form of post-traumatic stress disorder to varying degrees.

When doctors moved me to step-down ICU on August 19 and gradually decreased my sedatives, I felt like a canoeist slowly paddling through a diminishing fog. My surroundings slowly came into view, but still were not in complete focus. The crash had mangled my eyeglasses, so when I came to nearly three weeks later, I had only my nearsightedness to rely on. Anything more than three feet away was blurry. On top of that, my right eye was still swollen shut. And when it did eventually open, I suffered from double vision, as if the grogginess from the drugs hadn't made focusing difficult enough already.

I couldn't speak, as the tracheotomy had left a hole in my neck. Not until a few days later did I receive the tube that would allow sound to resonate from my vocal chords. That hardly mattered though, as the wires in my jaw kept me from enunciating.

My senses of smell and taste weren't an issue initially. I couldn't eat because of my broken jaw, so I had a feeding tube surgically inserted into my stomach. Additionally, the accident severed the nerves that send messages to the brain to perceive smells. I didn't realize I'd be without this sense forever until a couple of months later, when it simply hadn't returned.

Because of the drugs and the vast amount of surgical work, I felt numb physically. My facial surgeries were done through incisions inside my mouth. Even today, my sensation is dulled in places, including my lower lip, my upper gums, and chin. That can be a problem when I eat; I'm sure I've eaten many a meal totally unaware that macaroni and cheese or Fruity Pebbles were left dangling on my lip.

But, hey, my hearing? As good as ever, which had never been great. However, God was gracious enough to spare it injury. Therefore, I was able to hear the 3.1 million beeps from the various machines in my room that either fed me fluid or monitored one of my body parts during the two months of hospitalization. On top of that, I could still listen to my fiancée share her 3.1 million ideas on how to orchestrate the perfect wedding. You didn't think a little dive into a river was going to halt that, did you? Yes, God is good, and he has a twisted sense of humor.

I was hooked up to more tubes and wires than Frankenstein's monster. A machine did most of my breathing for me. If I needed assistance, I would try to point with my right arm to what I wanted. My family created a chart with common phrases that I could point to. "Yes." "No." "I have pain." "I am cold." "I have to poop." "I love Sonja." Yet with double vision, even reading that bulletin-board-sized chart proved difficult.

I recall that my nurses in step-down ICU were very kind, gentle, and accommodating. I suppose you have to be when working with those who have just moved out of ICU. I recall one of them, a young woman with blond hair, telling me about her lost dog. I felt really bad for her, but had no real way of showing it.

While they were nice, my nurses had a job to do: get me back up on my feet. Rest was important, but it wasn't all I would be tasked with.

"Oh, and by the way? Therapy starts tomorrow," my physical therapist told me at the end of her initial visit that day I had woken up for good. "We'll see you bright and early, Mr. Ebling."

****

Recovery happens in several stages, the first being survival. When people are in terrible accidents and are severely injured, they aren't initially worried about their emotional well-being, or how their moods affect their relationships with their spouse, family, or friends. No, the only focus is on not dying. Are my basic needs being met? You start at the top of the checklist:

Question 1: Am I breathing? If yes, proceed to Question 2.

Question 2: Can I feed myself, or if not, is there somebody who can feed me? If yes, proceed to Question 3.

Question 3: Am I capable of using a restroom, or if not, is there somebody who can assist in making sure that I can cleanly relieve myself?

Initially I couldn't do any of those three things on my own. Our bodies instinctively react to stressful situations with the fight-or-flight response. But what happens when you can do neither? I wondered about that as I lay there, unable to move.

The accident derailed me from the beginnings of middle age. I now required constant care, like a baby just arrived in its new world, or like a hospice resident watching life's sunset fade. At this point, I wasn't thinking about what this journey of recovery would look like. I had no blueprint. There was no timeline. This was a recovery made from scratch, with the recipe created by intuition and advice rather than precise directions.

Rehab began almost immediately upon my arrival to step-down ICU. Step-down wasn't anything fancy, simply a section of rooms for patients who had recently left ICU and were still too unstable to be transported to other hospital beds. Having newly regained consciousness, I felt rushed to the base of this mountain called recovery. I had only recently come back to life, even though eighteen days had passed since the accident. I desired respite and a chance to catch up.

I had stopped while the world kept moving. I wondered what I had missed. "President Bush came to the Twin Cities to view the collapse site," my mom informed me. "San Francisco Giants outfielder Barry Bonds broke the all-time career home run record," my friends remarked, something I had been following right up until the accident. More than a year later, during a conversation about game shows, I found out that Merv Griffin had passed away during the time I was in my medically induced coma.

Two physical therapists arrived the morning of the first full day I was awake. My hospital room was abuzz with nurses and family members. Each shift brought with it strangers and new nurses. If I needed an IV bag, it was one nurse. If I needed my vitals checked, it was another. If I needed to use the bedpan, it was still another nurse who wiped my bottom clean. (Now that I think about it, I'm glad that the oral thermometer and bedpan duties were held by different people.) Because I had so many needs (medication, vitals, blood-sugar checks, incision wound cleaning, etc.) my mother feared that mix-ups would inevitably occur. She made sure she was always around when a new face came through the door.

The two physical therapists were an interesting team. One was a middle-aged man with what sounded like a Greek accent. The other was a younger, dark-haired woman with a cheerful disposition and a beautiful face. I really liked her. She was a University of Wisconsin–Madison graduate like myself. During one of our first few meetings, she told me that she would be returning to Wisconsin's capital for the weekend to take in a Badgers football game at Camp Randall Stadium. She said she'd bring me back a gift, and she kept her word. I awoke one morning to find a Badgers doorknob hanger that read "Do Not Disturb. The game is on." I was surprised she took the time during her escape from the long, grinding days inside the hospital to hunt down a gift for a patient. It helped me realize that many of the people I had encountered did much more than just punch a clock. She recognized that healing involves more than time and drugs, and I'll never forget that.

The first trick they wanted me to perform was to sit at the edge of my bed. This was the first of dozens and dozens of things I didn't want to do. I had an eleven-inch incision that ran from my waist to my chest, held together with staples and tape. When twenty-four inches of my severed colon had been removed, the abdominal muscles had been carved up like the roast beast that sat upon the Who's Christmas dinner table. Any movement triggered an intense burning in my midsection. I preferred to lie motionless, but I knew that if I was ever going to leave this place, I had to be able to get out of the bed. With my good right arm, I grabbed the left railing and pulled myself up by rolling on my side. The IV lines snagged. I made a mental note to always to be careful of the half-dozen tubes and wires connected to me. I winced and fought through it. My stomach burned as if from a fresh stab wound. The therapists steadied my shoulders and made sure that my broken ankles did not touch the tiled floor. I sat there in a woozy stupor for a couple of minutes. Sonja and my mom applauded my accomplishment, as if I'd won a Tony Award instead of sitting at the edge of a bed in hospital-issued boxer shorts with little fishies on them. (Apparently, somebody at the hospital thought that putting adult patients in aquatic-themed underwear would make them happier, but I wanted to cry.) If sitting up involved this much pain, how would I be able to do anything ever again?

During the first few days in step-down ICU, my family and I felt like we were on a small boat fighting choppy waters. I slept most of the time, but when I was awake, there was a medical event to attend to. Early on, I started having intense back spasms, as if somebody had plunged a dagger into my spine. The pains were quite severe, so much so that I couldn't breathe. My face turned colors, and the nurses repeatedly asked me to breathe, but I couldn't. My body morphed into a boa constrictor, seizing itself so tightly I thought I was going to die. The nurses pinned me on my side and injected medication into my lower back. The pain subsided.

Additionally, the trauma that I endured during the collapse and the subsequent surgeries had fried my body's thermostat. I couldn't maintain my internal temperature. At its height, my fever hit 105 degrees. My family members tried their best to make me as comfortable as possible by keeping the hospital room's temperature low. They soaked cotton towels in cold water and kept them pressed to my forehead. Hours later, I would be soaked in sweat, asking for a change of bed sheets and a fan. Hot. Cold. Sweats. Shivers. It was a miserable state that took weeks to end.

These stark transitions were incredibly difficult to tolerate. Why all the shots? The blood draws every few hours? The temperature readings and the blood-pressure checks? They were all done so that I didn't flatline, but there were times when I felt I would have enjoyed the permanent rest. I felt like a guinea pig who wanted to scratch, squeal, and bite every time the hand darted into the cage, but, for whatever reason, froze and accepted its fate. I wanted to burrow away. Darin had lent me his iPod Nano and loaded it with music. When the lights went off each night, I curled in my white linens, inserted the ear buds to drown out the beeping machines, and cried myself to sleep as Tim McGraw crooned, "Live Like You Were Dying."

The good thing about the fevers was that they could be treated easily with medication. This allowed me to continue my therapy. The doctors wanted me to use a sliding board in order to move from the bed to a wheelchair. To slide down from the bed to the chair, I had to wiggle my butt along the wooden board. It was sliding up, from the wheelchair to the bed, that brought the pain. At first, it was the doctors doing most of the work, grabbing me under my arms and hoisting me into bed. But, more and more, I worked through the pain and figured out a way to leverage my weight with my one good arm.

Two days after starting therapy, feeling better and fueled by my little successes, I took another significant step toward leaving step-down. Thirty-minute therapy sessions were helping, but I knew it would take more than a daily sit-up if I wanted to see significant recovery. I decided that I would sit up on the edge of my bed, unassisted, for as long and as safely as I could. I knew it would exhaust me, but I had to start building stamina. I had spent three weeks in a bed, my energy sapped by the healing process. Alone in my room, I rolled back and forth from my back to my side, building momentum to pull myself up. I wiggled to the center edge of the bed. I began to feel somewhat dizzy, and made a conscious effort not to lean too far forward; otherwise, I would tumble onto the floor. I was up for a minute or two when my mom came into the room.

"What are you doing?" she said, astounded and angry. "You shouldn't be doing that without doctor approval!" It was the first of many times she'd say that during the following few months.

With my tracheotomy tube, I was now able to speak, though it was in a tinny, whispered vibrato. "I—I feel okay," I said, not letting on that I was growing more woozy.

A few minutes later, Sonja came through the door with a similar reaction. According to her CaringBridge entry, "I walked into Garrett's room this morning to find him sitting on the edge of his bed, holding himself upright! I just about peed my pants! It was such a great sight. If there's one thing I know about my man, it's that he's persistent, and it seems that his shorter, more painful stint in the bed-chair the other day only fueled him on."

I didn't tell her, but she was right. And I'd use the word "stubborn" rather than "persistent."

The next day, the doctors changed my trach tube so that my voice was clearer. Sonja and I had our first real conversation. She told me that even though she hadn't been able to talk with me these past three weeks, she still felt closer to me than ever, because it was through this horrible accident that she really got to know my mom, my sister, and the rest of the family. (Before the accident, Sonja and my mother had only met twice.) She added that she felt God was using this event to bless our future married life. To her, what we were going through was an amazing blessing despite its tragic nature, and we'd be better people for it. Less eloquently, I told her what I remembered right before the bridge collapsed. I suppose we both got to hear what we needed to hear.

****

I hadn't drunk anything in three weeks.

The inside of my mouth was a desert cave: hot, cracked, and dusty. My lips had hardened. They were chapped, swollen, and scabbed. And they were buried in an unkempt, salt-and-pepper beard. The doctors didn't allow me any liquids for fear that I would aspirate—that any water I consumed would end up in my lungs instead of my stomach. But I begged for anything moist. About three days after waking up, I was told that a nurse would be coming to check on how I was handling my trach tube and would maybe try giving me some ice chips. Ice chips! Frozen nectar from the gods!

The nurse arrived later that morning carrying a cup. The ice chips inside it were colored blue to make it easier to track the liquid once it entered my body. She dipped the red, plastic spoon into the cup and chiseled at some ice. I couldn't wait for the airplane to fly into the hangar. The chips slid through my puffy lips and onto my tongue in glorious ecstasy. I relished the tingle as the chips melted and the water seeped down my throat. I coughed. She stopped.

"Perhaps it's too soon," she remarked as she pulled away.

Too soon?

"We'll try this again in a couple of days," she decided. A couple of days felt like a U.S. Senate term. I wanted to cry, collect the tears, and drink them. But doctor's orders are doctor's orders.

Meanwhile, I was sitting up more and more. And because I slept intermittently, there were often times when I'd be wide awake in the predawn hours while my mother or Sonja was fast asleep upon a piece of furniture in my room. I recall one evening—a few days after therapy had begun—in which I could not fall asleep and felt an unprecedented burst of energy. The off-white walls frustrated me. The incessant beeps of the IV and feeding machines annoyed me. For the first time, I yearned for freedom and a little adventure.

"Mom," I said in my loudest, raspy voice. "Mom." She jolted from her light sleep. My mom never was a deep sleeper. She can't ever completely relax, and when this whole saga began, she became like a sentinel guarding the jail door. Sleep? Perhaps a little, but she was always aware.

"What's wrong?" she asked as she rose to her feet and walked over to the bed.

"I want to go for a wheelchair ride," I said, fully aware of the time.

"It's not quite 5:00 a.m.," she replied, but she stepped into the hall to get a nurse working the graveyard shift. The female nurse unplugged my IV from the wall so it could be pulled along with the wheelchair. She capped my stomach tube, and I was ready to rumble. Mom pulled the wheelchair to the side of the bed. I pressed the button on the bed rail to raise myself up. She located the sliding board and situated both the board and the wheelchair in order for me to slide onto the seat, like a kid down a banister. With a few grunts and a slide, I was in the driver's seat. Like two prison inmates who realized their escape plan had worked, we took off down the halls.

"Where do you want to go?" Mom asked, wiping sleep from her eyes.

"Take me somewhere new."

We rolled down corridors, past the rooms of slumbering patients, she in her flannel pajama pants, T-shirt, and half-inch-thick glasses, and I wrapped in a blanket. The nighttime ride was so different from the day's. No rushed footsteps; voices barking orders; panic and chaos from families when their loved ones arrived; and distorted voices seeking physicians via intercom speakers. The only sounds were my mom's echoing steps and the metallic squeaks of the wheels on my chair and rolling IV stand. I could feel the unnatural calm of a hospital asleep.

Ma beautifully performed the role of tour guide as she directed the wheelchair. She reminded me of my grandfather, who relished sharing his vast knowledge of the local land whenever we drove through the countryside. "Over there is where the tornado came through in '83. You can see where the trees are smaller," my grandfather might say. Or, "The Brahms used to have a grocery store there before it became the meat locker." Mom didn't fall far from the tree.

We passed a collage of photos on a wall, where she pointed out the various staff nurses who had taken care of me. "This is so-and-so. She was here the first day you came to step-down. And that's what's-her-name. She got you the extra blankets." We continued on.

"You see those doors on the right?" she asked. I nodded. "That's where you had your colon surgery. We waited in the lounge down this hallway for nine hours." To her, this was a trip down short-term memory lane. For me, it wasn't even a memory. We reached the end of the hall at a bank of elevators. "Would you like to see more of the hospital?" she asked. Yearning for more adventure, I said yes. Mom turned the wheelchair ninety degrees. And then there was a pop.

Mom looked down. She had accidentally run over my urine bag. There we were: it was 5:15 a.m., and we were surrounded by an ever-growing pool of pee. "Don't go anywhere," she said. I wasn't planning on it, as I wasn't exactly in shape to make a run for it. If somebody had come by, I'm not sure what they would have thought, seeing this invalid parked alone in a yellow puddle in a vacant part of floor 3. My mom grabbed about seventy dozen paper towels from the nearest restroom and asked a nurse to contact the overnight janitor for some predawn mopping.

During my eight weeks of hospitalization, my mother and I shared a million moments. I don't remember all of them, but I recall this night well. Even though my mom had barely left my side since she had arrived at the hospital the morning after the accident, I had never felt closer to her than at that moment. Sure, I was thirty-two years old, but that night, I was her toddler. We weren't in hospital corridors, we were at the park, the fair, or the zoo. She was the young mother pushing the stroller, pointing out the fountain, the Ferris wheel, or the monkeys. I was Mama's boy—eyes wide open and taking in this new world. And for the first time in three weeks, I felt safe.

Looking back, I feel bad about making my mom get up at that ungodly hour and travel the hallways of the hospital with me. But it really was the first time I felt "unstuck," and I had taken the initiative to unstick myself. I felt as though I had happened upon a slice of peace in a spectrum of pain and suffering.

****

KIM DAHL

Kim Dahl thrived on her hectic life. The thirty-two-year-old mother of three from Anoka always seemed to be on the go, and it was often in the driver's seat of a big yellow bus. Kim made her living driving school buses for First Student, North America's leading school bus company, according to its web site. She had worked for First Student for about ten years, and for the last four had bused youths from Waite House, which provides human services and community-building activities for residents in Minneapolis's Phillips neighborhood. And even though summer recess kept most kids out of school, it didn't mean bus drivers sat idle. Summer programs and field trips provided plenty of opportunities for people like Kim, and she took advantage.

On August 1, 2007, Waite House planned an afternoon outing at Bunker Beach Water Park. Kim, along with more than fifty children (two of them her own, Arrianna, eleven, and David Jr., five; Kim's other daughter, Brianna, nine, was not on the bus that day) and eight adult supervisors trekked some twenty miles north from Minneapolis—over the 35W Bridge—to Coon Rapids so the kids could enjoy some fun in the sun.

"They swam all day. It was a very hot summer day," Kim recalled. "Then we had a snack and packed it up and headed back to the Waite House. We were running late, actually, coming back, as some kids misplaced clothing, shoes, and things like that. This was common."

Kim also remembered that the bus's rear emergency door had broken earlier in the day. Normally, emergency doors stop short of opening all the way, but this had lost its braking mechanism and was now capable of slamming against the back of the bus. (Looking back, Kim wondered if this was foreshadowing of what was about to happen just thirty minutes later.)

Rides home from a field trip are very different from the trips there, Kim said. "Usually, the kids are pretty tired after a full day of swimming, so a lot of

50

them were sleeping or singing."

Kim planned to take an alternate route back, since she knew there was a Minnesota Twins game at the Metrodome that evening, and that the 35W Bridge was undergoing construction. But she changed her mind when she saw that southbound traffic leading to I-35W was flowing smoothly. "I wished I had done it the other way," Kim said regretfully.

It was on southbound I-35W that Kim encountered two other vehicles that received much media coverage when the bridge collapsed. As the bus reached the exit for County Road C, Kim noticed a UPS truck next to the bus and saw the Taystee Bakery truck merging onto the interstate from the entrance ramp.

"We got going and got past them," Kim recalled. "As we passed them, the kids on the bus would do a honking gesture to the trucks to see if the truck driver would honk at them. This was fun for the kids. Eventually, one truck slid behind me and the other was next to me starting to pass by me. We were near one another the rest of the way."

As with many tragedies, the moments leading up to this one were mundane. On the bridge, Kim was chatting with Julie, one of the adult supervisors. Julie was engaged, and as the two of them gazed over the bridge, they saw a boat coming through the lock and dam. "How cool would it be to have a wedding party on a boat on the river like that?" Kim said.

Then, life changed for every person on that bus.

"The next thing we knew, it was like someone took a blanket and lifted it up. It was like a wave or ripple effect," Kim said of the beginning of the collapse. "I didn't know what was happening. I thought that the truck to my left was hitting the side of the bus, pushing me over. And then we were dropping. I could hear concrete hitting the bus."

Julie was screaming at Kim, "Where are you going? Where are you taking us?"

"All I could think was, I have all these kids on this bus, and I had to make sure they'd be safe," Kim recalled. "I grabbed the steering wheel tightly and put my foot on the brake, because it was like, wherever we were going, I was going to have my foot on the brake and my hands on the wheel. Wherever we were going, I hoped we weren't going to roll or move."

It was like slow motion, she said. "I couldn't tell what was happening, everything fuzzed over. I have all these kids on the bus, and I didn't want them to get hurt; they are all like my own children. That is all I could think about the whole time."

The bus dropped roughly 45 feet before hitting the ground extremely hard, front first. Then it lifted again and slammed down a second time. It, along with the Taystee truck, landed on a section of the bridge. The screams of the children went silent as the cloud of dust began to rise and engulf the bus. When it settled, "the kids went crazy," Kim said. They started to cry and yell. They were scared and didn't know what had just happened. Neither did Kim.

> As I looked down in the doorway, I saw Julie upside down, in a tripod position, on the steps with blood coming down. Julie had been in the front seat sitting diagonally from me next to my daughter who was in the same seat by the window. When we hit, Julie went up over the seat and into the doorway. Her head was trapped between the door and the first step. I saw the blood and thought, *Oh my God. She's dead.*

At that point, Kim realized that her seatbelt had jammed and she couldn't move. Another staff member, Jeremy, came forward to see if he could get the kids out through the front door, but Kim told him to have the kids exit through the back. The front door couldn't be used, as the bus was up against the side of the bridge.

Kim added, "I looked down in the doorway and Julie began crawling up the steps. I said, 'Julie, Julie! Can you shut the bus off?' I couldn't reach the ignition because I couldn't move." She wanted the bus turned off because she didn't want those onboard to feel ill from the exhaust. Julie was able to turn the key to the off position.

While Kim repeatedly tried to free herself and the other adults and children exited the rear of the bus, she looked over to her left and noticed that the roof of the Taystee truck was peeled back, and the bread and buns were coming out the top. The truck was starting to smolder a little. "I didn't know still what was going on. I couldn't see the tractor of the truck. It was just the trailer sticking out of this big piece of concrete," Kim said.

The bus was now empty except for Kim and her children, who were frightened and didn't want to leave their mother. Staff members Angie and Jimmy got back on the bus and told the kids they needed to get off, as it wasn't safe. It took Kim's stern direction to get them to leave. "Get your asses off this bus now!" she yelled.

Now Kim was alone, and the inside of the bus was eerily quiet. Kim noticed that the bakery truck was smoking more and the heat emanating from it was intensifying. "I'm completely pinned," she recalled. "I could hardly breathe. My back felt like I'd fallen from a swing and knocked the wind out of myself. I started thinking, *This is it. I'm going to die. I'm trapped in my seat—I'm going to die here alone.*"

Jimmy returned and told Kim that she had to get off the bus immediately. In the intensity of the moment, Kim had forgotten that a cutter was stored behind the driver's rearview mirror. "The next thing I knew, the bus moved a little," Kim remembered. That sudden movement allowed Kim's seat belt to release. Using Jimmy for support, she walked off the bus, went over the side of the bridge, and stumbled five hundred feet further before dropping from the pain.

Remarkably, none of the children on the bus were seriously hurt, though some sustained head and back injuries from hitting the ceiling, windows, and seats.

As Kim lay on the ground, she could see that the south end of the bridge had fallen, but she had no idea that the entire span had collapsed. She recalled hearing sirens and helicopters, and then seeing people everywhere.

"I laid on the blacktop, but it was so hot, it felt as if it was on fire," Kim said. "My kids came and sat next to me and gave me some towels to lie down on.

"Somebody came up to me and asked me if I knew if there was someone in the Taystee truck. The truck's cab had been crushed by bridge debris. I said, 'Yes, there's somebody in there. Please go help him.' I was crying at this time because I knew the driver was in there. The person said, 'I yelled in there, but there was no response.'"

Another stranger grabbed Kim's hand and said he'd stay by her until somebody came to transport her. She asked him if she could use his cell phone to call her husband, Dave. She told him, "The bridge fell. I'm hurt but I'm alive and going to the hospital. I don't know which one yet. I have to let you go. I need to call my work. I love you. Good-bye." Her second call was to First Student, and she left a message. The phone lines jammed shortly thereafter.

Paramedics arrived and asked Kim about her injuries. "I said I was having trouble breathing but that I wasn't bleeding. I said, 'If there are others that are worse off than me, please take them away first.'"

Shortly thereafter, the entire Taystee truck burst into flames. Firefighters grabbed Kim by the armpits and dragged her farther away from the truck because they didn't know if the truck and the bus were going to explode. She was placed in an ambulance about five minutes later. She guessed that, at this point, about ten minutes had passed since the collapse.

Arrianna and David Jr. climbed into the ambulance with her, along with another girl from the bus who was hyperventilating. Paramedics put a neck brace on Arrianna, who was complaining of face and neck pain. Kim held the hand of the girl to comfort her as a paramedic inserted an IV into her arm. The ambulance headed to Abbott Northwestern Hospital in Minneapolis.

Once at Abbott, Kim underwent a series of examinations. Nurses pumped her with drugs to alleviate her severe pain. "They had me so high that I couldn't move my feet," Kim said. "The doctor initially thought I was paralyzed." The doctors had difficulty examining her, because she couldn't remain still due to the pain.

Kim remained at Abbott for three days and was released on August 4. Her injuries included fractures of her T12 and L1 vertebrae, a vertical tear of her right rotator cuff, and a stretched supinator nerve in her arm that caused numbness and carpal tunnel syndrome. She didn't have any surgeries performed during her stay.

In February 2008, Kim had surgery on her right shoulder to remove bone spurs. Doctors also tried to heal her back using a brace and a great deal of physical therapy. However, bone continued to rub against bone, and in August 2008, she elected to have her thoracic vertebrae fused. Kim hoped that this would alleviate the pain for good, but that wasn't the case. The next two levels of her vertebrae have since collapsed, and specialists have tried multiple approaches to ease the pain, including a rhizotomy, a procedure in which pain-sensing nerves in the back are burned to numb them. That offered little help, though. She also has had steroid injections that provided no relief. And in 2010, she had a pain pump inserted into her spine via her buttocks. She uses a remote

54

control to trigger the Dilaudid (a narcotic analgesic). Every five years, she will have to undergo surgery to replace the battery in the pump.

Even after all of this, pain is a constant occurrence. "When I inhale, I can have muscle spasm pain from that area. They say there's nothing left to do and that I have to live with it," Kim said. "For me, right now, the pain is an everyday reminder of what happened."

Kim has been told that working as she had in the past is likely impossible. The metal hardware installed in her back cannot take the constant vibration that comes with driving a bus. In addition, the medication can make her woozy—a definite driving hazard. She is restricted to lifting no more than twenty pounds, and any type of repetitive work with her hands, like typing, causes the carpal tunnel to flare up. She hasn't worked since the bridge collapsed.

"So, basically, I'm thirty-four and disabled, which sucks, but I'm not going to let this bring me down," Kim stated with determination. Her upbeat outlook, though, is often tempered by the daily reminders of what she can no longer do:

> It's like everything's been taken away, things like planting flowers, and it drives me crazy. I loved going tubing and waterskiing with the kids. I can still ride in the boat, but now I can't ride over rough waves. Snowmobiling was my favorite thing in the world. Now I only can ride if trails are groomed, and I get so sore. Riding a bike kills me. Hitting a bump while driving in the car kills me...Then I'm not able to function. I just want to lie down because it feels so much better to do that than it does to do anything physical.

The disability extends to helping the family tend to the home. "I was pretty much the cook and cleaner in the family," she noted. "I have to have the kids do most of it, or Dave has to cook, or we have to eat out, and that gets expensive. Laundry, housecleaning—I can't do it anymore. It just causes my pain to worsen."

The family has accepted it, for the most part. "Kids are kids, but my husband has been really supportive," Kim said. "Dave totally understands my situation but does want me to start focusing on moving forward in my life. He's not pushing me. He understands it's not going to happen tomorrow or two months down the line."

The emotional side of Kim's story began the day that Minnesota governor Tim Pawlenty signed into law a bridge victims' compensation bill at the capitol in May 2008. "I didn't start getting PTSD until that day. I lost it right there," Kim recalled. "I hit the wall completely that day. I went outside. I was hyperventilating, thinking, *I need help. I need to deal with me now.* I was there for everybody, too, but now I needed to work on me."

The post-traumatic stress disorder hit Kim and her family as hard as her physical disability, if not more so. "I was really nasty to my family. I couldn't concentrate or focus on anything," she said. "I would just sleep, lie in bed, cry, and feel sorry for myself. It turned into depression. On top of that, I was dealing with the pain. Doctors then put me on Cymbalta, an antidepressant."

The PTSD affected her relationship with her children:

> I treated them bad, didn't have time for them. Pretty much hated them, and I knew that I couldn't hate them. They are my children. I love them. That, too, was when I knew I needed help. I spanked—and I had never spanked before. It was anger coming out. I was angry about what happened and I took it out on them.
>
> They wouldn't do naughty things; they would do kid things. I would scream. I had to get help ASAP. I took it out on other people too: family and friends. I wasn't the old Kim. I had to get used to the new Kim.

Kim feels better, but the PTSD ebbs and flows. "Some days I'm good. Some days I'm just a mess. Emotionally, it comes and goes."

One positive result of the aftermath is that the past couple of years have brought Kim and her husband, Dave, "a lot closer, which surprised me," Kim said. "I've seen the collapse cause a lot of relationship issues in others. We've always been open and talked a lot, but we're even more so now and we're able to make decisions together. There's much more togetherness."

According to Kim, other members of the family had emotional battles they needed to fight as well.

> We were having the best year of our lives [in 2007]. We were financially stable. Everything was going the way we wanted it to, and then this happened. It was just a shock to all of us. My husband didn't get [emotional] until after my back surgery. He completely lost it. He cried, was very upset, angry. I'm sure it was a lot for him because he had all of us to deal with. It was so much on him that he finally lost it. He says, "I wish it would have been me instead of you. I wonder how I would have been had I gone through that instead of you." I say I'm glad it wasn't you because I need you. You are my backbone.

One of the challenges for Kim is that she's not able to be as independent as she was before the bridge collapsed:

> If I needed to move a couch, I moved it. We were both that way when we got married. When this happened, I turned into this "girl" who couldn't do anything, and he's okay with that. He just steps up and does it for me. He understands that I have pain a lot and tries to help me out. He says, "Let's do this together" or "Let's go sit in the hot tub together." This has changed me in that I have to let others help me and be okay with that. It's a hard transition. I was a single mom with two kids before marrying Dave. When I got married, it was the hardest thing to let somebody else help me, and I could still do some things

independently. But when the collapse happened, it became "we," not "me" anymore.

Some habits die hard, though. "There are days where I still try to do something myself even though I know I shouldn't," she said. "I always pay for it. An hour later, I'm always miserable. I need to not do that. I need help. I got to have help. I can't do some things myself."

****

The school bus was a media magnet when the bridge fell. The TV news reports focused on it, and when everyone emerged from the bus alive, some called Kim a hero for putting the children's lives ahead of hers. The media inundated her from early on.

"I wasn't the only one on the bridge. Other people lost their lives. Other people got hurt," Kim said. "The hero thing drives me crazy. I wasn't a hero. I did what anyone else would have done. I'm thankful that I kept my composure and was able to do what I did, put the brake on and not let the bus roll. I feel like God was there with me. He gave the bus wings to land safely. That day the back door to the bus broke. Why that day? It allowed the kids to get off the bus faster. I believe it was fate and God. I really do."

Thoughts of the collapse pop up from time to time for Kim's kids. Her son makes a remark each time he sees a Taystee Bakery truck driving down the road. Her daughter spent time in counseling, dealing with anger issues.

As for Kim, she thinks about the collapse less and less often, but she still steers clear of the new 35W Bridge, saying, "I get sick when I get near the collapse site. I find other ways to get downtown. I don't feel I have a need to ever cross the new bridge. I just can't do it. I have no ambition. I was underneath the new bridge for the anniversary though, and that was hard for me."

Kim wants everyone to realize that "we're all not at 100 percent. We're all not back at our jobs and living our lives. The money thing [bridge victims' compensation] drives me crazy. Just because you have money means you're hunky-dory, happy, and living life to the best. Not at all. I'd rather have my life back in this situation. I'd rather be struggling to make it than be broken. There's quite a few of us who aren't moving forward, but many people don't see or know that."

The bridge collapse jolted Kim both literally and figuratively. Up until that point, she sprinted through life. Struggle couldn't stop her, even with stress all around.

"I grew up fast, moved out of my house when I was fifteen," Kim said. "I stayed with friends and family. I moved into my girlfriend's house during my junior year and stayed there until my senior year. I've pretty much raised myself since."

Now her life moves at a snail's pace. While Kim cannot work, she realizes she can't spend the rest of her life doing nothing. When her counsclor suggested she think about volunteering and public speaking, particularly to troubled youth, her ears perked up.

"I can speak to them; I've been where they are. So I'm excited to do that," she said. Kim also expressed a desire to volunteer at libraries and schools.

Physically, the future likely holds more pain for Kim. She believes that, at some point, she'll have to have rods inserted into her spine. She also figures she'll need surgery on her other shoulder, which has been forced to compensate for her injuries. "This is how my body is going to be; I'm going to have to live with it," she said.

What has Kim learned through all of this?

"To not take life for granted," she said.

> When I wake up in the morning and put my two feet on the floor—whew!—I made it another day. I'm willing to help others more. I'm willing to sacrifice my wants and needs. I donate tons and tons of stuff. I've learned to be nice to people. I used to be a very tough person. I was very hard to get along with. I don't know why, but I was pretty stuck on myself. I thought I was indestructible.
>
> This could happen at any time. It could happen to anybody. But it happened to us because

God knew we could handle it. I feel that's the truth. He needed those people up there to help him, and we needed to be down here to help others.

4

EVEN THOUGH I HAD ONLY JUST BEGUN THERAPY, I was about to leave HCMC. In the next few days, I'd be well enough to exit step-down ICU, and HCMC needed my bed for the next unfortunate soul. I was several weeks away from being able to go home, so I needed a new place where I could heal. Mom began scouting for a long-term healthcare facility where I could stay until I began full-time physical therapy. She and Darin toured a place that seemed like it would be a good fit: Regency Rehabilitation Center in nearby Golden Valley, an inner-ring suburb west of Minneapolis. A room was available, and on Friday, August 24, I was transported by ambulance to what would be my home for the next month.

The nurses prepared me for my move. This included a shave, my first since the accident three weeks earlier. I'd grown quite a beard since then. One note: hospital-issued shaving cream and razors are not nearly as nice as the kind professional athletes sell on TV. No, these are the cheapest disposable razors you find on the bottom shelf at Walgreens. The only saving grace about all the scraping, tugging, and nicking was that my face was completely numb from the surgeries and pain medication.

EMTs wheeled me on a gurney from my bed to the awaiting ambulance. I had never been in the back of one before. Correction: I'd never been conscious and alert in the back of an ambulance before. As the technicians loaded me in, I felt like a UPS package, about to shift a bit with each bump in the road, and stamped with the word "fragile."

Rhonda, my only sibling, had come up to the Twin Cities from her home in New Ulm to be part of this six-mile journey to Regency. She asked the ambulance drivers if she could ride along with me. I'm not sure if it was ambulance policy, but she has always been able to use her good looks and flirtatious manner to her advantage, and they didn't fail her this time as she chatted with the two young male drivers. Rhonda is two and a half years younger than I am and married with six young children. The two youngest are twins who were born about six weeks before the bridge collapse. She had her first when she was seventeen. Personality-wise, Rhonda and I each follow the path of one of our parents. Like my mother, I am introverted, codependent, observational, and play by the rules. My sister is like my father in many ways: casual, scattered, unfazed by what others think, crafting the rules as she goes along.

When our parents divorced, I was five years old, and Rhonda and I lived full-time with our mother. Because Mom went to school to get her teaching degree, Rhonda and I were latchkey kids. We learned how to take care of ourselves, and while our personalities differed, we always supported and stuck up for each other. Each week, I'd hike across town to her ballet studio after school and do my homework in the lobby as I waited for her to leap and twirl her way to the end of class. Then I'd walk her home, often stopping by the local dairy for a vanilla cone paid for with some coins I happened to find in couch cushions or street gutters. When other boys bullied me on the playground, it was Rhonda who marched up to the miscreants and told them to knock it off. We always knew we were different, but like marines, we never left each other behind.

Rhonda sat next to my gurney in the back of the ambulance. Normally she has no problems making conversation, but not much was said as we wound through downtown Minneapolis side streets en route to Golden Valley. Not much really needed to be said, however, as I could read the expression on her face and the tears she held back. Unlike my mother, Rhonda hadn't been with me around-the-clock. She had a flock of children to tend to back in New Ulm.

I could tell that it hurt her badly that she couldn't be in the Twin Cities more. She relied on phone calls with Mom and Sonja to find out how I was doing in between her visits. As I lay there, eyes toward the ceiling, I could feel her gaze on me. I could sense her sadness and concern. She knew much better than I the road that lay ahead.

Rhonda had always seen me as big brother, full of advice (whether she wanted it or not), strong and independent, the guy who moved 1,200 miles from home and worked hard to succeed. Now she saw me in a new light for the first time: vulnerable, frail. Physically, I looked like a different person. What I saw in her expression was that I might be fixable, but I wouldn't ever be the same. That scared her, and it scared me too. I swallowed hard. Rhonda wrote in a CaringBridge entry on August 23, 2007,

So here is what it's like to be me. With my active family, I can't stay up here all the time. I wish I could, but I can't. I hate leaving Garrett, and coming back scares me. When I come back I get horrific butterflies in my stomach the closer I get. Anxiety swells up in my body, as I don't know what to expect. It's scary to be away and hear secondhand what's going on. And I read the CaringBridge and get an image and an idea of what's going on based on how other people perceive things. But reality isn't always as kind.

Face to face, things are a little different. Face to face, the guilt of not being able to protect someone you love from this devastation is severe. Face to face, the pain of each movement, word, and breath is more noticeable. Face to face, the anger toward an inanimate object is much clearer. Face to face, the fear of the unknown I feel when I have to leave again is more intense.

With that said, don't get me wrong or be discouraged. We are definitely moving forward. Today, I wasn't disappointed. Today felt good. Today was the first time I saw the Garrett we all love. I got to hear the compassion in his voice for others, hear the wisecracks he cracks so well and the sincere love he has for all his family and friends. To have that back made me cry.

We arrived at Regency, and the two ambulance drivers pulled me out of the rear of the vehicle. Sunlight. I hadn't felt it in three and a half weeks. Those three seconds in the sun nourished my soul and gave me the fortitude to keep on fighting. I imagined being a prisoner who was locked away for years and then, suddenly and unannounced, pulled from the blackness of his cell and led into an outdoor courtyard. The artificial, air-conditioned climate evaporated, if only for a moment, and the sun soaked into my pores. I could have laid on that gurney in the driveway forever and never complained.

I began getting nervous as I was wheeled through Regency's front doors. While I had only been alert for five days, I felt comfortable at HCMC. They knew who I was. If there was a question, the surgeons were right there. My follow-up appointments were there. There was a three-week routine to my care. Now I was in a foreign place. New doctors and nurses. A new room. New procedures.

There were positives, though. Regency was much closer to my apartment, as well as the home of a family friend, which became Mom's base of operations when she needed a place to shower or just get some rest. The care center's environs were breathtaking, part of a rich residential oasis tucked among more urban settings. We were told that Minnesota Twins pitcher Johan Santana lived in the area, so I could add "all-star pitcher's neighbor" to my resume. From a bird's-eye view, there was nothing wrong with Regency.

Because I arrived on a Friday afternoon, I wouldn't be starting therapy or seeing my new doctor until Monday. I'd be met by one of the rotating physicians instead. I had mixed feelings about this. On one hand, it was a tangible step forward. If my health hadn't improved, I would not have been allowed to move there. I was also happy to have a couple of days to settle in. On the other hand, I was charged up about beginning my therapy, and Monday seemed like a long way away. Moreover, neither Mom nor I felt particularly comfortable about the absence of my doctor. I wasn't just there for a broken bone—I had twenty of those, not to mention all of my other injuries. I was a World Series medical case, and I felt they were bringing in a minor-league pitcher.

After a few minutes of waiting in the hall, the ambulance drivers rolled me into my new room, which, coincidentally, was just a few doors down from another bridge collapse survivor, a construction worker. In a very well-practiced maneuver, the two men from the ambulance slid me onto the bed. A while later, a nurse came into the room to check me in. Because I was a new patient, any freedom I had acquired at HCMC would be temporarily revoked until I was given clearance.

All this free time on the weekends did, however, provide ample opportunity for visitors. Not surprisingly, I had plenty of them. Being part of a high-profile tragedy makes you a pseudocelebrity. I wasn't ready for it. It felt very strange to me that so many people wanted to drive to Golden Valley and stare at me as I lay there. There were times when I couldn't tell if people came to visit out of genuine concern or so they could tell their friends and family they now had some direct connection to the bridge collapse. I saw myself as simply a guy in a car accident, but the world saw my injuries as much, much more.

Of the dozens and dozens of visiting family, friends, and clergy, a couple really stood out. One of them was my best friend from my Washington, D.C. days. Ron and I spent five years as roommates inside the Beltway. We had survived the September 11 attacks, the D.C. snipers, and apartment cockroaches the size of mice. Although we hadn't lived together in more than a year and a half, we still made sure we got together every few months, throwing down pints of beer at an Irish pub in Minneapolis or Alexandria, Virginia. But I hadn't expected to see him for at least another nine months, because Ron was set for deployment in August to Baghdad as a member of the Maryland Air National Guard. Unbeknownst to me, Darin had been filling Ron in on my recovery, and Ron wanted to come out to visit. He was home for a week between the end of training and his departure for Iraq, and, since he wasn't supposed to leave the area when so close to a deployment, he asked for permission to travel to Minnesota for a couple of days. (Only later did he find out that his request had been denied, but due to miscommunication, he didn't get the message in time. Sorry, Uncle Sam!)

When Ron and Darin walked into the room, I was caught completely off guard. There we were, the Three Amigos reunited. Immediately, the jokes and putdowns began—something us good friends do often and well. If I closed my eyes, the three of us weren't in a sterile hospital, but in a filthy watering hole, making wisecracks about each other's favorite pro sports teams, laughing about embarrassing moments from our twenties, and playing our "Ladies and Gentlemen" game, in which you pick out somebody in a bar who looks remotely like a celebrity and proclaim, "Ladies and Gentlemen, it's [insert celebrity name here.]"

It was one of those rare moments when my mind was able to transcend the broken, near-dead body it was trapped inside of and almost think that the old times had returned. I felt as if I could just stand up and walk out the door with my best friends and go play trivia at the nearest Buffalo Wild Wings. But I couldn't. As soon as my friends left, the frustration returned.

Ron couldn't stay all that long. He had to be back home the next morning. The three of us mugged for the camera with a "hear no evil, see no evil, speak no evil" pose, and Darin and Ron left. It really hurt to see them leave. I said a prayer for Ron after he walked out the door. I asked God to bring him back from Iraq safely so that he could see me on the other side, when I'd be back to normal: laying down the sarcasm like a thick steak sauce and throwing back beers in front of a sports game on a big-screen TV. There was no doubt in my mind I'd reclaim all that had been taken from me. I wanted him to be there for that.

In addition to a plethora of visitors, I received new eyeglasses, thanks to the good folks at LensCrafters. I'd had my old pair for only about a year when they were mangled in the collapse. The doctors at HCMC kept them and gave them to my family when they came to see me that first time on August 2. The spectacles were twisted like a pretzel, and one of the lenses was missing. Darin took the pair over to LensCrafters to get another pair made. When they found out that I had been on the bridge, they gave him a new pair at no charge. Darin returned, and I slipped them on. I was able to see clearly for the first time in a month.

One of the more frustrating things about my care at Regency was the inconsistency compared to HCMC. When I had left HCMC, I was given permission to drink liquids. Once I was at Regency, that was revoked, at least through the weekend. This made me quite ornery. In another instance, my orthopedic surgeon at HCMC required that the boots I wore on both of my feet only be removed to change socks. At Regency, they said that I could take the boots off during the day when I was in bed. I was ecstatic about this, because the black boots were obnoxiously hot. My feet would continually sweat. The boots were held together with several straps that attached tightly around each calf with Velcro. They took several seconds to remove and a minute to fasten. I absolutely hated them. I fought viciously with my mom, who demanded we confirm with HCMC that removing the boots would be okay. "Mom, please, don't do this," I said. "Things are so miserable right now and this is one thing I can have." I thought I had successfully tugged at her heartstrings, and it almost worked. But, in the end, I lost the battle. Mom confirmed with my orthopedic surgeon at HCMC that the boots should not be removed, and they were kept on for weeks, until I could again apply pressure to my ankles.

Regency's employees were diverse. The nursing staff looked like a random sampling of the cafeteria line at the United Nations. I was at Regency for nearly a month, and I can only recall having one nurse whose native language was English. I didn't care where my nurses were from per se, but it's a little disconcerting to be so reliant on somebody who doesn't speak the language all that well—especially since *I* couldn't speak the language that well, what with my jaw wired shut.

Additionally, I felt that the nursing staff's response time was slow. One could argue that the staff in any post-ICU ward would be more responsive than in a general inpatient facility. Yet I'd hit my nurse call button and wait thirty minutes or more for somebody to come to the room. I learned quickly to ring for a bedpan way before I ever needed it. The same applied to pain medication.

There also seemed to be a disregard for the medical instructions that accompanied me from HCMC to Regency. One of the rules was that I always had to lie at an incline, so the feeding tube that went directly into my stomach didn't back up. There were several instances in which Mom would stop a nurse who was reclining my bed too far. Also, linens, towels, and washcloths were scarce. Because I had trouble controlling my body temperature, I often required cold, wet washcloths or extra blankets. Mom got tired of trying to hunt them down, so she stopped at Target one day to purchase extra towels and washcloths. Mom would bring up her frustration with the nurses, and then with family members of other patients. The former told her, "It is what it is." The latter told her the problems weren't unique to my hospital room.

The straw that broke the camel's back was found in the hallway. As days turned into weeks at Regency, my therapy progressed to the point that I could "walk" with my walker. The walker had an elevated left arm rest. My orthopedic surgeon at HCMC allowed me to begin putting pressure on my right heel. In a multistep maneuver, a therapist (if I was lucky, it was a pretty, young one) would wrap a belt around my waist and help me rise from my wheelchair with the walker in front of me. I'd grab the walker with my right hand and place my left forearm on the arm rest. I'd step with my right foot, then push the walker a few inches forward. The next step was a little hop, pressing down with my right hand and my left elbow. It was extremely painful. The first few attempts were measured in inches. But, as with everything, I pushed myself hard. I'd count the number of cinder blocks in a row along the hallway and set goals in my head. *Yesterday, I made it ten blocks. Can I do fifteen today?* On one particular day, I made it my quest to hop to the end of the hall. I felt confident that as long as I had somebody with me and took a few breaks, I'd make it.

I asked Sonja to follow me with a wheelchair. We began at the end of a hallway in a more quiet and secluded area of the care center that had no patient rooms. For several minutes, I hobbled and stopped. Hobbled and stopped. About three-quarters of the way, we approached a drinking fountain. Parched, I bent over and took a few deep drinks. Then it happened: the water made its way down my windpipe rather than my esophagus, and I began to choke hard. I coughed furiously. Sonja panicked and finished my jaunt for me by running to the end of the hall to the nurse's station to get help. When she got there, she tried to explain what was happening but had trouble finding the right words. The nurse, either misunderstanding or just not wanting to be bothered, told Sonja she would have to go to the other nurses' station near my hospital room to receive assistance, as that was my "home base." Sonja didn't know what to do. She ran back to me as I was hacking up water. Luckily, I was able to start breathing normally again on my own, without the assistance of a nurse.

The growing list of incidents culminated in a request for a "care meeting." Mom, Sonja, and Darin—who, along with Rhonda, became known as "Team Garrett" on the CaringBridge web site—met with the hospital staff, along with Kristen, my qualified rehab consultant. Kristen was responsible for ensuring that I was getting adequate care under the guidelines of workers' compensation. The meeting led to staff promises to pay greater attention to my care. However, we saw little change. Mom began looking into alternatives in the Twin Cities and beyond—including returning home and having a nurse visit the apartment (which I wholeheartedly supported!)—until I was ready to return to HCMC for intense therapy. However, there was no suitable alternative, especially since I was a mere couple of weeks away (we hoped) from being released back to HCMC. Sonja recorded the experience in a CaringBridge entry on August 29, 2007:

This is gonna be a long haul. I took Garrett for a wheelchair ride today, and we stopped on the outside patio for a few minutes and sat there in silence.

It felt like the words "this is gonna be a long haul" hung in the air as heavy as the humidity.

The first few weeks were such a rush—little sleep, fervent prayer, and lots of surgeries, procedures, and progressions. Now life is slowing down and restless legs, long nights of sleeplessness, and slow but steady improvement are the status quo. It's a bit of a shock to the system to downshift so fast...

I really thought when we got to the point where Garrett could talk and move around, it would be so easy. Our relationship would be up and going again, and I'd have my boyfriend back. But what I forgot is that recovery comes in stages, and even though a person's physical capacity returns, their emotional capacity can be on another track completely.

I miss talking with Garrett. I want more than anything to spend quality time with him again, instead of feeling like I'm sitting and staring in a hospital room, unaware if it makes any difference. I can't understand what he's feeling, if he's angry, depressed, sad, or hopeful. But I know this too shall pass, and the Garrett I know and love will come back to me.

****

My family relied heavily on Kristen's expertise, and I felt incredibly fortunate to have her direct us through this vast unknown. Her mere presence was a blessing. Had workers' compensation not applied in my situation, we would have been on our own, not knowing what we needed or how to go about getting it once we figured it out. She answered all of Team Garrett's questions:

- *How do we get a care meeting scheduled?*
- *How do we know Garrett's situation even calls for one?*
- *How do we go about getting Garrett admitted back into HCMC for intense, short-term rehabilitation?*
- *How do we get medical equipment Garrett might need once he goes home?*
- *What kinds of equipment will we need?*
- *How do we make sure the workers' compensation insurance*

*company pays for the equipment? The prescriptions? The doctors'
appointments?*

- *What about continuing therapy after he's released from the hospital?
  How is that paid? Where should he go? How do we know who is best
  qualified?*

The questions piled up like boxcars in a train derailment.

Kristen knew the ins and outs of workers' compensation. If she
encountered any resistance from a physician or an insurance company, they
stood no chance. Her mind was a steel trap matched only by her tenacity, and
when she had to push, she did it gladly. I admired her considerably. A mom
herself, she reminded me of my own mother. Kristen was a fighter. If she was
ever going down, she'd do so swinging, but to the best of my knowledge, she
was the undisputed, undefeated heavyweight champion of the health care realm.

Legally, Kristen was required to see that my needs were met until I
returned to work full-time. She attended nearly all of my physicians' appointments
from late August until May of the following year. I can't even begin to tell you
how many appointments there were—simply dozens upon dozens. If she was
running late, she called to let me know. One time, she was recovering from laser
eye surgery. Anyone else would have stayed home. Not Kristen. She arrived at
the hospital appointment with her preteen son. "He told me when and where to
turn," she said, describing her drive over. *You're crazy*, I thought.

Through the course of the ten months she worked with me, I learned that
she was an avid downhill skier, taking on tall peaks from Montana to Colorado.
That didn't surprise me one bit.

During this time, I also got to know my general physician, Dr. Herrera.
Ultimately, Dr. Herrera would determine when I would return to work full time.
While normally stationed at HCMC, he made a trek to Regency each Wednesday
to evaluate patients like me for discharge. Thus, I was always on my best behavior
when he came to visit, showcasing my progress in the hopes that he would answer,
"Next week" when I asked about getting released. Leaving Regency wasn't quite
that simple, however. In order for me to enter the Miland E. Knapp Rehabilitation
Center at HCMC, there had to be an open bed. I was put on the waiting list.

****

I'll never forget the first time I looked into a mirror following the accident. It was in the bathroom of my hospital room at Regency. I was becoming more mobile, so one morning, I decided to get into my wheelchair and roll to the sink. Up until that point, I had used an electric shaver and brushed my teeth while sitting up in bed.

All I really knew about my appearance was what people told me. "You're looking great, honey" or "The swelling has really come down." Of course, this was all subjective. My close friends and family had seen me since day two. To them, I was miles beyond where I had been when I started my path of recovery. They could say that I looked great and genuinely mean it.

I first became concerned about my appearance when my nieces and nephews briefly visited not long after I had arrived at Regency. Young children will react instinctively. They'll tell you what they feel by their movements and expressions. I knew my nieces and nephews well enough to interpret their half-smiles and quizzical looks. There was no rush for a hug from Uncle Garrett. Their big eyes, hidden behind ratty tresses, revealed confusion. I wondered if the smaller children even recognized me. Surely Rhonda, their mother, had explained my injuries? Perhaps they didn't fully understand. I told them who I was, that this was temporary, and soon I'd be chasing them around the playground equipment just like before. I really think they wanted to believe it, but the physical evidence proved otherwise. I was lying in a bed hooked up to IVs. Both of my feet and one arm were in casts, my jaw was wired shut, and I had a hole in my neck. I was about as useful to them as a bicycle with a flat tire.

I feared I had just discovered another thing that the bridge had taken from me: my close relationship with my nephews and nieces, a big reason why I'd moved back to Minnesota less than two years prior. But as that afternoon wore on, they warmed to me. They began to see that I was, indeed, inside that banged-up body, way deep down. I promised them I'd be back, but the reality was I had no idea how far from normal I was physically.

I rolled across the tiles, bumping into the door frame with the bulky wheelchair before squeezing through and into the bathroom. I plucked the electric shaver from my lap, turned it on with the press of a button, and looked into the mirror above the sink.

I now understood what my nieces and nephews had seen when they first came into my hospital room. It wasn't me. It was the face of a different man. This man's nose was puggish; mine had a sizable bump on the ridge. His jawline protruded; my bottom jaw fit snugly underneath my upper, creating an overbite. This man's face, unlike mine, was swollen and quite asymmetrical. One eyelid drooped far lower than the other. One pupil remained fully dilated. There were gashes and scabs around his brow. His temples were sunken in. His teeth were either missing or horribly out of place. This man should be living up in Notre Dame's bell tower.

My stomach turned over. I wanted to vomit. Was this it? Is this who I now was? This wasn't normal. It was anything *but* normal. I wouldn't be able to go anywhere in public without attracting stares of repulsion mixed with pity, I thought.

I didn't know what else to do, so I started shaving. Tears began to lubricate my cheeks as the razor passed over them. I couldn't come to grips with this. Everyone said I would be fine, but if this was "fine," I couldn't accept it. I could better understand if I had done something to cause the accident—if I had swerved while trying to reach for a dropped cell phone, or even if I had simply been daydreaming and veered over the center line. But I hadn't. I had done everything I could have reasonably done on that bridge not to be involved in an accident, and it had still happened.

I crawled back into bed and didn't leave for the next two days, avoiding my therapy exercises and visitors. I did not know when, or even if, my physical appearance would improve. To me, this was as good as it was going to get. Since the day I awoke from my medically induced coma, my goal was to return to normal. This was my first sign that reclaiming normal would be as likely as reclaiming virginity. Could I cope with a different appearance, especially one that was considerably less attractive than before?

We are so defined by our appearance. If asked to describe somebody, I would probably start by mentioning their skin or hair color, or maybe how short/tall or thin/thick they were. I would mention what I thought were their defining physical characteristics. I wouldn't initially describe them as intelligent or modest or caring, even if they were very much those things. I could be the greatest person in the world on the inside, but that wouldn't matter to strangers if

I looked like a freak on the outside. Surely I'd frighten others. I was frightening to myself!

Sonja used a video camera to record an interview with me in my bed at Regency shortly after I arrived there. I've shown it to other people to give them a better understanding of where I was at that time in my recovery and to gauge their reaction. Most say, "I can tell it's you, but you're buried deep down inside that body." It's true. In the video, my movements are slow and robotic. My voice comes out in a long, raspy mumble. I'm wrapped in a blanket and prayer shawl given by a local church I've never attended. I stare rather than look. I'm trapped.

When I go back and look at that video and accompanying photos, they hit me especially hard. No doubt I was in much poorer shape prior to that moment. But it was at this time that the mountain of recovery became so apparent, and I had only begun to climb its foothills. I ache, today as then, when I think of that daunting journey.

In retrospect, I am glad that the video was recorded, because it provides a benchmark of how far I've come since that time. The scars on my face and under my chin fade a little each day. Today, the swelling in my face is gone. My jawline and nose are different, but if you hadn't known me before, you wouldn't look twice. I'm no longer Quasimodo, just subtly different. When I watch that video, it's as if I'm looking at the stranger once again, but like my nephews and nieces, I can see Garrett deep inside. It's very creepy, and I get quite emotional each time I view the video. Physically, I've rebounded as far as I can. Today I can look in the mirror, shave and walk away, mostly okay with the result. Would I prefer the old Garrett face? In a heartbeat. Of course, I don't have that option. I can't go back. But there isn't a day that I don't wish I could.

****

As the weeks progressed, so did my therapy. My strength continually improved. I relied less and less on the feeding tube, opting instead for cans of Ensure Plus, better known to me as "senior citizen slurp." In order to stay off the tube completely, I had to drink twelve cans each day. In the hopes of getting out of Regency, I sucked down those cans and actually fooled myself into enjoying such delicious flavors as chocolate, vanilla, strawberry, and butter pecan. It must have worked: Tuesday, September 18, was my last day at Regency. I was headed back to HCMC. This time, there would be little rest. I had major rehabilitative work to do.

In preparation for my move, I was given the opportunity to take a shower. It was the first time I had taken one since the bridge collapse. I'd had to make do with a rag dipped in soapy water once every couple of days. To say I felt grimy would be an understatement.

My favorite nurse, Monte, wheeled me over to the shower room. Monte was one of the few nurses who had worked at Regency for a while. He was a large man with an equally large personality. A self-deprecating jokester, he always kept his patients' needs first. Regency desperately needed to clone him. He repeatedly claimed to be a superior athlete, but based on his physique, I found that improbable—unless the event was competitive eating.

We entered the shower room. It was spacious, covered in tiles. A curtain divided two stalls, and Monte pushed me to the far one. He helped me into a chair made of PVC pipe, turned on the shower, adjusted the temperature, and left me with a bar of soap. Sitting there under the cascade of hot water was the most physically comforting thing I had felt in six weeks. I sat there for a long time, letting the water stream over my bandage-covered incisions. I thought about my journey so far. I tried to figure out which was more daunting, the pain or the waiting. My stay at Knapp would be between one and two weeks, I was told. I avoided thinking about being back at home. I was focused on putting the pedal to the metal at Knapp. I wrote on Caring Bridge on Monday, September 10, 2007,

Today was a really good day. I haven't felt as positive as I did today in probably a week. I accomplished some things…I also have been testing myself, rightly or wrongly. I had to use the commode this morning. Nobody was around and the wheelchair was on the other side of the room. Sure, I could have called the nurse, but I thought, *Darn it, you can do this. It might not be pretty, but you can do this.* So I lowered myself to the floor and scooted myself over to the portable commode, which sat next to an ottoman. I crawled up onto the ottoman and then scooted over onto the pot. When I was finished,

I got down and crawled back over to bed. This was probably not nurse endorsed, but I did it. I proved to myself that it could be done…I'd say that if I can slide across a hospital room to use the crapper then I should be ready for rehab!"

****

THE OLSONS

White Bear Lake residents Brent and Chris Olson joke that they're joined at the hip. So it is no surprise that when the 35W Bridge collapsed on August 1, 2007, they were on it—together. The two fifty-eight-year-olds rarely stray far from one another, so when Brent called his wife that afternoon and asked if she was interested in taking in the Minnesota Twins game that night on the eve of their wedding anniversary, he pretty much already knew the answer. Brent recalls,

> That morning, I golfed with a friend of mine, Dave, who worked at the [Metrodome] fundraising…He was going to be working that night. That afternoon, I went into the office and did some work before giving Chris a call to make sure she wanted to go to the game. I went online, and I bought the tickets and printed them out. I remember that the time printed on the page said 5:01 p.m., August 1.

Brent raced home, and the husband and wife quickly cleaned up and bounded out the door of their residence in a northeast suburb and into Brent's baby, his 1997 Jaguar XJ6. Since they rarely drove into downtown Minneapolis, the Olsons were mildly surprised at the heavy traffic heading south on Interstate 35W into Minnesota's largest city.

As they reached the University Avenue exit, traffic became very slow. "There was construction; we were crawling, bumper-to-bumper," Brent recalled. "I'm going max five miles per hour."

They approached the start of the bridge, and Brent and Chris felt the deck below begin to sway from side to side. Chris said to her husband, "Brent, what is it? Is this an earthquake?" Decades earlier, the couple had experienced a temblor while living in California.

"All of a sudden—*boom!*—it started going," Brent said. "It went really quick, but it's all slow motion in my mind. I could see this thing breaking away. I couldn't see the south side, but did see the main part [the middle section] starting to go."

The bridge was collapsing right before their eyes. It fell in sections, like dominoes headed straight for them. Brent thought there might still be time to act. "I quickly looked over my shoulder to see if I could do a U-turn onto the northbound exit ramp onto University Avenue, but there were concrete barriers blocking the way—we were stuck," he remembered.

The slab of roadway in front of them dropped. "I looked at Chris, held her hand, and said 'I love you.'" They braced, but nothing happened to the concrete beneath them. "I looked in my rearview mirror and I could see that the bridge deck behind us dropped," said Brent. "Talk about the angels working overtime holding us up!"

Wasting little time, the Olsons left their vehicle, fearing their section of roadway was unstable. While their slab, which rested on the embankment short of the river, hadn't moved, the terrain surrounding it was steep and dangerous. They needed to find a way off. Brent walked behind the car to look for an escape route, while Chris headed in the opposite direction. As she surveyed the scene in front of her, a large cloud of dust and debris roiled from below. She was wearing a tank top, and the hot, ashy particles settled on her unprotected face and chest.

"It was hot. I blistered all over," Chris recalled. "It got into my contact lenses. When I went back to the car, I couldn't see anything."

Brent discovered a spot behind the vehicle where they could get down onto the ground, and he returned to the Jaguar, which had escaped major damage, to fetch Chris and lock the car's doors. The duo slid down the steep descent, "getting raspberries on our butt," Brent quipped.

At this point, Brent and Chris encountered other survivors, who asked them what they should do. Brent's succinct advice: "Get off the bridge!" That suggestion was manageable for some, but not all. One man had fled his truck as he saw the bridge folding ahead of him, and got caught up in the collapse.

Because he couldn't walk, Brent and Chris helped carry him off to the side. Brent later went to assist a second survivor.

Roughly ninety seconds had passed since the collapse. Brent and Chris now stood with a few others alongside the remains of the 35W Bridge. Of these survivors, none had come from the roadway ahead of them. The Olsons wondered if any of the people in those vehicles were still alive. (Brent later learned that the people in the cars ahead of his had crossed over the median and escaped onto the northbound side of the interstate, which had remained intact.)

"And then it was quiet. You could have heard a pin drop," said Brent. "There's no car noise. There's no honking horns, engines. There were no birds, nothing. You're looking, saying 'What the hell?'"

The Olsons' view was obstructed. The only thing they could see was the far, southern end of the bridge. The section in front of them had collapsed on a downward slope, crushing train cars on a railway below. (There was worry at the time that the train cars might have been carrying toxic materials, which proved unfounded.)

Ambulances showed up pretty quickly, Brent noted, but of their group of huddled survivors, only the man who couldn't walk needed one. During this time, Brent and Chris met two female nurses and one of the nurses' husbands, who had come to the site to see if they could assist. Chris, also a nurse, wanted to help, as did Brent. Police had told these nurses that a triage was being set up at the American Red Cross building directly across the river. The Olsons accepted the nurses' invitation to carpool there, being unfamiliar with the downtown Minneapolis area. In order to reach the car, the group had to walk from the collapse site to near the Third Avenue Bridge, a distance of roughly nine blocks. They all piled into the car and crossed the Mississippi River into downtown. "All I could think of was we had to get to the Red Cross building to help," Chris recalled. "The fact that we were crossing a bridge didn't really cross my mind."

Immediately after they traversed the river into downtown, they pulled into the lone empty parking spot along West River Parkway, a scenic road that runs along the west bank of the Mississippi. From there, they would need to hoof it to the Red Cross building, as streets heading toward the 35W Bridge were now blocked off. "I'd never seen so much yellow tape in my life," Brent exclaimed. "I didn't know that much existed! It was all over the place."

It took ten more blocks of walking before Brent and Chris reached the steps of the Red Cross building, which sat only one block west of the south entrance to the 35W Bridge. When they arrived, they found a group of children who had been in the school bus when the bridge broke apart. "We talked to some of them to help keep them calm, escorted them to the bathroom," Brent said.

More and more people showed up at the Red Cross's doors to help, so many that a Red Cross worker asked Brent to monitor the entrance and not let anyone in that didn't need to be inside. "I did let some of the parents of the children on the bus in," Brent said. The kids had put together a makeshift list of student names to see if they could account for everybody on the bus. Brent used this list when parents arrived.

Outside, people began to assemble into distinct pools in the parking lots surrounding the Red Cross. In one group were members of law enforcement and government agencies, including police and sheriff's departments from all over the region, the highway patrol, the U.S. Department of Homeland Security, the FBI, even the U.S. Treasury Department. A second group comprised doctors, nurses, and off-duty EMTs. A third group was made up of members of various fire departments. Brent estimated that there must have been about two hundred people who just showed up wanting to help in some way.

One set of volunteers, in particular, stuck out in the Olsons' minds. Two young soldiers showed up in their fatigues carrying their bags. They were combat medics who had just returned that day from Iraq. "Hadn't even gotten home. They came ready to help," said Brent. "Didn't get their names, but I was like, 'Wow. You guys have been through hell; you don't need to go through hell here.' But they didn't bat an eye."

It had now been nearly an hour since the Olsons had arrived at the Red Cross. Though it was supposed to be the triage area, they had yet to encounter other survivors.

"My God, is that it? Are we the only ones to live?" Brent and Chris wondered. Survivor's remorse began to creep into their minds.

"We had no other survivors to talk to," said Chris.

"Finally, word came while we were outside that survivors were being taken directly from the bridge to hospitals," said Brent. "We waited a little bit longer just in case."

As they hung around, rumors started flying that the north side of the bridge was going to collapse further, Brent recalled. The Olsons met another nurse, who lived in a high rise along the river's west bank not far from the Red Cross. She invited them to her apartment, where she had a telescope she used for bird watching. From there, they could get a better look at the north end of the bridge. The trio crossed over I-35W via the Washington Avenue overpass. While doing so, they ran into a Minnesota Public Radio journalist seeking eyewitness reports. She asked Brent and Chris how close they were to the collapse. "Well, we were on it," Brent said sheepishly.

Coincidentally, two friends of the Olsons who work for the U.S. Army Corps of Engineers and had heard about the collapse were watching the news with the volume down and listening to public radio. They recognized Brent and Chris's voices. "That's how they found out we were on the bridge," said Chris.

They reached the nurse's apartment and rushed to the telescope to take a peek at the north side of the bridge. It was still there, though Brent was thrown for a loop when he noticed that an SUV near their vehicle had its emergency flashers engaged. Brent and Chris stayed for a few moments before deciding they needed to reach their original destination: the Hubert H. Humphrey Metrodome. Because their friend Dave, a.k.a. Slick, was manning a concessions booth, they knew if they got there, they had a ride home.

They returned to the Washington Avenue overpass, only to find that, by this time, it was under the control of law enforcement. "We got to the bridge, and now there are cops there who won't let us cross," Brent recalled. "I said, 'Look we were on the bridge and we are just trying to get the hell out of here. If we can get to the Dome we have a ride.' He says, 'No, I can't let you cross.'"

The Olsons needed to find a detour. Dusk was descending upon Minneapolis, and they didn't feel safe.

"I did know that there is the road from the university that goes underneath I-35W and past the Dome," Brent said. "I thought, *Maybe we can get there by walking that route.*" Brent and Chris walked to that road, but quickly realized that there was no sidewalk. It was too unsafe to attempt walking in the road after sunset.

They were then informed of a Hiawatha light rail station at Cedar-Riverside. They headed in that direction, cutting through a parking lot in a part of town known for its high Somali population. "We got a lot of weird looks," Brent noted.

As they approached the light rail station, the train departed like the punch line to a cruel joke. "I go to the platform to see when the next train comes," Brent said. "Not for another twenty minutes. I'm thinking, *Is it really going to come?*"

Not feeling safe standing around waiting, Brent and Chris located a path along the tracks. As they approached the end of this path, a car made a turn and came directly toward them. Frustrated, Brent raised his arms and yelled to the car, "What are you doing?" The emergency lights on the car's roof activated. "Come right through," Brent said graciously as he invited the police squad car to drive past.

Finally, the Olsons reached the entrance of the Metrodome. Naturally, Dave's concession stand was on the far side of the Dome. By the time they reached Dave's booth, it was the bottom of the eighth inning, and the food stand was no longer open. Brent asked for his friend Slick till they found him.

Upon seeing Brent and Chris, Dave uttered, "Oh my God, how close were you?" sensing immediately they were involved somehow with the collapse.

"Well, we need a ride home," Brent answered.

Dave gave them each a beer and a brat. At that moment, a police officer walked in the door and gave Brent an odd look, but didn't say anything. A couple of minutes later, Brent and Chris decided to walk across the concourse and find a place to sit in the stands and rest. Exhaustion quickly began to set in, and Brent asked Chris if she was ready to go. "Yeah," she said.

Dave's vehicle was on the opposite side of the Metrodome. They trudged to his car. As they were walking, Dave noticed a blood spot about the size of a grapefruit on the right shoulder of Brent's shirt. Brent realized it must have come from one of the people he assisted at the collapse site.

Brent and Chris spilled into their home and turned on around-the-clock television coverage to see if anything new had been reported. It didn't take all that long for them to decide to go to bed.

****

Brent and Chris are staunch Catholics, but even the priest was surprised when he saw them sitting in the third row on a Thursday morning at St. Mary of the Lake. They'd decided that they should attend Mass because it was their wedding anniversary and they had much to pray about considering the prior day's events. Not surprisingly, the worship service focused heavily on the I-35W Bridge collapse. Prayers were given for those who perished—the number at that moment was unknown—the survivors, the missing, and the rescuers. The clergyman recounted two stories. A friend of his had crossed the bridge only seconds before it tumbled into a heap of twisted metal. He discussed how it could have been anybody on that span. He also mentioned somebody else who had visited the collapse site to offer assistance.

When Mass ended, Brent and Chris approached the minister.

"What brings you two here today?" the priest asked.

"Well, today is our anniversary," Brent told him.

"Which one?"

"Thirty-eighth. Say, when you were talking about second-hand accounts of the bridge collapse—if you want a first-hand account, you can talk to us," Brent revealed. The man of God's jaw hit the floor.

Brent took the next few days off from work. Prior to the collapse, Brent and Chris had taken daily, mile-long walks along the parkway adjacent to White Bear Lake. Now, they walked in the morning and in the afternoon. "We'd meet people we knew, but didn't tell anybody or say anything about the collapse," Brent said. But, eventually, people began finding out, most likely from pew to pew at church.

It took about three weeks for the Olsons to come in contact with other bridge survivors. They received a letter from Minneapolis Police Department Lieutenant Kim Lund regarding a group of bridge collapse victims that had been formed through Survivor Resources.

At first, Brent and Chris were hesitant about attending. Was it really for them? "We're okay. We didn't get hurt," Brent reasoned.

"Was this just for people who really suffered with the physical and the mental stuff?" Chris wondered. Yet some force pulled them to attend the second meeting of the group.

"There weren't very many people there initially," Brent noted. "Many were still in the hospital, and others hadn't been contacted yet." A few weeks later, the number of attendees ballooned. At one point, as many as forty attended the meetings.

Certain survivors who attended the group session made it known that they didn't think Brent and Chris should be there. Others defended their right to attend the gatherings. Brett reflected,

> After we went to that first meeting and reflected on it, my thought was *I'm not okay* [*and we needed to be there*]. It was wonderful because everybody could open up, spill their guts, bitch, do anything they wanted about the bridge, and nobody is going to judge. These people understand.
>
> I told [Survivor Resources executive director] Margaret McAbee that this group is really great. But at some point, it is going to start winding down. Whether Chris or I need to be here for therapy, as long as this goes on and people are showing up, we're going to come, because it gives somebody else somebody to talk to. This is not a group otherwise.

Brent and Chris also saw a psychologist a couple of times to talk about their feelings about the bridge collapse.

While the Olsons found plenty of support at Survivor Resources, some of their relationship with friends became strained shortly after the tragedy. Chris acknowledged,

> The bridge collapse was everything we talked about for the first two weeks…When I went into work [at Twin Cities Oral Surgery] and talked about it, at first it was news. A couple of weeks later, a group of us friends planned to get together. Something came up about the bridge and they just rolled their eyes. A dear friend even said, "Come on. It's been a couple of weeks. Get over it."

They'd ask, 'How's it going?' or ask about the bridge," Brent said. "I'd start talking, and you could see their eyes glass over. They asked the question, but didn't want to listen."

"That was very hurtful," said Chris.

"So we pulled back big-time," Brent added. "This reinforced that maybe we weren't okay and needed Survivor Resources, because our friends didn't get it, whether they wanted to or didn't want to."

After those incidents, the Olsons pretty much limited their discussions to family, a few trusted friends, and other survivors. "We have to be careful what we say," Chris said. "It's old news and nobody wants to hear about it."

Over time, Brent found that the effects of the bridge collapse were still prevalent, especially with his job as an accountant.

"It was hard to concentrate and get into my work. I really began to notice this in 2008 when I started doing tax returns. I found it difficult to dive in and focus on what I was doing," he said. "I was also working in the house at the time. Chris wasn't working, and there were distractions."

Brent would come out of his home office to get coffee, and Chris would inform him that she had errands to run. "Would you like to go?" Easily distracted, Brent would accept in a heartbeat. "I did get my work done, but it was more difficult," he says.

****

"One hundred ninety people you never knew, but you now have one thing in common."

That's how the Olsons sum up the other survivors of the bridge collapse. The Olsons have grown close to a handful of survivors they've met either through Survivor Resources or through lobbying efforts to pass a state victims' compensation law. They have hosted get-togethers at their home and joined other survivors for dinners at bridge collapse anniversaries.

Brent described the uniqueness of the survivors' situations. "Out of a setting like that—you're not going to become best friends with everybody. Whether a friendship develops or not, it isn't anything you can set out to accomplish. It's just something that happens."

Brent and Chris got to know fellow bridge survivor and Texan Omar Abuabara well. The three traveled separately to Washington, D.C., in November 2008 to hear firsthand the findings of the National Transportation Safety Board on the causes of the bridge collapse. To save money, the three of them shared a hotel room. "We hit it off with Omar really well," said Brent.

Brent also spoke briefly at the ceremony on the first anniversary of the bridge collapse and mentioned the camaraderie that had developed among survivors. Brent's words were brief and to the point: "I wish I had never met you—under these circumstances. But I'm happy that I have."

To further illustrate the bond, Brent brought up a point made by filmmaker Dan Kenney, who created the 35W Bridge collapse documentary "One Day in August." At a lunch following the film's second public showing on August 1, 2010, Dan mentioned that collapse survivors were a lot like war buddies.

"I guess that's what war buddies are," said Brent. "People you randomly meet, who you may never see again, and a traumatic event brought you together."

A 35W Bridge memorial will stand along the Mississippi River in downtown Minneapolis come August 2011. For the man whose license plate reads "35W-C27"—the designation sprayed in orange paint on the Olsons' car by authorities who found it amid the rubble—it will be a welcome sight. Said Brent,

> There should be a memorial, but not just a place for survivors or victims' families. So many people in the city were affected. The thousands who had their commutes rerouted. The gawkers who came for months to look at the site. It burns a memory into their brain, too. They weren't part of it, but they were, in a sense. We need a spot where people can meet and think about that day.

Brent and Chris both said that the collapse didn't lessen or strengthen their faith, but it did reaffirm it. "Special things have happened as a result of this tragedy," said Brent. "We've made good friends. With every bad thing, there is some good that comes from it. And I'm glad that they're paying more attention to bridges, and that's huge. And it's not just the survivors but the whole public. My cousin lives in Las Vegas, not a lot of bridges there. But when she crosses over a dry riverbed she shakes her head: 'This shouldn't ever happen.'"

For personal reasons, Brent and Chris decided not to participate in the consortium lawsuit against URS, the bridge inspector, but when it was announced that a press conference regarding a settlement would be held on August 23, 2010, at the law offices of Robins, Kaplan, Miller and Ciresi, Brent decided to attend because the process and results were important to both him and his wife.

"I felt I needed to be there," said Brent. "I listened and cried as the survivors recounted how their lives have been forever changed."

Of special note to Brent was the fact that the attorneys at the Robins, Kaplan, Miller and Ciresi firm decided to donate the $1.5 million they were to receive from the settlement to cover costs incurred throughout the three-year process to the 35W Bridge memorial. The attorneys had also worked pro bono for their bridge clients during that time.

"God bless them all," Brent exclaimed.

On the morning of the third anniversary of the bridge collapse, Brent and Chris decided to reclaim a small part of their lives. They hopped into the Jaguar intent on finishing the trip that was cut short that day in 2007.

"I held back just ahead of the group of cars behind me, allowing more distance between the cars ahead of me," Brent said, making sure that nothing would prevent him from driving over the span on his own terms. "If a cop had wanted to give me a speeding ticket, he would've never caught me," said Brent with a laugh. "It was tense, in a sense. Afterward, it was a relief."

"It felt good to be able to take it back," Chris recalled, admitting that she cried as the Jaguar sped across the span.

The couple joined at the hip continues on, like two youngsters in a three-legged potato sack race. And while they were already close, the tragedy brought them closer. Neither can imagine having been on that bridge alone.

"Initially, I would have said that it would have been better if Chris hadn't been there, because then she wouldn't have had to go through it. But I think it was good in the sense that I can relate to her emotions and she can relate to mine," Brent said. "One can empathize, but if you weren't on it, you weren't on it. We know how each other feels."

5

MY JOURNEY HAD ENTERED ITS SEVENTH WEEK. It was my first day at Knapp Rehabilitation Center, and as during my arrival at Regency, there was a mound of paperwork and countless examinations to tend to first. While this phase of recovery would prove to be the most physically and mentally exhausting, it was also the most exciting.

Though I still had the stomach tube protruding from my midsection, I no longer used it. I was sucking down cans of Ensure Plus like Popeye consumed spinach. My jaw was about to be snipped loose, and I was looking forward to that more than anything. I had more energy—maybe it was because I was getting stronger, or perhaps it was pure adrenaline. I think it was likely both.

Knapp was a private section of HCMC, with a security door that required patients to be buzzed in and out. I later heard stories that the doors were there to stop AWOL patients from escaping. I felt a tad uneasy about entering a place from which people tried to escape, but I put that out of my mind. This was the final stage before going home, and home was all I could think of.

The ambulance drivers rolled my gurney through the doors and into my room. It was situated right next to the nurses' desk, so in addition to my button, I could raise my voice if I needed anything. On the wall was a giant dry-erase board with the weekly schedule written in marker. The days were filled with activities, unlike at Regency. Other than the sixty-minute lunch, most of the hour-long blocks of time were filled with physical therapy (twice a day), occupational therapy, recreational therapy, cognitive testing, etc. Any napping would have to wait until after supper.

My nurse on most days was Janet. Janet was middle-aged, tall and slender, with straight, dishwater-blond hair. She had an accent that was South African or perhaps Australian—I couldn't quite make it out. She was as strict as Monte was tubby. If I needed anything, I was to ring her. Of course, I wanted to do everything on my own. At Regency, if I wanted to go to the bathroom, I'd sit up in bed, reach for the walker, and hop the ten feet it took to reach the portable toilet. The first time Janet caught me heading to the bathroom on my own, she read me the riot act. If I wanted to get the blanket draped on the chair across the room, I was supposed to ring Janet. If I wanted to go brush my teeth, I had to ring Janet. If I wanted to inhale, exhale, and repeat, I had to ring Janet. I learned to wait until I knew Janet was busy with other patients or was on her break before I tried to do anything. I wasn't about to let this not-so-merry Poppins slow me down, even if she was following protocol and I wasn't.

My first full day of therapy was Wednesday, September 19. Not surprisingly, Mom wanted to attend each and every session with me. The first stop was to see a doctor and participate in some mind puzzles to determine whether I had any lasting problems with cognition. The first exercise was to repeat an ever-growing series of numbers. I did just fine until the string of numbers surpassed ten. Ten numbers are used in phone numbers, so that wasn't difficult, but throw in several more, and I simply couldn't do it. I feared the doctor would think this was the result of brain damage, even though I knew that I had never been good at remembering long lists. The next exercise involved a series of drawings. In each drawing, something was either missing or awry. For example, the drawing could be that of a boy on a bicycle, except that the bicycle was missing a chain. It was my job to identify that the bicycle had no chain. I breezed through that. The exercise seemed rather elementary to me, and as I quickly pointed out the error, I'd give my mom a raised eyebrow, signaling, *You've got to be kidding me. Were these tests made for five-year-olds?* Lastly,

I was shown a complex drawing that contained many different shapes. I was asked to look at it for about thirty seconds. Then the drawing was taken away and I was given a piece of paper and a pencil and told to re-create what I had just seen. I did fairly well on that also. Leaving that doctor's office, I felt confident that I would pass this section of therapy with flying colors.

Next came recreational therapy. This was really nothing more than a lecture on the dangers of drinking. The doctor was a guy a few years younger than my mom, who swore like a sailor. He used the scare tactics employed by high school drivers' ed teachers: do this and you will die! Drinking, he told me, would cause seizures. He advised that I not drink for a year, or better yet, ever. I think it came out as, "If you get goddamn hammered, it will fuck up your brain and you will fucking die." I felt he must be a hypocrite; no guy who cursed this much could be completely sober all of the time.

Physical therapy was a different story. It took place in a large gym filled with mats, ropes, horizontal bars, and other pieces of equipment meant to get patients back on their feet. I had physical therapy twice a day, and it didn't vary much. I think the main purpose was to build stamina. My therapist's favorite activity was to make me lap the gym with my walker, concentrating on keeping my left foot off the ground with each hop-step. It was exhausting, as each lap took a couple of minutes to complete. I started with a half lap, but within a few days had rolled my way up to three laps.

Occupational therapy mattered most. In order to go home, I had to be able to do certain things. I had to be able to cook myself a meal. I had to be able to enter and exit the shower safely. I had to be able to go up and down stairs. I had to be able to get in and out of a vehicle. I learned to do these things there. Knapp was fully equipped to teach these tasks. "Easy Street" was a section of the building that therapists used to help patients learn. It included an actual vehicle (coincidentally parked in front of a mural of a bridge) that I practiced getting in and out of. There was also a replica of a grocery store. In another section, a real kitchen provided the setting for my final exam, where I had to heat a can of soup on the stove. To most, this would be a simple task, but it sapped my energy completely. I wasn't used to standing for fifteen minutes straight, or reaching or bending over. I had to learn to make sure the pot handle wasn't in a position where I could easily knock the hot soup onto me or the floor, and I had to remember to turn off the stove. I successfully cooked my soup, but was too tired to wash the dishes. The therapist didn't seem to mind, and besides, I had a dishwasher in the apartment.

By the end of that day, I was sore and ready to sleep.

****

On my first full day of therapy, September 19, 2007, I wrote on CaringBridge,

The sounds don't go away for many of those who were on or near the 35W Bridge when it collapsed. The crushing thunder of concrete and steel, the shrieks for help from those pinned under debris or sinking into the muddy soup of the Mississippi River. Many victims were unscathed or minimally injured, but the sounds continue to haunt. I can't begin to imagine what they are going through, even though I was right there in the middle of it. My mind went black the instant I had impact. I didn't hear the wailing sirens, I didn't hear the cries of distress. I didn't see the plume of smoke and dust.

In that respect, I feel lucky that I don't remember anything after the bridge gave way and I started my plummet. I'm sure many will have to receive counseling to help untether them from all that happened that rush hour evening of August 1.

As I hop along on my walker, panting and sweating after one hundred feet of dragging my recovering body from here to there, I can't help but feel blessed. That I'm alive. That I'm here. And that I'm loved by a God who saves, and family and friends who buoy me through this.

****

"She's eating lunch in the dining area down the hall," Mom said to me in a hurry-up-and-go manner. It was my second day at Knapp.

I had met many people along my journey thus far, but there was one person I had heard much about that I had yet to meet. Paula Coulter was, like me, one of the more severely injured survivors, and also a patient at Knapp. I had met Paula's husband, Brad, and two daughters, Brianna and Brandi, a month earlier. My family had gotten to know their extended family during their long hours in the hospital waiting room, while both Paula and I were in ICU.

This family became the face of the bridge collapse victims, whether they wanted to be or not. The four of them were driving northbound and were almost off the bridge when it collapsed. Their van tumbled down an earthen embankment. Brad and the girls suffered back injuries and other injuries. Paula's fate was much worse. She suffered major injuries to her head, torso, and hips. As in my case, doctors feared Paula wouldn't survive, or that she would suffer permanent brain injury.

I really wanted to meet Paula. I felt she was the one person who could truly understand all that I had gone through. She knew what it was like to be chained to a hospital bed, to worry if she would ever regain her preaccident appearance, her mind, her life. She knew what it was like to be pumped with medications and poked endlessly with needles, like a lab rat. Paula knew how desperately I wanted to go home, close my eyes, open them up, and have the past two months erased. Can't we just go back and have a do-over? Take a different route to our destination?

I hopped into my wheelchair—without Janet's aid—and rolled myself to the dining area at the end of the hall. It was a large, open room with floor-to-ceiling windows overlooking the Metrodome. There was only one other person there: Paula. I rolled closer. She was seated in a wheelchair and had just finished her meal. She stared at her food tray as if she didn't really know where she was or what she was doing. Because she'd had surgery on her skull, doctors had chopped her hair down to a butch cut.

"Hi, Paula," I said. "My name is Garrett. I was on the bridge, too. I met your family. They're really nice people."

Paula turned to look at me, but her expression didn't change. She muttered, excusing herself I assumed, and rolled away down the hall. I wondered if Mom had mistaken this woman for Paula.

I sat there in my own wheelchair, disappointed. I'd expected a smile from her, some sign of relief in recognizing a comrade. Perhaps I'd expected too much. After meeting Paula that first time, I held out little hope that she would regain her normal mental faculties. Paula was buried somewhere deep inside of her wrecked body, too. I just feared that nobody would ever find her again. I feared that Paula would never find Paula again.

****

My relationship with Janet was love/hate, but she became my new best friend whenever she uttered a certain phrase: "day pass." I was given clearance to spend that next Saturday at home in my apartment in Minnetonka. I hadn't been outside of a hospital—other than in an ambulance—in nearly two months. Home! Words could not express my joy. Home felt normal. Home felt comfortable. I was headed home.

While Mom filled out the paperwork, a visitor came to my door. He was a teenage boy who happened to be a long-term patient at Knapp. He started asking me questions as if he was Geraldo Rivera. "How did you get a day pass?" he demanded. "How come you get to leave?" I didn't have the answers. All I knew was that I was going. He grew increasingly irritated. When Mom returned, he blurted, "Why does he get to leave?" Mom slid a few steps over and got a nurse's attention. The boy was retrieved.

"So that's why the main doors were locked," I said to her afterward.

Darin cleaned the apartment in anticipation of my arrival. It was late Saturday morning, and Mom and Sonja rolled me down HCMC's labyrinthine corridors to the parking ramp. A series of twists, turns, and hobbles was required for me to get into the backseat of Sonja's Saturn Vue, but I wasn't going to let that stop me from going home. We pulled out of the ramp, and the bright sun hit the windshield. It was an abnormally warm, windy, late-September day. I stared out the back window. Scenery whizzed by surreally. For whatever reason, the bridge collapse wasn't on my mind, even though being in a moving vehicle should have triggered my fear. I thought about time, how so much of it had passed as I'd lain still. I made a point of ignoring the overpasses and underpasses as we traveled. I was simply happy to be moving again.

We pulled into the apartment building's parking lot. Sonja pulled the wheelchair out of the car, and Mom assembled the foot pedals. I twisted, turned, and hobbled into the chair, and we made our way up to the fourth floor.

The two-bedroom, two-bath apartment looked just as I remembered it, except that my roommate, Darin, had moved some bedroom furniture to make it wheelchair accessible. I switched from my wheelchair to my walker to survey my surroundings. My last stop was the couch. I plopped myself down. Hot air blew in from the open windows. I felt the need to do something normal.

"Sonja, can you get my guitar?" I asked. Sonja brought the instrument over to me. I had purchased the guitar a year and a half earlier and had taught myself a few basic chords, enough to play some of my favorite songs. The guitar felt unfamiliar in my hands. I quickly discovered that I couldn't rotate my left wrist enough to properly press the strings on the neck. I attempted a few chords, but failed to play cleanly. Disappointed, I set the guitar down and turned my attention to the college football game on the television. This, too, proved unsatisfying. I had watched enough TV in the hospital, so I decided to take a nap. Mom pitched a blanket over me, and I slept while Mom, Sonja, and Darin sat around and talked about what needed to be done before I returned home for good.

Technically, my day pass allowed me to stay away from the hospital until the evening. Team Garrett fully expected that I would use up every last second, but when I awoke in the late afternoon, I asked if they could take me back. Just as with my introduction to Paula, my expectations didn't match up with reality. Home did not feel normal. Home was not comfortable. I didn't want to be home if I couldn't remain there permanently and reclaim those feelings. Little did I know that "normal" was being redefined.

****

I learned on Friday, September 21—the day before I'd used my pass— that on the following Monday, all of my therapists and doctors from Knapp, as well as Dr. Herrera, would meet with my family and me to discuss my possible discharge. I was optimistic that their decision would be favorable, but tried not to get excited.

Even with the meeting, I was still scheduled for all of my various therapy sessions on Monday. The morning began with physical therapy in the gym. When I got there, I saw a familiar face. Paula was on one of the mats with a therapist. They were working on her flexibility. As the therapist gently rotated her legs, Paula winced and moaned. After that, the therapist brought Paula over to the parallel bars so she could work on standing and sitting. My therapist instructed me to begin my laps with my walker, and as I neared where she was standing, I received a surprising greeting.

"Good morning, Garrett," said Paula. Her voice had inflection, a marked change from our last encounter.

"Hi, Paula," I replied. "You're looking better. Keep it up, and we'll soon be having races with our walkers!"

I continued on. I'd see her once more before I left Knapp for good.

After therapy, I went to the meeting. It was in a small room, and the chairs were arranged in a circle, as if for an intervention. Nearly a dozen physicians, nurses, and therapists attended. One by one, they gave glowing accounts of my progress. My cognitive tests were normal, my physical stamina was excellent, and I was able to cook and clean myself as long as I was careful and didn't rush things.

The doctors asked me what I thought. I had mentally prepared for this moment. My speech went something like this: "I want to thank you all for your help in getting me to where I am today. I never expected to get this far this fast, and that's a testament to you. I really feel like I'm ready to go home."

I didn't tell them that I had been feeling that way for the past six weeks. I just said, "I want to go, so that somebody else who really needs your help can have my bed."

It turned out that there was no waiting list at that moment, so the bed was a moot point. But the doctors agreed. There wasn't much more that they could do for me. Well, there was one more thing.

I returned to my room. My afternoon therapy sessions were cancelled. Mom began filling out the discharge paperwork. I was ready to go, except that I still had a rubber hose sticking out of my belly. My stomach feeding tube had to be removed before I could leave. I had assumed that I'd be put under, but that wasn't the case. Dr. Herrera walked through my door and put on a pair of latex gloves.

"I'm going to remove your feeding tube," he said in his heavy Hispanic accent.

"What does that mean?" I asked, with a hint of panic in my voice.

"Well, there is a tiny inflated balloon at the end of the tube inside your stomach. I'm going to deflate it. Then I'm going to count to three, and then I'm going to pull."

"Um, is this going to hurt?"

"My guess is that it shouldn't be that bad."

"Your guess?" I asked, growing increasingly anxious. "Have you ever done this before?"

"Well, not exactly," said Dr. Herrera. "But I've done similar procedures."

"Uh-huh."

When Dr. Herrera said "pull," he actually meant "yank." He counted to three and yanked as hard as he could. "Ack!" I yelled. The tube came out partway.

"One more time," he said.

Dr. Herrera put all of his weight into it, and the tube sprang loose. I felt an intense, warm pain, as if I had been shot. The doctor gave me a hand towel filled with ice cubes to numb the pain.

"Aren't you going to sew me up?" I asked.

"Nope. That hole will close up by itself in a matter of minutes," he said as he made his way out the door. The pain gradually subsided.

When it was time to leave, Mom grabbed her camera and documented the entire event as if she were the paparazzi and I was Celine Dion leaving a high-end shoe store. Rolling out of the room, leaving Knapp, exiting HCMC, and rolling down the parking ramp to the car—we have a scrapbook's worth of such images.

The quickness of my hospital release surprised me. I'd chafed for freedom for seven weeks before rehab, even cried with homesickness, but rehab itself had seemed to end as quickly as it started. In a weird sense, I felt cheated that I couldn't take the time to savor the experience when I was physically and mentally most able to do so. On the other hand, I was going home, and Dorothy, with her ruby slippers firmly planted in Oz, was right about home.

****

The day of my discharge, September 24, 2007, I wrote on CaringBridge,

> Greetings from—home!
>
> Yes, oh yes, I came home from the hospital this afternoon following a "care conference" with all of my doctors and therapists at Knapp. They said that cognitively I was doing excellent, and physically and medically I was ready for the big move. They took me off all my medicines except for a few minor ones. They also removed the feeding tube from my stomach (yeowch!), so I'm now officially not connected to any tubes. Yes, it has been a very good day.
>
> So what's next? Obviously, this journey is far from over. I have to put on special boots every time I get out of bed. I use a platform walker that allows me to hop on one leg to get from here to there (it's incredibly tiring to do). I use a wheelchair. It will take time to get used to life at a slower pace for a while. In a month, I have an appointment with the orthopedic surgeon, who will likely then allow me to bear weight on my left side. From there, I'll be walking again and will feel normal. A new "normal," but normal nonetheless. I'm alive and loving it.

****

6

"I'M GOING TO FIND YOU A DATE," I told Darin as we sat in his vehicle and drove the two miles from our apartment to the local Target store.

My best friend and roommate chuckled.

"C'mon, I think we can use this whole wheelchair thing to your advantage. Think about it," I said, trying to get a rise out of him. "When women see you pushing around a wheelchair-bound person, not to mention a 35W Bridge victim, they'll melt like marshmallows in a campfire. You'd be like the single guy walking the cute little puppy. It's a chick magnet!"

Darin laughed as if he hoped I wasn't actually serious. He pulled into the Target parking lot and rolled me inside. The discount mega-retailer was in full Halloween mode. We spun up and down the aisles, checking out the holiday costumes and decorations. I was still in no shape physically to join in any spooky celebrations, but at least I could get in the spirit. We continued on down the main aisle, and I spotted an attractive young woman ahead of us. As we came up alongside her, I stomped down with my good right foot abruptly. Darin, pushing the wheelchair, ran into the back of my seat and let out an "ungh!" The woman turned around to see what the commotion was all about. I giggled.

"Knock it off," he said. I laughed even harder.

It felt so good to be out and about, even on a shopping trip. I'd developed severe cabin fever in the two weeks I'd been home. Darin and I found ways to kill time, as he'd lost his job as general manager of Applebee's while I was in the hospital. His bad luck was my gain, because he generously became my at-home nurse (or gofer), and that allowed my mom to return to her teaching job in New Ulm.

When I first came home, much of my time was spent in bed sleeping. More than half a dozen surgeries and two months in a hospital pretty much saps all your strength and stamina. I couldn't do anything substantial. Even a simple shower was so strenuous that I would have to lie down afterward. I napped throughout the days.

The slippery shower stall was probably the most dangerous place in my apartment. I didn't have doctors' permission to bear weight on my left foot or left arm, and I was so weak that I feared slipping. At least the apartment complex's maintenance worker had installed metal grab bars, so that I had something to hold onto and lean against as I literally hopped in and out of the shower.

I recall the first time the new me tried taking a shower in my apartment. My mom was there and offered assistance. My instinct was to refuse; talk about embarrassing! But in the end, dealing with my pajamas and bandages (I still had the incision on my stomach protected with surgical tape) was such a hassle that I called Mom in. She helped get me undressed as I sat on the toilet seat for better support. Once my clothes were off, I stood up with my walker and moved toward the glass shower door. A shower chair had been placed inside. In order to get in, I had to back up with my walker, do a half pivot, hop, and grab the metal bar with my right hand—all without tripping on the chair and falling. This trick seemed like something out of Tony Hawk's book of skateboarding stunts. Halfway through my first attempt, I aborted. Mom saw my plight and held my arm as I tried again. This time I made it.

I was breathing heavily. *If it's this hard to take a shower, how will I ever do anything outside these apartment walls?* I thought as I soaped myself up, inspecting my bandages and incisions. The adage "that dog won't hunt" popped into my head, a saying I hadn't heard until I had moved to Virginia years earlier. This dog couldn't even stand. Maybe it was time for Mom to just take Old Yeller behind the building and end all the trouble.

Home life was one big, difficult adjustment. My apartment gave me a false sense of normalcy; I felt that I could just pick up where I'd left off. Yet attempting even the most basic tasks thrust me into the reality of my present situation.

Relearning to eat solid foods was also frustrating. When a jaw is wired shut for nearly two months, it forgets how to open wide. Eating something as thick as a cheeseburger became a tedious affair. I'd have to pry the buns off and eat it in pieces. Usually, I'd just opt for soup or scrambled eggs—soft foods that didn't require opening my mouth very far. Another issue was timing. Eating involves two parts: chewing and swallowing. Done precisely, they result in harmony and satiation. Done incorrectly, they result in spitting up and gasping for air. There was a time when more food hit the carpet than the pit of my stomach.

And then there was the drooling, which was also a side effect of my wired shut jaw. Now that I was home, with an unwired jaw, I had assumed the problem would correct itself. However, the surgeries to my jaw and mouth left my lower lip and chin quite numb. The drooling continued, as I could not feel the sensation of liquid on my bottom lip. Therefore, I had to keep my head tilted back slightly. If I ever tilted just slightly forward, it would unleash a tsunami that usually ended up in my crotch, soaking my pajama bottoms. I quickly learned to always carry a wad of paper towels with me, lest I appear to have wet myself. Over time, the numbness and drooling lessened, thankfully.

Getting around with my walker also proved difficult. The apartment was small, stuffed with couches, two chairs, and two tables. I drove my walker into furniture, corners, the fish aquarium, you name it. Additionally, the apartment had a thick carpet. It was like trying to ride a ten-speed through tall weeds.

Getting out of the apartment was also slow and difficult. One time, I ordered a pizza. After the delivery guy buzzed the intercom, it took me five minutes to get into my wheelchair, roll myself down the long, fourth-floor hallway, take the elevator to the first floor, and roll down the hall to the front door. The guy was completely annoyed; I made sure to tip him well. When I got back to the apartment, I feigned enjoyment while eating my now-lukewarm pizza.

Though disappointed and frustrated, I knew deep inside that I had the ability to move forward. Practice and continued healing would speed my progress. Soon, the walker and wheelchair would be replaced by an aqua-colored scooter. It looked like a three-wheeler with a platform. I rested my bent left knee on it and strode with my right leg. It worked well, except for its tendency to veer to the right. But I only had to deal with it for a few weeks. On the day before Thanksgiving, I was given the okay to start walking on my own. Like everything else, it was slow and awkward. I had an exaggerated limp. I kept running into things because I stared at my feet when I walked, being extra careful not to slip. Twisting my ankle would be hellishly painful.

The next step was attending weekly physical therapy at a sports medicine clinic in Minnetonka to help correct my limp and my lack of stability. Surely, part of my impaired balance was due to my busted ankles. Perhaps the traumatic brain injury I sustained was another factor. In any event, with the help of my therapist, I practiced walking heel to toe, walking backward, standing one-legged on phonebooks, and so forth.

In conjunction with the physical therapy, I had begun working out at a local chain fitness center. I spent countless hours standing on one leg to improve my balance, performing sit-ups to strengthen my once-sliced-open abdominal muscles, lifting dumbbells to restore power to my left arm. I also spent a lot of time in the swimming pool, where I could stretch and kick without fear of falling down. Over time, my strength and agility grew substantially, though never to preaccident levels.

While the physical therapy and workouts helped, I continued to experience soreness and frequent headaches. Kristen, my rehab consultant, suggested I visit a massage therapist. I was reluctant to do so at first. To me, massages were for well-to-do women who had time to pamper their bodies. Getting a rubdown while listening to CDs of babbling brooks and pan flutes wasn't my idea of working toward recovery. However, nothing really seemed to be helping my headaches, and I knew that they were due to muscle tension. I gave in and made an appointment.

Picture this: totally naive guy walks into upscale, suburban spa. Asian music plays softly in the background. Middle-aged women lounge around in white terrycloth robes and sandals, reading magazines and sipping tea. I'm the only person there with a penis. I approach the woman behind the desk. Surprise! She's middle-aged too.

"Hi. I'm here for a massage." *You know, the kind where I don't end up in jail because of a police sting?* I added mentally.

"Your name?"

I wanted to give a fake one, I really did. But workers' compensation was paying for this.

"Um, Garrett." As if I couldn't remember my real name. "This is my first time getting a massage. Ever," I stated, hoping she'd get the hint and tell me precisely what I needed to do and expect.

"Great!" she said, smiling broadly. I couldn't tell if it was genuine or sarcastic. "Take this robe and slippers and go into room three on the left. Put them on and lie down on the table. Jane will be with you shortly."

I did as instructed, but once I entered the room, I started to panic. *How many clothes, if any, am I supposed to take off?* I thought to myself. *I have no idea!*

I tried to deduce the answer. *Well, they gave me a robe, so I'm assuming some clothing has to come off. I guess it's safe to take off my shirt. But then they'll see all of my scars. Crap. I'll have to explain those, and then we'll get into a long discussion about the bridge, which will eat up my massage time. And what about my jeans and underwear? If I go nude and that's not policy, this Jane person will freak out, and I'll get kicked out or arrested! I'd better play it safe.*

I removed my shirt but kept everything on below the equator. I lay down, wrapped in my robe, and waited for Jane. I wondered what she'd look like. Maybe she was my age. Maybe she was younger. Maybe she was a University of Minnesota sorority girl who gave massages when she wasn't discovering herself on campus. There was a knock on the door, and in walked a woman who looked like she should be working the voter registration table at the local elementary school. With hands like George Foreman. Sigh.

What Jane lacked in youthful beauty, she made up for with her grip. Jane worked my shoulders like she was kneading dough. It felt sooo good. The soreness seemed to melt out of me. I swore Jane must have been a weightlifter for the 1972 East German Olympic Team.

Her hands continued to migrate down my back to my waist. "You know, some people find they store a lot of tension in their gluteus maximus," Jane stated as she ground her palms into my lower back. I'm pretty sure I didn't pay for that, nor did the woman at the counter tell me that Jane put the "ass" in "massage."

"Oooh! I didn't know that," I grunted. She finished my backside and asked me to turn over. I complied. I noticed that Jane saw the scars on my chest, stomach, neck, and arm.

"I was in an accident," I blurted out, even before Jane could ask, not that she would have. "That's why I'm here. There's a lot of soreness and tension that I think needs to be worked out of my body."

"You're correct," Jane said. "I'm going to start by rubbing your temples and sinuses. These are points where tension can hide." She began contorting my face with her Goliathan hands. I felt painful stings when she pressed on certain points, not because of stress or tension, but due to the metal hardware and craggy bone beneath my skin. My face had been rebuilt in August with an assortment of stainless steel plates, screws, and other pieces. The bone became uneven in areas where it had fused and regrown. Before, my facial bones were smooth; now, they were jagged and asymmetrical. I clenched my jaw and lay still until she was done. When that was finished, she moved to my shoulders and down each arm, twisting and kneading. I wouldn't mind having my arm twisted in this manner every day.

The time seemed to fly by, and before I knew, it my session had come to an end.

"I hope you come back and see us again," said Jane as she assisted in sitting me up.

"Thanks," I replied. "That felt really good. I had my doubts at first, but you made me a believer."

"You're welcome, Garrett." She paused. "Oh, and one other thing. Next time—lose the jeans. It's difficult to rub your lower back if I can't get to your waist."

I had my answer.

****

When I left Knapp in September, only one other 35W Bridge collapse survivor had yet to go home: Paula had more work to do at the Courage Center in Golden Valley. Though she had done well at Knapp, her body just wasn't ready for life outside of a medical facility. Her mobility, flexibility, and stamina needed to improve. She had an estimated timeline for recovery, but really had no idea when she would be able to return home.

I followed Paula's recovery religiously through her CaringBridge page, and I kept up with a few other collapse survivors I had gotten to know. While my own site had received tens of thousands of hits, Paula's count was in the hundreds of thousands. Was I envious? No. Well, maybe a little. But I understood; Paula's mountain was a bit taller than mine. Naturally, a bit more attention was paid to it.

I really wanted to visit Paula, and so my mom contacted one of Paula's sisters (they had exchanged e-mail addresses while getting to know one another during my time in ICU). Mom planned to come up to the Twin Cities the following weekend to take me to Courage Center in Golden Valley.

The day arrived. Thanksgiving hadn't arrived yet, and I still used my wheelchair to venture outdoors. Autumn leaves had already fallen, and leaden, gray clouds filled the skies. My stomach was strangely unsettled; was I nervous to see Paula? While I had felt a kinship with her, we hadn't really spoken to one another except for a passing hello. Would she be happy to see me? Or would she resent my faster recovery?

We entered the foyer, expecting to find a reception desk, but there was none. We'd have to find Paula on our own. Mom rolled me into the elevator and we went up one floor. We got out, meandered down a hallway, and hooked a left. There, Mom found a nurses' station and asked for directions. We made our way to Paula's room, but when we poked our heads in, she was nowhere to be found.

We heard sounds coming from a nearby waiting area. There, members of Paula's family were sitting, as youngsters ran circles around them. Apparently, Paula was in a therapy session. So Mom wheeled me to the table and grabbed a chair of her own, and we all talked. Mom and I provided a medical update from my end. In a couple of weeks, I'd consult with an orthodontist about my misaligned teeth. I feared I'd have to get braces (and this was later confirmed). I also had recently visited the doctor who had performed my colon surgery. He said everything looked good on that end and declared the surgery a success. And in a few weeks, I'd be walking again. While my physical recovery was far from over, I hadn't hit any bumps in the road or regressed. That, according to many, was the biggest miracle I had been given.

For Paula, the outlook remained positive, but there seemed to be more and more setbacks. Paula's mobility was being hindered by calcium growths in her hips, brought about by her lack of mobility early on in her recovery. Her bladder wasn't working correctly, and she was experiencing considerable back pain as well.

I could see it in her family's eyes—that same helpless exhaustion my mother felt. And like zombies, like Mom, they kept trudging forward, because there was no other direction to go. They relied on each other for encouragement and support. There was no doubt in my mind that they wanted to scream, "This is not fair!" but they kept it inside. It's as if they and we were cut from the same cloth.

When Paula returned, making her way down the hall with her walker, we clapped and cheered. Her pace was slow but deliberate. A nurse held a belt around Paula, a safety precaution just in case she lost her balance—something I wore many times during my therapy sessions as well. I could tell she was slightly embarrassed by all of the attention. "No big deal. I'm just walking," was what I could read from her face. But it was a big deal. It was a big deal to me. A few months ago, I'd seen her fighting through the pain to do a basic move like sitting up. She'd come a long way already.

I had hoped to have a deep, philosophical discussion with Paula, but all of the commotion and the throng of visitors prevented that. That was okay—I figured I'd get my chance to talk to her more at a later date. As Mom and I moved toward the exit, we passed other residents of Courage Center who had obviously suffered permanent brain injuries. They had huddled in front of a TV in one of the building's common areas. Their minds seemed to be like old, dying versions of the boob tube they were watching. There was a clear picture trying to fill the screen, but it couldn't overcome the distortion. What had happened to them? And why had I been spared a similar fate, been so lucky during my most unlucky moment? Inside, I too wanted to scream, "This is not fair!"

****

THE COULTERS

What was supposed to be a night of celebration turned into a life-changing evening for Brad Coulter, his wife, Paula, and their two daughters, Brianna and Brandi. The family's intention was to gather with relatives at Joe Senser's in Roseville to celebrate their oldest daughter Brianna's matriculation at Winona State University on a soccer scholarship.

By 5 p.m., Paula, Brianna, and Brandi had already packed in a full day. Paula, forty-three, had taken the day off from her accounting job at Mentor Network. She began her day with a five-mile walk/run and visited with her neighbors at the end of the driveway. (The neighborhood gossip? Somebody had gotten a new puppy. Paula, who owned two pugs, could easily relate.) After cleaning up, Paula and her daughters headed to the Southdale shopping center in Edina for lunch at P. F. Chang's, followed by a family favorite: shopping at the Mall of America, a few miles east in Bloomington.

Brad, forty five, finished his workday as a database administrator for Jostens in Edina and commuted home to meet the others for the family rendezvous in Roseville. The four piled into the Honda Odyssey. Brad took the wheel, with Brianna beside him, while Paula and Brandi sat in the back. Paula reminded Brianna to buckle up as Brandi pulled out her cell phone and began texting, the sport of teenagers.

The Coulters planned to meet Paula's two sisters and their families at 6 p.m. Brianna's cousin Tyler was also heading off to college, in Rochester. With the two kids leaving the nest, it was a time of excitement. Paula felt lucky to have such a tight connection with her nearby sisters and their families.

"Brianna was excited, but I was excited too," Paula recounted. "Brad and I felt [soccer] would give her an outside commitment from the academic side, so she would have some structure and keep her on task for what her plans would be after school."

It was apparent that Brad and Paula put education first, even with two daughters who had found great success as athletes. Even so, soccer played a prominent role in the family's life. The next morning, the crew had planned to leave for Muscatine, Iowa, for one of Brandi's soccer tournaments. They would never get there.

As they left for Roseville, the Coulters phoned to let the others know they would probably be a little late, since traffic was heavy. The trip was a familiar one for the Coulters. The girls often participated in tournaments at the National Sports Center in Blaine, the mecca for Twin Cities soccer. "We spent a lot of our summertime going that route," said Brad, who on that August day was just one month shy of celebrating his twenty-second anniversary with Paula.

And so they headed up Interstate 35W, tired and hungry. With Brad driving, Brianna daydreaming about her new adventures in Winona, and Brandi texting her friends, Paula found time for a little nap.

Like any midweek-evening commute through downtown, traveling was slow and brake lights inescapable. Brad estimated that they reached the 35W Bridge at a clip of 5 or 10 mph.

"We got just about to the other [north] end, and the bridge just started shaking," Brad recalled. He thought that the bridge's movement was due to the construction work. "I'm a little familiar with the concrete process, where you use shakers to settle all the concrete. I initially thought the shakers were kind of hitting the side, which would be vibrating the bridge," said Brad.

> First thing I noticed, looking across the lanes, was that there were construction workers running around. I didn't know what the issue was with that. As it got more shaky, I got a little more anxious to get going. I tried to speed up a little more, but with somebody in front of you, you can't go very far. I was stuck, and then we got taken for a ride.

With a whoosh, it all went down.

"The next thing you know you're riding the road down," Brad said. He thought, *Hang on! Here we go!* "I wasn't sure what was going on."

Brad had something to grab onto: the steering wheel. The other three in the car didn't have that luxury, and bounced around violently, even though they were all buckled in. "I think one of the girls yelled, 'What is going on here?'" Brad recalled.

The van fell sixty-five feet and hit gravel. It landed upside down in a mangled heap. "Once it happened, we were like, 'What just happened? Where are we?'" Brad recalled. He, like the others, was hanging upside down, held by his seat belt.

"I get claustrophobia," he said. "I'm sitting upside down looking out the window. The first thing I thought about was the earthquake in San Francisco [on October 17, 1989], when those bridges went down. I was waiting for concrete to come raining down and bury us, but it never did happen."

Relieved to be alive, the father of two gazed out the window and saw other vehicles scattered among piles of debris. Brad found a way to release his seat belt and climbed out his window. "I knew when we hit that my back kind of went, but adrenaline's going. *I gotta get out of here; I don't care what's wrong [with my body].*"

When the Odyssey landed, it crumpled, and most of the windows blew out. Brad described the car's shape as a "horseshoe."

> Right away there was dead silence. Then sirens. Kinda eerie. I saw a construction worker lying facedown in the gravel. He must have fallen while standing on the bridge. He was moaning. Then I heard another woman screaming because her leg was crushed. Then gradually more commotion. You're there to try and help them all, but you know you can't. I knew people were coming.

One by one, everybody climbed out of the minivan on their own—except Paula. Brad remembered how helpless he felt at the time:

> I tried to stand up, but I couldn't stand straight because of the pain. The girls started crying. Brianna was crying about her back. Brandi was wondering where we were. I looked back and Paula was hanging from her seatbelt. My first thought was *I can talk to her.* But she wasn't responding other than moaning. I saw blood. I didn't touch her because I didn't want to cause more damage, and I couldn't anyways because I was too hurt.

A few construction workers reached the family and told those who could to move to safety, as there were four lanes of highway hovering dangerously above them. Bridge debris and rocks intermittently fell from above. Workers sent Brad and the girls up a sand pile and escorted them to the triage area. As for Paula, some construction workers located a plywood sheet and used that to carry her to safety.

"As we got to the triage area, there were people coming out of the woodwork: doctors, nurses," Brad recounted. Where they came from, he had no idea.

Shock began to set in for Brad as he tried to comprehend what had happened and how badly he and his family were hurt. He knew that he and the girls had suffered back injuries as well as minor cuts and bruises. It was Paula they were worried about, because she wasn't moving. However, once in triage, Paula began to respond and spoke with Brandi, telling her she loved her and that everything was going to be okay. The family was laid in a row, with Brad and Paula as bookends for their daughters.

"I knew she was hurt pretty bad, but thought she would be okay," said Brad. The triage team assessed Paula and determined that she needed to get to the hospital immediately.

The girls and Paula were taken separately by ambulance to Hennepin County Medical Center in downtown Minneapolis, while Brad was sent to North Memorial Medical Center in the inner-ring suburb of Robbinsdale. Because of the shortage of ambulances, Brianna was taken by pickup and Brad by fire truck to the hospital.

Paula's sisters began to worry when the Coulters failed to show up at the restaurant or answer their cell phones. They backtracked to the bridge and looked over the scene in disbelief. Assuming the Coulters had been on the bridge when it collapsed, they began their search, eventually locating Brandi and Brianna in the emergency-room waiting area at HCMC. One of Paula's sisters had discovered that Paula was also there, when a nurse entered the waiting area holding Paula's rings. Paula had been taken into surgery.

As for Brad, his examination revealed fractures to his L1, L2, L4, T12, and C6 vertebrae. He would remain at North Memorial for five days, escaping surgery, but was told to wear a back and neck brace. However, there was no time to recuperate at home in Savage—his wife was fighting for her life.

Paula suffered a hematoma, a pooling of blood, inside her skull that required an immediate operation. She also required a craniotomy to remove a section of her skull called a bone flap. During surgery, her condition became too unstable to finish the procedure. In fact, her heart stopped at one point, but the doctors were able to revive her. It was two weeks before they could continue. Shortly thereafter, surgeons fused her spine from her T12 to her L2 vertebrae. She also had a crushed L1.

Paula's recovery was slow, as is often the case with traumatic brain injuries. "The first time I clearly remember anything following the collapse is probably around September 10," she recalled. "I remember Brandi, Brad, and Brandi's boyfriend coming to see me in step-down ICU. My sister was there. I remember a nurse being in my room. I just remember that one moment."

Paula remembers being told what happened. Her sister asked her how long she thought she had been hospitalized. "I don't know—a couple of days?" Paula replied. She'd been there for nearly six weeks. "It took a long time for me to realize how big of a deal the collapse was, and how many people got hurt," she said.

Initially, doctors had no idea if Paula would ever walk again or regain her mental capacity. The family was told to prepare, in case Paula would need to live out the rest of her days in a nursing home.

"Initially I was confused," said Paula.

> While there was part of me there, not all of me was there. I was obviously recovering from a brain injury. I was on a lot of meds. They weren't sure if I would walk again. My physical therapy time was spent trying to accomplish sitting, standing. Once that was accomplished, it progressed to trying to take a step.

As if brain injury were not enough, her spinal injury caused her plumbing to go haywire. She couldn't urinate properly on her own, and she had tremendous pain and difficulty with her bowels. She continues to suffer from this pain today.

Even while dealing with those ailments, Paula's most immediate issue was the tremendous pain in her hip joints. The condition was diagnosed as heterotopic ossification, or HO. HO is the development of abnormal bone in soft tissue caused by brain injury. The effects are excruciating, as pieces of bone form inside flesh and muscle.

"Here's me thinking, *Thank God we found the cause. I can get some medicine and the pain will go away*," Paula said. But that was not the case. She couldn't lift her right foot off the floor even an inch.

Her physician at HCMC decided not to perform surgery but instead see what would happen over time. That wasn't good enough for Paula and her family. They shopped for a second opinion and eventually found a doctor who agreed to help. He performed three surgeries on Paula and removed almost three pounds of bone. The result was a substantial reduction of pain for Paula in her hip joints, though she still suffers from stiffness at times. "There was a lot of trauma done in that area, the tissue. But it's a pain that comes and goes. If I stand too long, it returns," she said.

Paula stayed at HCMC until early October, then was transferred to Courage Center in Golden Valley, where she would remain until shortly before Christmas—the longest any bridge survivor remained under medical care away from home.

"I think what I hated the most was being alone," she said.

> I could handle it better when I got to know someone, be it a nurse or a fellow patient I had met in the lounge. I didn't argue about wanting to go home until they said I would be going to Courage Center, and I didn't want to go there. I worried I wouldn't have the level of help that I had received at Knapp. [Paula had been placed in HCMC's Miland E. Knapp Rehabilitation Center before being transported to Courage Center.] That nobody would help me go to the bathroom, for example. Courage Center was a place where the aim was independent living, but I feared that they would push too fast too soon. There was a fear of having to be on my own.

Except for five days, Brad was by Paula's side while she was at HCMC and Courage Center. Three months after the bridge collapse, he returned to his job at Jostens, where he had worked for twenty-two years. His first days back were filled with physical therapy appointments. He completed a twelve-week course at Physicians' Diagnostics and Rehabilitation in Edina, where he was put on numerous machines and practiced twenty different exercises. He also saw a physical therapist at Park Nicollet, as well as a chiropractor.

"My back is still very stiff," said Brad. "It takes a while to get going in the morning. When I turn my neck, it causes stress and headaches. I have to keep stretching it throughout the day. I think it's as good as it will get, and I feel older than I am."

When Paula did finally return home in December, Brad assumed the role of caretaker. "At night, she had to be put into bed, and she had all kinds of surgeries that required placing pillows and getting her in and out of bed because of her bladder issues," said Brad.

A year later, Paula returned to her job on a part-time basis, working up to thirty-two hours a week since then. "They've been wonderful to me," Paula said of her employer. "Very supportive. I've been able to be out for my surgeries and have been able to work from home when I need to."

However, her position at Mentor Network did require some changes. She had been in her new position for five weeks when the bridge collapsed, and the job required traveling out of state to administer software training. Because of her continued pain, Paula chooses not to travel. "You just have so much stuff that is affected by this," she said.

Emotionally, the family is doing quite well, all things considered. Because she was asleep at the time of the accident, Paula has no memory of what happened when the bridge deck tumbled. As for the other three, they somehow escaped the horrible flashbacks that often stem from post-traumatic stress disorder. "I'm grateful that we don't suffer from PTSD," Paula remarked. "I don't understand why Brad and the girls don't have it."

While physical recovery has ended for Brad, Brianna, and Brandi, Paula's continues. She must perform self-catheterization in order to urinate. "It's inconvenient, but it's not the worst way to have to go to the bathroom," she said. "If I had a list of what I'd most like fixed, it would be the pain in my rectum."

That pain can be unbearable for Paula. While the actual nerve damage is in the spine, the nerve communicates the pain there. "Certain things cause it to hurt more," Paula noted. "I can't sit on a heated seat. I have to be careful with spicy foods. I have problems with things not moving through my digestive system. My stomach gets bloated."

The discomfort is like a sharp gas pain in her intestines. "I had a colon/rectal specialist say, 'We can always put in a colostomy bag.' But I said, 'Hell no!'"

In June 2010, doctors implanted a pain simulator in Paula that modifies the discomfort. With a remote control, Paula can switch the pain so that instead of feeling a throb or a jab, she feels a tingle. "I generally always have pain," she said. "A lot of that has to do with the pain in my rectum from the pressure in my colon. Some days, I can do things that I know aggravated it, but other times, it comes unknowingly. It feels like I sat down hard on a rock." She keeps her humor on hand, though. She once half-jokingly asked her doctor if she could get a groin transplant.

Paula also had two InterStim implants put in to restart her bladder. The procedure was initially successful, but has since failed. "Sometimes, your body gets used to that stimulation and it no longer works, or it could be that the doctor didn't have it in the same spot as before when it worked," she said.

Despite her setbacks, Paula has been trying to get as healthy as she possibly can. She works out five days a week for up to three hours a day. She meets with a physical therapist who helps her with balance and core strengthening. She is training to jog a 5K. She works with a personal trainer two days a week for an hour, and she also works alone, doing cardio for up to forty-five minutes and stretching for an hour.

> I believe that as much as I hurt, and as much as I hurt after, I know that if I didn't do all the stuff that I do for recovery, I would not be where I'm at today. I believe God helps those who help themselves. I'm not satisfied with half-assedness. I'm not okay to just settle for something. I pray and thank God for giving me the motivation and the determination to do what I have to do…I don't want to get old and have things physically be worse because I had these issues.

Paula noted, though, that she "never thought recovery would take this long."

"At times I'd ask when I would get my old self back—and I thought it would take a year. "I think my expectations now are that I just keep doing what I'm doing."

Today, Paula can live independently in spite of some inconveniences. She's driving again, but she can't lift heavy items, and she has difficulty bending over. "It's difficult getting my socks on, because I can't bend over that way because of my back. I've found ways to get my bottom-half clothing on that isn't the way I used to do it. What I've found, works. It is what it is," she said.

Paula admits that the whole experience does bring about anger.

> I'm angry that this happened, but I've never blamed God. I believe someday I will understand the reason why this happened. It will take a long time and a lot of things to pull together.
>
> There are times where I wish I wasn't here. And that's gotten better. I'm so sick of waiting to get better. People look at you and think that you're fine. "Oh my God! You can walk!" People take for granted all that they have. You can feel your feet. You can cross your legs. You can get your own underwear on, your socks, your shoes. You don't have problems with going to the bathroom like you're ninety-five years old. There is so much that other people take for granted, that they don't realize—that they can just move without thinking about their balance. Sometimes my balance will get off, and I wonder if people in public see me and wonder if I'm an alcoholic! I think falling off the bridge and all the crap that happened to me was enough. I don't know why I had to have this other stuff on top of it.
>
> I don't think I ever seriously meant it, but

my life would be way easier if my life was up in heaven. I wouldn't have to work out three hours a day, but I'd have had to miss out on great times with my kids and husband. I told my family on several occasions, "You would have been sad for a long time, but you would have been grateful that I wouldn't be dealing with long-term stuff."

As slow as recovery has been, Paula believes it can continue.

> Physically, I'm getting better. Like I've said to a few people, "The survivor is the person who continues to suffer." You fight through all the injuries and complications, and all these things you've been affected by. The person who survives is the one who must continue with the struggle. I pray for those people who did not survive, that they died quickly and didn't have to suffer.

If Paula could rewrite history, would she?

> I just want my old self back, where I can just get up and walk to the cabinet and get something, where I don't have to think about getting out of the chair and walking over to the cabinet and reaching to get the item I want. They think you walk so they think everything is fine. They don't know about everything else wrong on the inside. I just want to have my old self back and have things be so much less effort and work and thought. If they would say, "Okay, your settlement is $5 million or instead you can find a doctor to fix everything and be how you used to be," I would do it, because no amount of money

is worth what I've given up.

Shortly after the accident, I had somebody say that, in five years, I won't even remember the accident. I don't think that that will ever happen. I don't think that I will ever function in a way that I won't recall that this happened. Every time I go to the bathroom. Every time I take a step. I've given up so much that I don't think I could ever just not be aware of it.

****

The day before the bridge collapsed, Brianna got a tattoo on her foot with Japanese characters that spell out the words for "believe" and "faith." When Brandi turned eighteen, while Paula was at Courage Center, she had the same characters tattooed on her foot with an addition: the date of the collapse. A year later, Paula followed suit with the same tattoo and date.

"I believe God was with us that day, and I believe he was with those who didn't survive," Paula remarked. "I know that I could not do this without him, and I thank him and praise him that he will help me keep moving."

Brad said that what stands out for him throughout this ordeal is his family's resilience. "Recovery was a blessing," he said. "Everybody worked very hard. We understand what it really takes to get back. You gotta do what you gotta do."

He added that he doesn't know why he, Paula, and their two daughters were on the bridge when it collapsed, and he doesn't expect to figure it out anytime soon.

"But," he said, "it would be nice to have that answer."

7

THE CHILL, DAMP WIND HOWLED as Darin and I exited his GMC Envoy one evening and stepped onto the parking lot asphalt in the industrial neighborhood of St. Paul. It seemed a strange place for the police precinct, tucked among lonely warehouses and untended semi trailers. Except for an occasional back-alley drug deal, the place seemed deserted.

Darin pulled my wheelchair out of the trunk and rolled it over to the passenger side of the vehicle. I had gotten pretty good at getting in and out of cars. With my good arm, I could grab the "oh shit!" handle above the doorframe and swing my body either into the seat or out of the car and gingerly onto my right foot. I rolled myself to the precinct's front door, and a lady standing there held it open for me as I scooted through. I felt nervous and excited. I'd be meeting some people with whom I had a shared past.

Survivor Resources is a group that evolved from a program begun by St. Paul to address the needs of families of homicide victims. Over time, it expanded to serve families in Minneapolis and elsewhere in Hennepin County who required support for a multitude of tragedies. When the 35W Bridge collapsed, Survivor Resources responded. Led by Margaret McAbee, the organization held weekly Wednesday evening gatherings for bridge survivors to meet and discuss their physical and emotional recoveries—as well as their often-desperate need for financial assistance.

I rolled my wheelchair through the door to find about twenty-five people seated in black, high-back, leather chairs around a long, wooden table. It looked like a board meeting, except people were in jeans and sweatpants. Most of them didn't wear any accoutrements of physical injury, but when it came to some, their pain was obvious. I recall one woman in a wheelchair, and another wearing a neck brace. They ranged from young adult to retirement age, and most were white. They chatted as if they all knew each other, and as Darin and I entered, we felt stares that asked, "Who are you, and what are you doing here?" I felt as if we had intruded upon a clique.

As the Survivor Resources meeting officially began, everyone took turns introducing themselves. Some of the names sounded familiar, as I had heard of them through Mom, Sonja, the newspapers, or TV. Most were complete strangers. I was one of the last people to speak.

"Hi. I'm Garrett Ebling." When I said my name, some of the expressions of mistrust warmed. Apparently, my story had made some of the rounds within the survivor community. "I feel very blessed and lucky to be here with you. I just got out of the hospital. I was hurt pretty badly. And I know that many of you have been meeting since the week after the bridge collapse. I just want to say that I want to help in any way I can, even though I'm still kind of physically limited."

Margaret passed around a sheet of lined paper and asked for each of us to write down our names and e-mail addresses so that she would have a contact list for the group. While I scanned the roster, matching names with faces, a policeman entered and explained the session's agenda. Those who wished to discuss a political strategy would remain in the room, and the rest would head to the basement to talk about their physical and emotional recovery in a more traditional therapy setting. I chose the latter, and Darin and I followed about a half dozen others to the elevator.

A ragtag assembly of sofas and chairs beckoned us as we got off the elevator. Just as we had upstairs, we sat in an oblong formation. The therapist explained the ground rules. "This is a safe place. We welcome any thoughts or feelings. Everything you say or feel has validity. If you want to speak, we encourage it, but you don't have to if you feel uncomfortable."

She opened it up by asking nobody in particular how their past seven days had gone. An introvert by genetics and an observer by trade, I sat back and let others talk. A young woman described a highlight of last week: it had been two months since the collapse, and she had made her first trek in a vehicle on an overpass. She said she was quite afraid as her car zipped above and across another road. Her stomach tossed. Her heart pitter-pattered. Her eyes watered. But she made it across, safe and sound.

By her side was a middle-aged woman. She hadn't been on the bridge when it fell, but her son had. Emotionally, he wasn't ready to attend the Survivor Resources meetings, but she felt she needed to be there, to collect information for her son and to find comfort in the shared experiences of others. Across from her, and to my left, was a blond young man. Of all those who spoke, his was the only name I remembered, because his words and attitude struck me so. He had been on the bridge when it fell, and he was mad. Not just mad, but "fucking mad." His contempt boiled over, directed at anyone and everyone who had been involved in the bridge's construction and maintenance. Darin admitted later that he felt uncomfortable sitting next to this ticking time bomb. We all heard him out and let him get it out of his system. I couldn't understand his anger, though. Sure, we were put into a bad position through no fault of our own, but I had been enveloped with love and care since the moment I fell into the river. I guess I thought everyone else had, too.

When it was my turn, I said that I felt lucky not to be suffering from any emotional trauma. I chalked it up to my amnesia surrounding the collapse. I had plenty of physical hurdles, but I wasn't angry or bitter. I was only concerned with getting back on my feet and reclaiming every little piece of my life that had temporarily been taken away.

The session ended, and everyone reconvened. A city official came forward and offered each of us a poster depicting an aerial shot of the 35W Bridge collapse site. I took one, but I found it an odd token. How would victims of the Hiroshima atom bomb feel if they were given a picture of the worst tragedy ever to befall them? Darin and I left the precinct with our souvenirs and headed back home.

I had mixed emotions about the experience. On the one hand, it was comforting to meet a group of people—the only group of people—who truly understood what I had gone through. On the other hand, the group's online message threads revealed tension between certain members. Some bridge survivors were accused of not being "hurt enough" to be involved in the group's activities. Others were criticized for being melodramatic and currying favor with the media. The back-and-forth became quite uncomfortable for me to read, and though Margaret responded to my e-mailed concerns by apologizing on behalf of the others, I asked to be removed from the list and decided not to attend any meetings in the near future. It was a stark reminder that, while we all went through the same experience, we were different people, with different physical and emotional traumas, backgrounds, lifestyles, morals, and opinions. We were all different fish in the same pond; some were guppies, others piranhas.

The differences didn't stop there. Most bridge survivors divided into two legal camps. The law firm of Robins, Kaplan, Miller and Ciresi offered their legal services pro bono. The attorneys of Schwebel, Goetz and Sieben provided their services for a fee. My family waited for me to recover somewhat before asking me to decide which law firm would represent me. After reviewing the options, I chose the Robins firm while I was recovering at HCMC. Phil Sieff, an attorney for the Robins group, paid a visit to the hospital and explained that the firm was committed to seeing the case through, that I wouldn't be charged at any point in the process, and that the firm's reward would be in finding the truth and giving back to the community. That seemed good enough for me, and I signed on, as did nearly one hundred others.

While each of us had different experiences, opinions, and agendas, one thing was certain: the media had lumped us in one group, the bridge survivors. Whether we liked it or not, we were going to have to move forward together. I didn't know what to make of this. Up until this point, my journey had been a solitary one. Prior to the Survivor Resources group meeting, Paula and her family were the only survivors I had met. I had been quarantined in various hospitals for two months, while most others in the group had met repeatedly and had been crafting a strategy to make their losses—financial and otherwise— publicly known. They had been on television and in the newspapers. They voiced the "group's" concerns, and I had missed out on what they'd said. I felt like I was in catch-up mode, but catching up to what?

All I knew was that I and others needed help. Medical bills began piling up for many. Injuries had forced dozens of survivors out of their jobs. Rents and mortgages weren't being paid. There wasn't money for groceries, phone bills, and insurance. These people had done nothing wrong by driving across that bridge, but the bridge had betrayed them. It had not only injured them, but was drowning them in financial ruin.

I, on the other hand, had escaped this fate. For me, workers' compensation had kicked in. My medical bills were being paid by insurance. The president of the company I worked for chipped in to help me pay my rent. The Salvation Army took care of a phone bill here, a student loan payment there. Family, friends, and strangers dropped off Target gift cards to pay for everyday necessities. To be honest, I can't imagine having to deal with it all and then also have to deal with financial fears. It would have been too much for me to handle. I said as much, publically, to help spread the word about how important it was to the futures of many bridge survivors that the state government step in and help.

From the moment the bridge fell, there were rumblings and demands for government support of bridge survivors. At first, city officials worked with the American Red Cross and the Salvation Army to see to it that the immediate needs of victims and their families were met. But while the immediate needs were addressed, the long-term ones would require government intervention. Two state lawmakers proposed legislation to provide compensation. Rep. Ryan Winkler (D-Golden Valley) offered up a bill that set no cap on the pool of money that would be provided. Sen. Ron Latz (R-St. Louis Park) brought forward his own version, which set a cap of $40 million. Whatever form it took, new legislation was urgently needed; under existing state law, the collective payout could not exceed $1 million.

The two lawmakers decided to announce their bills at the American Red Cross building near the bridge collapse site less than three months after the accident. I decided to attend the morning press conference. It was a big deal for me, because it would be the first time that I would drive (in my new Chevy HHR) solo into downtown Minneapolis. Despite using a wheelchair and having only two useable limbs, I was driving. I'd roll myself out to the back end of my car, stand up on one leg, and lean against the vehicle. Then I'd open the trunk, collapse the wheelchair, and toss it into the back of the car with my right arm. To get to the driver's seat, I'd shuffle my right foot—heel, toe, heel, toe—while keeping my left foot in the air until I reached the door. I'd crawl into the bucket seat and close the door. Voila! When I reached my destination, I'd reverse the process. It was cumbersome, and I probably amazed a few bystanders by "miraculously" standing up in my wheelchair and tossing it into the trunk, but it worked for me.

Up until this point, the media didn't know who I was. My family had avoided TV and newspaper interviews while I was hospitalized. Because I was a former journalist, they decided that I could talk to the media about my situation if and when I felt like it. I knew when I rolled into the Red Cross building that the media would be there, and that this likely was going to be my "coming out" party. This turned out to be true.

I rolled into the room where the press conference would take place. Behind a lectern, the windows looked out on the site of the bridge collapse. In front, a couple of rows of chairs lined a table with microphones. Perpendicular to this were several more rows of chairs. Throw in several dozen lawmakers, social services officials, attorneys, bridge survivors, reporters, and photographers, and there wasn't much room for me and my metal chariot. A man leaning against the wall made room for me, and I rolled into his spot. An official stepped up to the microphone and shared the ground rules. A few bridge survivors would make some brief comments about the necessity of compensation. Both lawmakers would then introduce their bills. Then, a few bridge survivors, including Paula's husband, Brad, and two who had lost their spouses would share their experiences.

As I sat there and listened to these stories of loss, I couldn't help but be overcome with emotion. Like many in the room, I was hearing these tragic tales for the first time. Even though I suffered from the same calamity that had befallen them, I felt more like the other spectators in the room. I think that was, in part, because I do not recall the events immediately following the collapse. In a way, it's like I wasn't there on the bridge—but I most definitely was. When the survivors and families finished speaking, the floor was opened to others who wanted to say something. I raised my hand and pushed my way to the front. Chris Messerly, an associate of Phil Sieff, shifted the table and microphone to accommodate me.

I don't recall my exact words, but I remember the room was quiet except for the rapid clicks of the cameras around me. I gave a detailed account of what I remembered when the bridge fell, along with a grocery list of all of my injuries and time spent in various hospitals. I spoke about how I had gotten engaged just four days before the bridge collapsed. I explained how I had come to meet Brad and Paula while at rehab. I finished my several-minute speech with a plea for help that went something like this: "I'm very grateful for all the kindness that the bridge survivors and widows have received so far, but the assistance can't end here. We have dozens of people facing permanent injuries and financial ruin because of something that was somebody else's fault. We deserve more. We deserve to be made as whole again as possible. We need your help."

I rolled back to my spot against the wall, but it had been filled in by others, so I moved on and out the door. There, I was met by several journalists from all facets of media.

"Can you spell your name?" one person asked.

"Could you repeat your list of injuries?" asked another.

"Do you think a law will be passed to help you and other bridge survivors?" queried a third.

I told the group that I didn't feel like answering questions now, but if they wanted to speak with me individually, they could write to me, and I provided my e-mail address. A couple of other reporters stopped me in the elevator and near the main entrance and asked if they could contact me to write articles about my experience. I gave them the same answer. On my way out, I ran into Bruce Lambrecht, the man who had offered up a bedroom in his Minnetonka home to my mom while I was hospitalized at Regency. My mom was good friends with Bruce's sister-in-law, who was once a fellow teacher in New Ulm. Bruce hadn't seen me since I had gotten out of the hospital.

"Where's Darin?" Bruce asked, assuming I had brought along my chauffeur.

"He's back at the apartment. I drove here," I said matter-of-factly.

"Ha! Good one," he replied.

"No, I'm serious. I bought a car. I drove over here from Minnetonka."

"What? How?" he stammered.

"Don't worry about it," I said with a grin. "I can manage."

"Well, then, can you give me a ride to the west side of downtown?" he asked. "I'll buy you lunch." I didn't turn him down.

****

With the proposed legislation for bridge victims' compensation officially on the legislature's spring to-do list, both the media and bridge survivors and family members of those who had died stepped into high gear. From day one, the bridge was a top-of-the-broadcast topic, and that didn't change as the months passed. The political aspect of the collapse was the poker that stirred the ashes of the conversation. Online newspaper message boards filled with anonymous criticisms of survivors. We were targeted as greedy and undeserving:

"Why should my tax dollars go to you?"

"Shouldn't your automobile insurance cover your damages?"

"Seems like everyone is getting a bailout. Where's mine?"

"All the money is going to end up in the lawyers' hands anyway!"

Some even remarked that they wished they had been on the bridge when it fell, so that they could collect a check.

Survivors and our families were angered and saddened as we read these comments. There was so much misinformation out there. Some of us tried to set the record straight on these online message boards, but we found they weren't venues for intellectual dialogue. They were more like kiddie pools in which two grown adults stand feet from each other and engage in mudslinging. How unfortunate.

Other survivors spoke with television, newspaper, magazine, and online journalists in the hope of sharing our stories. The results were mixed. Some reporters took the time to gather information, speak with several sources, and attempt to paint a fuller picture, with some success. Others relied on a quick get-in, get-out strategy for their stories. Their superficial, ninety-second bits on the 10 p.m. news propagated errors that could only be attributed to sloppy reporting and writing.

As for me, I tried to be selective with my interviews. If it was for a quick-hit TV story, I usually turned it down, although there were instances in which I appeared on TV. A reporter from KSTP came to Roseville Lutheran Church when a fellow bridge survivor and I spoke at a six-month-anniversary remembrance service for 35W Bridge victims. I also spoke to a TV reporter from WCCO later that spring at the state capitol following one of the votes that moved the compensation bill forward. Additionally, I—along with other survivors—was interviewed as part of a program for the Discovery Channel on the construction of the 35W Bridge's replacement.

I'll admit, I was more likely to speak with newspaper reporters or magazine writers, since my background was in print journalism. I appeared in articles for *Minnesota Monthly* and *Minnesota Moments*. Also, I conducted interviews for both the *Minneapolis Star Tribune* and the *St. Paul Pioneer Press*, as well as other publications.

One interview in particular stands out. I spoke with a reporter from the Associated Press. That newspaper article prompted the AP's multimedia division to fly a reporter from New York to the Twin Cities to interview me for a video/web story. This was a stark reminder to me of the bridge collapse's national and international scope. I tended to forget this; I felt my recovery was personal to me. The collapse itself was personal to me.

The young, female AP reporter had one day to shoot her story. She flew to Minneapolis and met me at Great Clips (I had returned part time in December 2007). She interviewed me and a coworker. My colleague, Katie, had headed home from Buffalo Wild Wings that fateful day in the same direction that I had gone. However, she and another coworker, Tiffany, stopped for gas just before reaching the 35W Bridge. When they left the gas station, they found themselves stuck in a traffic jam, but it wasn't the one I'd faced. The bridge had vanished; cars had nowhere to go. Their decision to refuel may have saved their lives.

When we finished the interview at Great Clips's corporate office, we ventured over to the site of the 35W Bridge collapse. This would be my first visit since the collapse. It was December and unbearably cold and windy. The temperature hovered a few degrees above zero. We parked about a block away, on the north end of the Tenth Avenue Bridge, which ran parallel and close to the 35W Bridge. I was content to conduct the interview there, but the reporter wanted a better shot. She wanted me to stand on the Tenth Avenue Bridge. I told her I didn't feel all that comfortable doing that, but she suggested we just get closer. So we walked to the edge where the bridge met the asphalt. She asked me to keep going. I took two steps. She wanted a few more. I took a few more steps. She wanted more. As a former journalist, I knew where she was coming from. She wanted an interview of me with the bridge collapse site as the background. I knew it would be the best framing shot, so I put my fear behind me and kept walking till I was about a third of the way across the bridge. I just kept repeating to myself that it was okay. This bridge wasn't going to fall.

The extreme cold was in my favor. The petite, young reporter from New

York asked a few questions, then hustled back to the warmth of her car. I, on the other hand, hustled out of anxiety. It took me a while to calm down. I breathed quickly, heart thumping. It wasn't that my visit had conjured up frightening memories; rather, I felt as if I had run up to a sleeping bear, poked it with a long stick, and run away. The golden boy had gotten away with it.

With my background as a former newspaper editor, I knew what journalists wanted to hear in interviews. I chose my words carefully to be quotable, spelled my name without being asked, and freely spoke on and off the record. I suggested topics and slants that I felt would make interesting story angles, as if I were writing the story. In fact, if I'd had my druthers I would have written the article myself and just handed it to them.

But I wondered what the interviews were like for other bridge survivors. They were probably very nervous. They probably didn't really know what to say. A camera lens and a microphone are very intimidating when you're not used to them.

As important as it was for me to share my story to educate the public, I cared even more about persuading the 201 members of the Minnesota House of Representatives and Senate to pass the compensation bill. As I recovered from my injuries at home that fall and early winter, I wrote letters and e-mails to each of those legislators. I told them of my journey, my recovery, and my luck in escaping the financial typhoon that was wreaking havoc in the lives of many of my comrades. I shared stories of my new friends and the difficulties they were facing: the mounting bills, the threats of foreclosure. None of this was our fault. The state had let us down. It was Minnesota's bridge that failed us. We couldn't afford to let our government fail us twice.

As a Minnetonka resident, I contacted my House and Senate lawmakers. Sen. Terri Bonoff and Rep. John Benson met with me separately, and I reiterated what I had stated in my letters to them. I recall both senators being quite moved by my story. As I bid each of them adieu at the end of our coffee shop chats, they told me they would support a bill for victims' compensation. When it came time to vote months later, neither let me down.

As 2007 came to a close, the interviews and the conversations with legislators cooled off in step with the weather. The waiting game continued until the spring, when the state legislative session began. It was then that Chris and Phil and their associates with Robins, Kaplan, Miller and Ciresi called me and their other bridge clients together. They told us what to expect from the legislative process. There would be meetings at the capitol—lots of meetings. The two bills (one from Representative Ryan Winkler and the other from Senator Ron Latz) would be taken up by various committees and voted forward. If they indeed made it to the full House and Senate, their differences would have to be ironed out in a conference committee.

We had to win not just one vote, but many votes. Killing the bill would take only one defeat. This wasn't about simply getting into the play-offs; we had to win the Stanley Cup. Therefore, the attorneys needed our help. We had to be visible, sitting in on those committee meetings. We needed to hand out literature and stop by our lawmakers' offices. To kick off our initiative, we would meet at the capitol in one large group. We decided we'd all wear red clothing that day to call attention to our cause. We'd hold a brief press conference at the capitol with our bill sponsors and then go visit the offices of our local representatives and a handful of other outstate (nonmetro) lawmakers.

I was able to maneuver my part-time schedule at Great Clips so that I could be in St. Paul for "Red Day" and for various committee meetings and votes. I watched firsthand the wheels of government spin—sometimes awed, sometimes embarrassed, sometimes astounded. I held my breath for each vote, and exhaled when it went the right way. It took several weeks, but eventually both bills found their way to the conference committee. This was where the real debate took place.

Few state legislators argued against financial relief for bridge survivors and families of those who had lost their lives. Both sides had essentially agreed on a process. A panel of lawyers would serve as the compensation panel that would review each bridge victim's case and calculate a monetary figure for total damages.

But the real issue at stake was whether the fund would be capped or not. Representative Winkler's bill did not cap the total amount of money the compensation panel could award. Senator Latz's bill did. We and our attorneys opposed the cap, stating that a limited fund would not adequately compensate victims whose medical bills were in the hundreds of thousands of dollars, with some even exceeding $1 million.

I sat through impassioned debates. One lawmaker spoke of his friend who'd died in the collapse. Another argued against setting a precedent by handing a blank check to bridge survivors. Each side went back and forth as I and others listened and prayed—doing both equally hard.

On May 2, 2008, well after midnight, the House-Senate conference committee reached an agreement. One of my attorneys sent me an e-mail at 1:30 a.m. The final agreement consisted of two funds. The primary fund would cap individual compensation at $400,000. For those with exceptionally large medical expenses, premiums, co-pays, or deductibles and future wage losses, the compensation panel could tap into a supplemental fund of $12.6 million. Three days later, both houses voted for the bill. Word spread quickly that Republican governor Tim Pawlenty would sign the bill into law on May 8. I planned to be there.

When I arrived at the capitol that morning, the governor's office was abuzz. Journalists, bridge victims and their families, and the governor's staff and security were all pressed into a small room. There were spotlights and TV cameras. My peers and I were situated around the governor, who was seated at his desk flanked by Senator Latz and Representative Winkler. The ceremony began, and the cameras rolled. Governor Pawlenty made a brief statement, scrawled his signature, and shook some hands. I got to keep a pen that read something like "Office of the Governor." The next day, the newspaper printed a photo of the governor, with me peering over his shoulder. Compensation was on its way. Sort of.

****

Those weeks at the capitol were physically and emotionally exhausting for me. I poured hours into meeting personally with lawmakers, writing letters, visiting committee meetings and votes, and speaking to the media. And the long walks from the capitol to the legislators' offices via the underground pedestrian tunnels (built for wintertime use) were draining. But the whole effort also felt truly rewarding when we won.

I recall one of my later trips to the capitol. It was an unusually warm spring day, and I and about a dozen other bridge survivors met and talked on the capitol steps. Each of us shared updates on our health. One person had recently finished a surgery. Another was getting ready to go under the knife. There were some laughs sandwiched by moments of silence. Somebody wanted to snap a photo. We gathered and put on our smiles. I sensed that we were all fighting, not just for our own future, but for the futures of the families who'd lost somebody on the bridge. And we were fighting for a sliver of justice for those who perished, because we all knew it could have easily been us in their place. For many of us, the process carried with it a sense of duty.

While we had won the right to compensation, it wasn't as simple as sticking out our hands and having a check land in our palms. A special master panel was convened, consisting of three attorneys: Susan Holden, Steve Kirsch, and Mike Tewksbury. In early fall 2008, it was the job of my attorneys and I to provide a complete file to determine my compensation. That file would include my medical records, which—when combined—were thick enough to be easily confused with the Minneapolis phone book. These included notes from doctor visits, surgeries, X-rays, hospitalizations, and follow-ups. Added to that were records from my auto insurance company, notes from my mental health therapist, my physical therapist, and my qualified rehab consultant, among others. We were also allowed to include impact statements written by me, Sonja, and my mom. An excerpt from my statement to the special master panel ran like this:

Ms. Holden, Mr. Kirsch, and Mr. Tewksbury:

Thank you for taking the time to read my letter and creating the opportunity for us to be able to meet...

Even today, the physical recovery continues. I wear braces on my teeth. There still is much dental work to do. My gums have receded around several teeth and need to be repaired. My feet feel sore when I walk, and some days the limp returns. It is a daily, frustrating reminder of the bridge, and it begins with the first step out of bed. Through all of this, however, my physical recovery—considering the severity of my injuries—has been overwhelmingly positive...

I firmly believe that when this is all said and done, I will be standing, but as somebody different than I was before. I don't look the same. I don't feel the same. My beliefs have changed along with my values. That safety net I believed was always there to catch me turned out to be a mirage. I have been damaged by this bridge: physically, emotionally. And I, like 140 others, did nothing to deserve it.

Since that single moment on August 1, we survivors have learned a lot about falling and rising. This compensation package graciously put forth by the Legislature and for which bridge survivors and victims' families had to fight hard is likely the only monetary retribution we will ever receive. I support the spirit of the law and understand that you must and should follow it to the letter. I only ask that you do so with grace and compassion…

Lastly, I want you to know that I understand the tremendous amount of work this panel must undergo to provide justice to the 140 survivors and the families of those who died. I appreciate all you've done and will do. We need your help, and above all, we need to be heard.

Thank you,
Garrett Ebling

****

Compiling all of my information took countless hours, and the law firm that represented me was tasked with the same assignment for the nearly one hundred other bridge victims it represented. Other attorneys were brought in to help gather the information rapidly, as there was a deadline to meet. Each of us victims was paired up with an attorney. I happened to get one whose expertise was in defending large companies facing lawsuits over workplace catastrophes. Up until this point, my lawyer, Jason, hadn't been affiliated with the 35W Bridge lawsuit. His line of work had him flying all over the country, rescuing corporations from the blazing litigation that accompanied oil-tank explosions or pollution spills. Now I was knocking at his office door to discuss how we'd acquire the thousands of pages of documents we'd need.

Jason was a likable guy, a husband and a father a handful of years older than I. He looked like an everyman, the type of person you'd meet in a coed softball team or neighborhood church. He always made sure I had a soda in my hand (the law firm provided free sodas from the vending machines; all you had to do was press a button, and a Coke was yours at no charge). The only mark against him was his apparent lack of organization. Piles of folders, binders, and boxes were scattered willy-nilly across his office floor. The walls were bare. I wondered if he had just moved into the office (which, it turned out, he had), and worried that my file might end up in a pile under his desk rather than in the hands of the special master panel.

Over the course of a few visits, though, I found that my worries were unfounded. Jason effectively hunted down all of my doctors and surgeons and got them to write their prognoses and speculations on what future medical needs I might have—not an easy task. He also convinced me to speak with an expert who helped decipher what my future wage loss might be due to my status as partially, permanently disabled. (My doctors had determined that I was somewhere between 5 percent and 10 percent permanently disabled due to the injuries to my ankle, left arm, and face.)

Since I was legally entitled to a meeting with the special master panel, Jason accompanied me there as well. Even though I'd written my impact statement for them to read, I wanted to meet the trio personally for a few reasons. First, I felt meeting them would have a greater impact. I wanted them to see the person behind the letter. Second, I wanted to emphasize my most critical points. Third, I wanted to know who they were and what their temperaments were.

The meeting occurred a week before Christmas. It was brief, less than an hour. Like a good reporter, I jotted down a few notes so that I'd be sure to hit my main points. We shuffled into a board room and waited for the attorneys' arrival. One by one, they entered, removing their winter coats and shaking hands. We sat down at the long, wooden table. I took a deep breath and prepared to defend myself against a battery of tough questions. To my surprise, their questions were gentle, even compassionate: "How are you feeling today? Tell me more about what it's like to not be able to smell anything. Your letter stated that you look different now than before the collapse. How does that affect your mood?" I quit reading from my notes and simply spoke from within about my experiences, my feelings. I wouldn't be lying if I said a box of tissues was passed around the table as I shared my experience.

It was never my intent to broadcast my injuries in the hope of having a few more dollars sent my way. To me, compensation wasn't about money, but justice. It just so happens that, in this country, justice is provided in the form of cash. As Jason and I left, I felt that I had said what I wanted to say. I had done all that I could do.

Eleven weeks later, the compensation offers were made. And a couple of weeks after that, my "justice" arrived at the law office in the form of a check. Jason called me, and I told him I'd drive downtown and pick it up. It was about 8:30 p.m. We met in the skyscraper's lobby.

"This is my favorite part of the job," Jason said as he held the check in his hand. "I remember one time I won a case for a guy and handed him a check for $3 million." My check was nowhere near that amount. In fact, it was maybe one-sixth of the total amount of damages that the special master panel had deemed I had suffered. (The entire amount designated for bridge victims' compensation was nowhere near the amount needed to cover everyone's total damages.)

"I appreciate all you've done for me, Jason, I really do," I said. And then I left. A chapter in my recovery—a goal that had given me purpose—was done. On the surface, I appeared ready to move forward, but an emotional dam within me was about to burst.

****

OMAR ABUABARA

They say that everything is bigger in Texas, and for Dallas metro resident Omar Abuabara, those words certainly rang true. In 2007, the thirty-three-year-old bachelor was living the big life. A lead systems engineer for Cisco, Omar was happy to spend most of his time on the job. He worked exclusively on the company's Wells Fargo Bank account, helping the institution streamline its technology processes. He was constantly on the road between his home and San Francisco, Minneapolis, Des Moines, Phoenix, and other hubs.

Omar had the bug for travel. He always had reward miles to use, and he took every opportunity to do so when not working. He'd visited more nations than a person has fingers and toes, and he relished the chance to see and learn something new. Texas is big, but the world is bigger, and Omar wanted to see, hear, taste, smell, and touch every bit of it.

In all things, Omar had an insatiable drive, and that included networking. His job environment allowed him to build and maintain relationships as well, if not better, than he did security solutions. In his five years as the Minneapolis account lead, he had become close friends with a handful of Wells Fargo employees whom he had helped. One week every month, Omar visited Minnesota's biggest downtown, meandering the skyways and making a difference.

"You build relationships and become an extension of that company," said Omar, who was born in Michigan and grew up in San Antonio. "I'd rarely, if ever, work in the Cisco office. I'd rarely, if ever, work from home. I'd rarely work in my hotel. My job was on-site with the customer. You kind of live and breathe their environment, find where they struggle, and help them through it."

But like all good things, this job was coming to an end. Having survived one of Cisco's more complex accounts for more than five years, he was ready for his next challenge. Omar had just been promoted and would soon be in charge of international financial accounts at Cisco's headquarters in London. He saw the opportunity as an adventure, even though he would miss his friends.

"That week that the 35W Bridge collapsed was the last week on the account," said Omar. "Because I'd recently gotten a promotion, I was in town to get my replacement up to speed and say my good-byes."

Omar's final Wednesday in Minneapolis got off to a normal start, with a morning workout and two bottles of juice provided by his friend Frank, who worked at the shop inside the Hyatt Regency. After that, Omar took a call concerning his new job, in which he would be the consulting systems architect for financial verticals in emerging markets: Africa, Russia, developing nations in Europe, South America, and Mexico. He followed that with a quick jaunt through the skyway to grab a new pair of jeans at the Saks Fifth Avenue outlet, before meeting his good friend and Wells Fargo teammate Mark Warner for lunch. At one point, Mark had mentioned to Omar that the Powerball lottery jackpot was high and that they should go pick up a couple of tickets. They agreed that if they won, they'd split the pot.

"I have a habit where every time I buy a ticket, I sign it," Omar recalled. "I handed Mark my ticket and said, 'Watch the numbers tonight and let me know if we in.' Mark says, 'If we win, what makes you think I'll tell you?' I then flipped the ticket over to show him my signature, and we had a good laugh."

Omar also remembered seeing another good friend of his, Scott Roeglin. Omar, ever the jokester, decided to announce his arrival with his car's engine.

"He was crossing the street in front of the office, and I hit the gas to try to scare him. He waved at me and we chatted for a bit," he said.

As Omar left Wells Fargo that afternoon, he stopped to chat with another good friend, Andy Solin, the manager of the labs at Wells Fargo where Omar had spent a lot of time. Omar knew it was important to spend an extra minute or two to chat with his friends, since he'd soon be closing the chapter on his job here. Those extra minutes were going to change the course of his life.

Omar hopped into his rental car, a silver Cadillac CTS, and headed east on Washington Avenue in downtown Minneapolis. He dialed both Mark Warner and his brother, Tim Warner, and the three of them chatted about where to meet up for dinner. They debated meeting at a restaurant or at one of the Warners' homes in Chisago or Hugo on the Twin Cities' northern fringe.

Omar said that, as he turned onto northbound Interstate 35W,

> I remember…traffic stopped initially but began picking back up. That was my third time crossing the bridge that week. I had an eerie feeling about the bridge. There was a lot of work being done on it. When I first crossed it, two lanes were closed, two were open. When I came back [on the return trip], three lanes were closed and one was open. They were working hard on it, and stuff was everywhere. It's easy to say now, but when it fell, I knew it wasn't an earthquake and didn't feel that it was a terrorist attack. Immediately, my reaction was that they hit something that caused a chain reaction because so much work was being done.

As Omar crossed the bridge, he continued to chat with Mark and Tim.

"I was above U-10 [the gusset plate that the National Transportation Safety Board concluded was where the collapse initiated] when it broke," Omar recalled.

I really struggle knowing that I was above it when it collapsed. Part of me actually believes that I was the weight that pushed it over.

I remember one incident where someone I had just met—a friend of a friend—made a comment to me that "no wonder that bridge fell, you're a big ol' boy." He was just an idiot that didn't think before he spoke. I almost ripped his head off, I lost it.

Am I dead? Am I in heaven? No. I'm still alive. Okay. Am I missing my limbs? Have my brains oozed out of my head?

As the bridge began to break apart, the first thing Omar noticed was the cars ahead of him disappearing. "I slammed on the brakes, and for a split second I thought, *Wow maybe I'm going to stop before*...but then I realized I was right in the middle. As I'm stopping, I'm falling."

Still on the phone, Mark and Tim heard about eight seconds of screaming, a thud—and then the line went dead shortly thereafter.

This is it. I'm dying, Omar thought. "I got into a fetal position, closed my eyes, and screamed. I felt the impact after falling 116 feet. I don't know how long I was out, or if I even was out, but I thought I had died."

Upon landing, Omar remembered going through his mental checklist to determine his fate. "Am I dead? Am I in heaven? No. I'm still alive. Okay. Am I missing my limbs? Have my brains oozed out of my head?"

The car landed in the brown, murky Mississippi River water, nose angled down and to the right. "I don't know what's under me," Omar recounted. "It's dark because the car is underwater and the water is nasty."

Despite his plight, Omar managed to find a moment of relief, mentally noting that he had just survived a near-death experience. "But then I realize this car is filling with water, and if I don't get out of here, I'm going to drown."

Omar pressed his seat belt button, no avail. He tried to open the driver's side door, but it wouldn't budge. He repeatedly flung his fists into the driver's-side window to smash the glass, but even that didn't work. "I hit that window with everything I had about ten times, and it wouldn't break." Trying another tactic, Omar reached behind and pounded on the backseat window, which still peeked above the waterline. With one swing of his fist, the glass busted.

He began to lose his composure, but at this point, his seat belt—for some reason—broke free from its latch. Omar, now unrestrained, swam to the backseat and climbed through the opening and up to the water's surface. He flung himself on top of the car, now a tiny island of crumpled metal. "I had blood pouring from my hands, with the scars to prove it," he said.

For the second time, Omar found some sense of relief.

"I just fought hard to survive again, and I did. All of a sudden, I'm looking around and it's eerily quiet," Omar recalled. "I saw people moving around. I didn't hear much. I saw a car angled up [on debris] with two front wheels hanging on [a remnant of] the bridge and the rear wheels hanging over the water. The car was still running, and the wheels were trying to turn. It was causing smoke. There was a tanker nearby, and I worried that the combination of these could create an explosion. *Great, now I'm going to blow up and die*."

Omar once again channeled his survival instincts. As if he were a trained soldier, he assessed the situation and determined that he had four options. One, he could swim back toward that tanker and onto a patch of debris. Two, he could swim toward the car with its engine running and to another section of bridge. Three, he could swim out to a third piece of bridge on which there was another man. Four, he could swim over to the lock and dam where a ladder protruded from the water, the most difficult option to reach, but likely the safest.

Concerned about the safety of the man on the piece of bridge, the Texan chose option three. The man was twenty-five-year-old Brian Sturgill, a sales manager for a home security company from San Diego who, like Omar, was in town on business. He picked up a two-by-four and told Omar to grab it so the current wouldn't pull Omar away.

"I remember feeling excruciating pain once I got back into the water, having to submerge my huge, open wounds into that mix of gasoline and water. I basically had to swim through gasoline to get to safety," said Omar. "To this day, when I smell gasoline, it takes me back. I hate it."

Omar quickly found that it became easier to walk toward Brian than to swim. "There was so much crap below me that I could walk once I got about halfway," he said.

"I begged Brian to let me use his phone. I called my Dad. [Omar's mother had passed away when he was eighteen.] I said, 'Hey, I just want you to know

I'm alive. Don't worry.' And my dad is thinking, *What did you just go through to begin our conversation like that?* That freaked him out. 'Dad, a bridge fell in Minneapolis, and I was on it, but I'm alive. Turn on the TV.' And I told him I loved him and then hung up the phone."

Brian fetched some towels from his car (which was also on the bridge piece) and gave them to Omar to wrap his bloody hands.

It was at this point that emotion overtook Brian.

"Brian starts bawling. I looked at him like he was the weirdest person in the world," Omar recalled. "I just didn't get it. *What the hell is wrong with you?* I thought. 'We just survived, dude!' I told him, 'You shouldn't be crying! You should be happy! I just survived three near-death experiences!' To see Brian losing it, it just didn't click."

Two other women swam over to the same chunk of debris where Brian and Omar now stood. Brian pulled two pairs of shoes from his suitcase and gave each woman a pair. Shortly thereafter, a rescue boat picked all four of them up and headed downriver.

"I remember there weren't enough life vests. I gave mine to one of the women," said Omar.

As the rescue boat headed for the east bank of the river, it passed beneath the Tenth Avenue Bridge, which ran alongside the 35W Bridge. Omar became very agitated and moved to the side of the boat, preparing to jump if he had to. The rescue worker, feeling the boat rock, began yelling at Omar. "Sit your ass down! What are you doing?"

Omar seethed with anger. "Think about what you're doing!" he screamed back. "You're taking people who just fell more than one hundred feet off a bridge that collapsed under another one!" At this point, the other survivors in the boat realized this as well and began to panic. The boat driver apologized and sped up. "He got it—it just didn't occur to him right away," said Omar. "I was in survival mode, and he wasn't."

The boat reached the shore. The victims needed an ambulance, but none was easily accessible. They faced a long walk up a winding road to the top of the hill. "We're walking, we're drenched, and we're hurt," said Omar. Someone spied a City of Minneapolis truck, and a worker standing outside of it, gazing at the devastation.

"He kind of looked like a taller, balder version of [former actor] Chris

Farley," Omar recalled. "He was driving a white city truck with some tanks on the back. We go right up to him. 'We need some help. Can you take us to the hospital? Can you get us up to the road?'"

His response?

> "No, I can't. There's no room in the truck." He refused to help us. The guy was evil. He was smiling and laughing and wouldn't help us. I had never seen an evil person like that. You hear stories of people on death row who have that look, but I had never seen that before. He was somebody who looked inhuman and just evil.
>
> I started cursing at him. "How can you not help us?" Thinking back, it probably wasn't a good idea, but I even pleaded with him originally to just take the girls. He sped out of there, so we just started walking. Then a cop flies past us the other way. We tried to wave him down but couldn't get him to stop.

By sheer will, the group arrived at the hill's summit. The male volunteer accompanying them flagged down a Toyota pickup with a topper. Inside, the couple happily agreed to take the four to the emergency room at the University of Minnesota Medical Center. "I remember using the shop vac in the back as a pillow," said Omar. The Good Samaritans dropped off Omar and his three new friends at the emergency room door, where they all but collapsed.

In a flash, Omar found himself surrounded by a dozen folks in white coats when less than an hour earlier, he had been alone. Doctors were accompanied by residents and students, and the room suddenly felt crowded and claustrophobic. Let the poking and prodding begin.

"I was getting IVs in each arm, tested for internal bleeding, getting X-rays, a CAT scan—everything but MRIs—lots of bloodwork and other tests, and medicine. It felt like a couple of hours went by," Omar recalled. "They moved me to surgical post-op so I had a place to rest before a room became available."

When the hoopla began to die down, Omar called his father a second time, and his dad—a retired doctor of internal medicine—talked to Omar's doctor. Omar also called his sister, Heidi, in Cincinnati and told her what had happened. Then the shock hit:

> I got off the phone and it was quiet. I had a little angel of a nurse, the sweetest little thing, taking care of me. At that very moment, I knew exactly what Brian had felt. I cried uncontrollably for about thirty minutes. I got it. I totally got Brian. He was just that far ahead of me. I was late to the game.
>
> She held my hand and wiped my tears. Just sat by me and didn't say a word. I don't know who that was, if she was an actual nurse or a resident, or a student. I wish I did so I could thank her. That was one of the worst few moments of my life: so alone, scared, weak, helpless. It was a feeling I never want to experience again.

Medical staff wheeled Omar to his now-ready hospital room, and the nurse informed him that he had two visitors and asked if he'd like to meet them.

"Hell, yes! I have no family here. Of course!" Omar replied.

Friends and Wells Fargo coworkers Andy Solin and Joel Waldon stepped into the room. "Never have I been so happy as when I saw Andy and Joel's faces—and they're ugly faces!" Omar laughed. "You go from feeling so alone to seeing those two guys."

Andy and Joel found Omar after hearing from Mark and Tim, who had started calling others to try to locate Omar following their cut-off phone call. Andy and Joel then informed Omar's former boss, who had just transitioned to another job two weeks earlier, and his client director for the account. Andy also talked to Omar's dad. In addition, they sent e-mails throughout the Wells Fargo system. Soon Omar was receiving cards, letters, flowers, cookies, even a raspberry pie—one of Omar's favorite Minneapolis desserts—from Murray's Steakhouse. On top of that, one of the new account managers at Cisco drove up from Des Moines that first night and was in Omar's hospital room the next morning. That commanded a lot of respect, Omar noted.

It seemed as if everybody from Wells Fargo wanted to know how Omar was doing. Wells Fargo team members all the way up to the chief information officer were constantly asking about Omar, calling him, and visiting him. Wells Fargo senior vice-president Steve Brown even sent a $100 gift certificate to one of Omar's favorite restaurants, Fogo de Chao.

"I can't tell you how much respect I have for that company. I felt like I had been a twenty-year Wells Fargo veteran," said Omar.

The calls and the visits got so frequent that Omar's roommate, who was also a bridge collapse survivor, finally pulled back the curtain that divided them and said, "Okay, let's talk. Since I'm not going to get any rest, I might as well get to know you!"

Mark Warner, who had been on the phone with Omar when the bridge collapsed, stopped by the hospital every day. The two of them would watch DVDs, although Omar didn't stay awake through many of them. During one visit, Omar remembered to ask Mark about those lottery tickets.

"Hey, did we win the huge jackpot?" asked Omar.

Mark gave Omar a look he will never forget. "I believe you used all of your luck the other night!" It was then that it hit Omar just how lucky he really had been.

Omar's injuries included a bruised sternum, a bruised lung, a bruised clavicle, a sprained ankle, ten herniated discs, bruised ribs, and lacerations. The CAT scans and X-rays came back negative. Omar would remain in the hospital until Saturday, August 4, because he was extremely dehydrated and his lactic acid blood count was very high as a result of the internal bruising. "Because of how hard I fought, that makes perfect sense. I gave it everything I had!" said Omar.

Once released from the hospital, Omar flew to San Antonio for nine days to rest at his dad's home. "For three weeks, it looked like I was a boxer in a bad fight, with my hands all wrapped up," Omar recalled. "Each day, I had to wash them and put prescription ointment on them. People would say, 'If you were in a fight, I'd hate to see the other guy.'"

It didn't take long for Omar's father to realize something was going on inside his son. Omar's mood had distinctly changed:

Dad noticed I was out of it. I wasn't the same person. I was more of a zombie. I wasn't me. I wasn't happy-go-lucky like everybody was used to. I was a shell of myself. I was there, but I wasn't.

My dad sent me to a psychiatrist. [The doctor] said, "Look, it's post-traumatic stress disorder, the same thing the troops come home with. You're not going to have any symptoms for a while, as it takes a couple months to develop. But I'm going to give you some quick-acting antianxiety pills."

Omar returned to Dallas to continue his recovery at home, but he couldn't just lie around. He missed his friends and his coworkers. Cisco was holding its annual sales conference in Las Vegas, and Omar was eager to attend, even though it was barely two weeks after the bridge collapse. He was out of the wheelchair and hobbling around with an ankle brace. Medication numbed the pain enough for him to board the plane to Vegas.

"Whenever I fly, it's first class," said Omar, and this trip was no exception. In 2006, Omar had flown more than 208,000 miles thanks to his job and his desire to see the world. As a result, he was constantly upgraded. On this trip, he was seated next to a male passenger glued to his laptop computer.

The flight attendant hands me a glass of water over his laptop. He freaks out, "Be careful! That's my life!" I look over at him and say, "No it's not." He replies, "No, it is." And I say, "No, really, it's not," and I left it at that. This guy was never going to get it. I realized that I used to be that guy. I lost many things that day at the bridge, including my laptop in the river, with all of my mp3s. I had probably ten thousand mp3s.

When Omar arrived in Las Vegas, he hoped to room with his former boss, Johnny Pak; however, because of his outstanding performance that year, Johnny got upgraded to a suite at a different hotel.

"I just wanted to hang out with him and those people that I was closest to. That was disappointing," he admitted, although he was able to spend many hours talking with Johnny.

Omar also met others in Vegas with whom he felt a strong bond:

> My close friends Greg Hobbs and Bruce Sedlak were waiting at the airport for me with a car. I don't think I've ever been as happy to see those two guys as I was that day, and I know they feel the same way. My Aunt Marina [Omar's mom's only sister] who lives in Los Angeles came with my cousin Michelle to see me as well. I also got to see many other work friends—it was a very emotional few days.

Omar didn't feel well enough to attend many events at the conference, and when he discovered that he had missed a speaking event hosted by *The Pursuit of Happyness* author Christopher Gardner, he was very disappointed. However, fate put the self-made millionaire and motivational speaker in Omar's path.

"Chris walked over to talk to our table at lunch after his engagement," Omar remembered. "He looked over at me and asked what happened."

Omar told him he had just survived the Minneapolis bridge collapse a few weeks back. Chris responded with a hug, pulled him aside, and spoke to Omar for a few minutes, encouraging him to read his book.

"I bought it and read it, and was like, wow! It meant a lot that he did that," said Omar.

Christopher Gardner wasn't the only author who had a significant effect on Omar. Four months before the collapse, he was watching one of his favorite channels, Fox News. Part of the show was about a U.S. Navy SEAL named Marcus Luttrell who had written a book, *Lone Survivor: The Eyewitness Account of Operation Redwing and the Lost Heroes of SEAL Team 10*. Marcus was part of a four-man SEAL team in Afghanistan that was discovered by goatherders, who disclosed its whereabouts to the Taliban. Almost immediately, the SEALs were under attack by enemy fighters numbering between eighty and 150. Marcus was the lone survivor. A rescue mission failed when a rocket-propelled grenade hit a U.S. helicopter and killed sixteen military personnel. Marcus evaded capture by walking wounded for seven miles before being taken in by Pashtun tribesmen, who sheltered him and eventually contacted the U.S. military in what can only be described as a miraculous event.

"That story really touched me," Omar said. "I'm a huge fan of the military. I appreciate what our boys do for us. When you live in Texas, you serve if you can, but at the very least, you have a strong appreciation for the military." Omar's uncle retired a colonel from the U.S. Air Force, and many of his friends either have served or continue to serve in the navy, coast guard, army, and marines.

"To see these SEALs and to hear their stories, you understand the meaning of 'hero.' It was the first book I had ever bought and read without putting down. I ended up reading it twice and buying seven or eight copies of the book for good friends of mine."

It was the mindset of a SEAL that helped Omar make it out of the river on August 1.

"God had put that book in my hand to read," said Omar. "If Marcus could survive all he went through in Afghanistan, I sure as hell better be able to get out of a river in the United States of America. Marcus's story really helped me that day."

In 2010, Omar got the chance to tell Marcus firsthand how his story affected him when he attended a National Rifle Association event in North Carolina at Charlotte Motor Speedway.

> I look over and see a couple of military guys and another guy standing next to them in a pair of jeans and a shirt, and it's Marcus Luttrell! I went over to him and shook his hand and said, "I'm sorry to bother you. I read your book, know your story and wanted to thank you." I wore my 35W pin and told him my story and he's like, "Welcome to the club, brother." I told him what it meant to me, and sorry about the boys that he lost and that I understood what he went through. I got

my picture taken with him. I keep this tableside.

One of the friends to whom Omar gave a copy of the book was Rod Dozier. Rod is a former SEAL who used to work for Wells Fargo. In fact, Rod was on the SEAL team that Marcus had been a member of, but at a different time. He knew of the story but had never read the book. One day, Rod showed up at a barbecue that Andy Solin held on the anniversary of the bridge collapse. Omar spoke with Rod for a spell, but later realized that Rod had left without saying good-bye. Andy then approached Omar and handed him a gift. It was from Rod. In Omar's hands was a gold Navy SEAL trident pin that belonged to Rod. It signified that the wearer was a Navy SEAL—the best of the best.

> I was out of words. I called Rod when I got back home. "I'm speechless. I can't tell you how much this means to me." He said, "Look, I just didn't want to make a big deal about it so I asked Andy to give it to you. You don't know it, but you helped me through some tough times in my life. I know you're going through some tough times in your life, and I want you to know that people are thinking about you."

When Omar returned from the conference in Las Vegas, he continued his physical and emotional recovery, but it wasn't without trial. The physical pain continued, especially in his right knee, even though the doctors had initially ruled out serious injuries. MRIs of his knee later painted a different picture: a torn medial meniscus and a torn lateral meniscus that was poking into the patella. That required surgery and a microfracture procedure.

The knee improved, which allowed Omar to focus on the pain in his right shoulder. Doctors kept telling Omar that they couldn't find a problem with his shoulder, but his pain was telling him something different.

I was so frustrated with my shoulder that during Thanksgiving 2007, I met with a good friend I went to Texas A&M with, Kelly Wunsch, [a left-handed pitcher who played for the Chicago White Sox and then the Los Angeles Dodgers from 2000–2005]. He was home in Austin, and I stopped by, something I did every year since he moved there. We were having a couple beers on his porch, and I was telling him how my shoulder was killing me even though doctors were saying nothing was wrong with it. He's had about twelve surgeries and has had just about every procedure there is! He asked me how I think I hurt my shoulder. I told him that I remembered my shoulder slamming into the passenger seat during the collapse. He said, "I think you have a [major labral] slap tear. Get an MRI and have them inject the dye."

Omar took the southpaw's advice. His shoulder underwent an MRI, and it showed exactly what Kelly had predicted. A surgeon suggested an operation, but urged Omar to seek physical therapy first. Omar did so, but he got a second opinion as well. He had surgery in August 2008.

"The arm feels a lot better, compared to what it was," he said. "It was a lot worse than what they thought when they went in. I needed to be immobile for about two months after surgery, and it took about a year to heal the best it could. The shoulder made my knee feel like nothing."

Omar still sees doctors and attends physical therapy. "At first, I had really bad doctors who misdiagnosed me, radiologists who misread MRI reports," said Omar, still bitter about the inadequate care he received. His ankle still gives him fits. He's had physical therapy for three years and a slew of cortisone shots to address the pain. However, his knee surgery led to overcompensation that aggravated the ankle injury.

Omar knew he had emotional battles to face as well. PTSD had latched onto him tightly. He suffered from depression, panic and anxiety attacks, recurring nightmares that prevented a full night's sleep, and a racing heart. He began seeing a psychiatrist once a month and a psychologist once a week. More or less, that continues today.

"That's something that's tough for me. You grow up mentally tough in Texas. You don't talk about your feelings," said Omar. "It's different, 'the cowboy way.' I still really struggle with that aspect of it."

For some time, Omar tried to discount the validity of his emotional struggles by comparing them to what others went through—and what he assumed were greater struggles.

"Something that really hit home was when my psychologist—who has treated patients of abuse, violence and veterans of every war since Vietnam—said that my trauma is every bit as traumatic as anyone else he has seen. I would always compare my situation to others and downplay what I went through; he made it clear I was wrong," Omar noted.

Fighting physical and emotional injuries can be tough in themselves. Trying to take on workers' compensation is a whole other battle. Omar's situation was unique. Workers' compensation kicked in for Omar because he was in Minneapolis for his job. Unfortunately, a tug-of-war began between insurers in Texas and Minnesota over who would be responsible for paying the bills. The result was delayed and subpar treatment.

"Insurance companies will fight all they can to make you try to give up so they don't have to pay for it," Omar opined. "That was exactly what I've gone through. I don't want anybody to have to go through what I did. They fight you every step of the way."

As an example, four months after shoulder surgery and two months after he started physical therapy, the insurer sent Omar's case for review to a different doctor, one who had never seen him and who didn't hold the same credentials Omar's surgeon had. This doctor determined that Omar didn't need to go to therapy anymore. Omar said,

> They find doctors who will diagnose
> in their favor and keep giving them business.
> It's a joke. That's the way the system is. One
> of my case workers said it best: "The system
> is set up so the people who need help don't get

it, and those who take advantage of the system do." You lose a third of the pay and get horrible medical [coverage]. I'm at well over half a million dollars in subrogation I'll have to pay back. [In subrogation, an insurance company attempts to recoup expenses it paid out in a claim.]

As of October 2010, Omar had still not been cleared by doctors to return to work.

****

A painting titled *Thirteen Flowers* sits on a ledge above the fireplace in Omar's home in a suburb northwest of downtown Dallas. It shows the new 35W Bridge over the Mississippi River, with the Minneapolis skyline in the background. In the river are two figures on a slab of debris, one reaching out to help the other. In the forefront are thirteen flowers, each representing one of the people who died in the bridge collapse.

Created by Minnesota artist Marni Tobin, the original painting was auctioned off at a benefit for Survivor Resources in 2008. Omar decided he had to own that painting. "Money was no object," he said. "Even though the painting depicts a victim and a rescue worker, to me, that was Brian and me on that piece of bridge." To Omar's surprise, he was the only bidder on the painting. "It was important for me to have. Others who live around the Twin Cities have so many resources to connect with—family, friends, places. Being in Dallas–Fort Worth, I don't have any of that. This painting is really it."

Feeling isolated in Texas has worn on Omar:

> The reason I struggle, and it's been harder on me, is that my support structure was blown up. While I got to move home to Texas, I have no family in the Dallas–Fort Worth area. I have no coworkers in the area. I have no other bridge

victims in the area. As I deal with this, I am all alone. I'm a single guy who is not married, doesn't currently have a girlfriend, doesn't deal with bridges on a regular basis. I should be happy to be alive, and I get that, but you get so caught up in your day-to-day treatments, and the depression, the PTSD, just sucks. And it's tough when your family and friends just don't understand. And it hurts. They don't get it. Nobody truly understands unless they have been through it. Others dismiss it. There are some who don't want to get it. There are some who are afraid of it. There are some who want to understand it and never will, and there are some who pretend this can't be him anymore. It has affected some relationships. I have lost three old good friends because of this. It is what it is. It's sad, but there's nothing I can do about it.

I've lost three years of my life. My life has been in limbo. I'm about to be thirty-seven years old. I figured by now, I'd be married with family! My life has been wasted, and I've let it. We can't control what happened to us, but we can do as much as we can with what we've got, and I haven't done that. There's regret, but it seems it's uncontrollable to me. I call in to the Survivor Resources group meeting in St. Paul every other week because it's my only tie back to the bridge.

Like the scars that mar Omar's hands, there are other reminders that life is different now—and not for the better.

I feel like a ninety-year-old man every time I wake up and get out of bed. I also feel like I died that day. I'm not the same person, and I never will be. I was somebody who was carefree, wasn't afraid of anything. Now I wouldn't know that person if I saw him. Omar died, and what's left of him is what I'm trying to figure out. And the toughest part is accepting that.

I am trying to deal with what I have and realize I can't do what I used to do. I haven't run in three years. I haven't skied in the snow. I haven't played golf or tennis, and I miss that tremendously. I used to live life to my fullest. I used to think that the beach was the place where I could recharge and my problems would go away. After the bridge collapse, a friend of mine got married in Mexico. I couldn't wait to spend time with all these close friends on the beach. That's when it hit me. Those problems don't go away down there. They stick with you. I realized that in my most ideal place in the world, on a beautiful beach, none of this crap has gone away or been minimized. It's been tough.

There are a few "wins" however:

The one thing I was able to get back in 2010 was hunting. It had been three years since I last hunted, and my good friends Matt Thigpen and Matt Brown took me duck hunting New Year's Day. I shot two ducks with one shot, something that is pretty rare. It definitely hurt my shoulder, and it was difficult with the other medical problems, but it was worth it. Mentally, it was a huge win for me!

Omar finds his comfort in the strength of others, be it Christopher Gardner, Marcus Luttrell or thirteen-year-old Abby Elmore. Abby is the daughter of a friend who used to work at Wells Fargo. Omar got to know the family over time, visiting them on several occasions. In 2009, just before the second anniversary of the bridge collapse, Abby gave Omar a poem she had written that she titled, "35W, The Truth." The poem hit him just as hard as that bridge had struck the surface of the river on that fateful day.

> As I went to dance on the beautiful day,
> I didn't know it would soon be my most dreaded,
> As I walked up those stairs and saw 35W on the screen,
> I thought to myself this must be a dream,
> But I went to class not knowing the truth that on that bridge,
> One of the people was you,
> Class had ended and I walked outside,
> Not knowing all Minnesota had cried,
> I got in my car as Mom told me the truth,
> That surely you were on the bridge that collapsed that afternoon,
> I thought to myself you were dead,
> But when I got home my dad told me you where a survivor instead,
> A thousand tears I cried that night,
> But now I see you with all my sight,
> I know you will come back each year,
> To play chicken feet and tell your story for all to hear,
> You are an amazing person,
> And I know it's true that without you on earth I wouldn't know the truth,
> That life passes us so quickly you would be surprised,
> That one sunrise can be gone in the blink of an eye,
> So keep the people you love close to your heart,
> Because someday...
> Unlike that day,
> They won't have a choice if they really want to part.

"There isn't a day that goes by that I don't have this poem with me. That thirteen-year-old girl made a thirty-five-year-old man cry like a baby," Omar admitted. "She's an amazing little girl."

Omar realizes that there may not be a happy ending when it comes to the aftermath of the bridge collapse:

I always thought the finish line would be that once everything was done, we'd get two pieces of bridge. I would save one and the other, I would take to one of my friend's ranches and shoot the crap out of it, let some anger out. I always envisioned the final chapter, closing it out, shooting the bridge. That's me letting out my anger and frustration on something that tore my life apart.

Every time I think there is a check mark, that I'm closing something out—anniversaries, surgeries, milestones—it doesn't go away. I'm afraid I have false expectations. Part of me wants to think I still have things to do, so I don't feel that relief yet. But the other part of me realistically thinks that if I'm not going to feel lasting relief when I reach these milestones, then there really is no "here."

For Omar, justice can only happen if somebody admits fault for what happened on August 1, 2007:

I want somebody to say, "Yeah, we royally screwed up," and more importantly, say, "I'm sorry" and accept responsibility. I need to hear that. PCI [the construction company repairing the bridge when it collapsed] gave their insurance money, and said we're not accepting fault but we're settling, and URS [the company tasked with inspecting the bridge] did the same thing. In this country, settling is just part of the cost of doing business, and that is very sad. So, I don't think justice will ever be served. I've been struggling with that. I really have. That's more important to me than anything.

8

"I'VE BEEN HAVING A LOT OF VIVID DREAMS LATELY," I said, as I looked over at the alarm clock sitting on the wooden desk. It read 4:06 p.m.

"Well, tell me about them," Dr. Laura said, perched on her leather chair. Laura was near my mother's age, tall and thin with hair that I guessed had gradually gotten shorter as she had gotten older. I wasn't sure if she wore glasses because the snobbish psychology community demanded it, or because she really had poor eyesight. She shared the bottom floor of a small office building on the western side of the Twin Cities with two other therapists, and they all shared a unisex restroom and waiting area. A compact boom box could always be found sitting on a small table in the lobby, setting the mood with Eva Cassidy, Enya, or some other soothing crooner. The walls featured framed drawings for purchase from local artists; some featured farm buildings, others lush meadows or meandering streams.

Laura's office itself was a small, beige rectangle with a window that poked out of the sloped landscaping, so that all one could really see was the lawn. It contained a desk, a shoulder-high, exotic potted tree, which always seemed on the verge of dying but never did, a love seat for patients, and a comfortable chair for her to pick the minds of her clients.

Across from her, I had worn through the cushion of the love seat during more than one hundred sessions of mental health counseling. It was November 2009, and I was feeling as though I had reverted to the condition I was in during my very first (somewhat involuntary) visit—even though she had been gazing at me from that same chair and interpreting my life for the past twenty-one months.

"Two weeks ago, I had a dream that I was competing against NFL quarterback Brett Favre in a bicycle race in my hometown."

"Really?" Laura exclaimed. "That must have been exciting."

"It was. I almost had him. But right before we reached the finish line, he pulled ahead and beat me."

"Hmm." Laura's face contorted.

"Well, I can't imagine all dreams mean something," I said, praying she wouldn't come back and suggest it was a cry from deep within.

"What about your other dreams?"

"Well, there's one I remember very clearly."

Laura leaned forward.

"I was back in Eyota at my grandparents' house and preparing the house to get it ready to sell. [This was actually something that was going on in my life at that time.] My grandparents had all these animals—mostly farm animals, you know, sheep, goats, what have you—and we penned them up. Well, one night, they all got loose, and when I returned to the house in the morning, the animals had scattered across the town."

Laura nodded.

"Most of the animals gathered around the outdoor pool of a home a few blocks away. I guess they thought it was a pond or an oasis or something. Well, I called a couple of friends and they came over, and I decided that a few of us would attempt to round up these animals. The problem was that we had no place to put them, and there were hundreds of them. I decided that—one by one—we would carry them back to the house and put them in a room in the basement."

"Interesting," Laura said as she sat back into her chair. "Go on."

"Well, we started grabbing the animals. Things were going okay until we got to this flock of ducks. They were super mean, and they had sharp teeth inside their bills. They'd bite my friends as they tried to pick them up. My buddies refused to transport the ducks, so I told them to grab some of the furry creatures and I'd take care of the ducks. So I did. I grabbed a duck and it clamped onto my hand with its vampire teeth. It kept letting go and clamping down again as I walked the three blocks back to my grandparents' house. The pain was incredible, but I didn't stop. I didn't look down. I just kept my focus until I got the duck into the basement room. We got several animals into the basement, but there were just too many. We couldn't collect them all."

"You know, Freud has a lot to say about basements," Laura said as she again leaned forward. I raised my left eyebrow. All I knew about Freud was that he had a dirty mind. "The basement is your subconscious. It's where you stuff away your thoughts and emotions, where you don't have to deal with them."

Laura did this a lot, say something that nailed my situation. It was like playing psychological Battleship, and she knew exactly where my vessel was most of the time.

"The animals are your thoughts. You instinctively want to corral them, shove them in the basement where they can sit and you don't have to deal with them. Before the bridge, you could complete the task successfully, and probably with little difficulty. But now your brain has lost that ability. It can't cope. And you're mentally exhausted and fatigued."

Bingo. Laura had done it again, even though she didn't give a reason for the vampire ducks.

"How was your weekend?" Laura then asked. "You had a friend flying in to visit, right?"

Laura did have an amazing memory. I guess that's important when you have several clients.

My good friend Ron—who had gone to serve in Iraq shortly after my hospitalization—had flown out from the Washington, D.C., area to Minneapolis to celebrate Halloween. There's an unwritten pact between him and me that we celebrate two holidays with each other: Halloween and St. Patrick's Day. When Ron and I were roommates in Virginia, we always made a point of celebrating these two events with pints of beer in hand. When I moved back to Minnesota in late 2005, the tradition came along in the U-Haul.

"That reminds me," I told Laura, "there was an incident at one of the downtown Minneapolis bars Halloween night."

"What happened?" she asked, leaning forward with pen in hand, ready to jot down notes should the need arise.

"Well, Ron, two friends, and I went to this bar. It was packed full of customers wearing every kind of dress imaginable, and I mean every kind." (I had shaved my head the day before, purchased a tan-colored Snuggie, and went as a monk. Ron had taken his outfit to an extreme. We stopped at a Target before heading to the bar and he bought a gray bathrobe and a red sheet that he draped over his shoulder. He then put on sandals and pinned signs on his chest and back that read "I have no small apples." He also carried a handmade map to Damascus. His costume? Mini, apple-less St. Paul. Not surprisingly, none of the tipsy women at the bar got it.)

"Well, one of my friends turns to me and says, 'I just want you to know that I just saw a guy walk in wearing a costume of the 35W Bridge collapse. I figured you'd see it anyways, but I wanted you to be prepared.'"

Laura put her hand to her stomach. "You're kidding me," she said.

"I wasn't entirely shocked, Laura. Earlier in the night I saw some guy dressed as one of the World Trade Center towers, complete with an incoming toy plane attached to his torso. Nonetheless, I was pretty put off."

"What did you do?" Laura asked, still holding her gut.

"I approached him. I acted as though I couldn't figure out his costume. He looked to be in his early twenties—just a kid—and he was with a young woman, probably his girlfriend. I asked him who he was supposed to be. 'I'm the 35W Bridge collapse,' he said in an almost proud way, like he'd just thought of the most clever Halloween costume ever. I pointed to a Matchbox school bus glued to his chest. 'You know, thirteen people died and dozens more had their lives forever changed on that bridge just two years ago—and you're looking at one of them.'

"His girlfriend quickly jumped into the conversation. 'I told him we'd probably run into somebody connected to the bridge.'

"'Well, consider the mission accomplished then,' I said, and I walked back to my friends."

Laura was aghast. "I just can't believe that somebody would even think that would be acceptable," she remarked.

"Well, I really did want to punch him," I said, "but I didn't feel like getting the crap kicked out of me by a six foot three, 290-pound bouncer."

"If it's any consolation, I think you did a pretty admirable thing," Laura replied.

"Thanks," I said, and shrugged my shoulders, as I don't take praise very well. "At first, I was really angry, but then I wondered if it was just because I'm at the epicenter of the bridge. I mean, if I was a woman who was raped by a man wearing an orange ski mask, and then saw a guy in the bar dressed as an axe murderer wearing an orange ski mask, I would take it much differently than anybody else in the bar. Was I being oversensitive?"

"Garrett, I had a physical reaction when you told me this story. It wasn't just you. It was a stupid kid not using his head."

"I suppose. I just don't know how to trust my emotions anymore," I explained. "I'm just so tired. It's been over two years, and the cloud still hangs. The bridge is still front and center, and I can't shake it."

I started seeing Laura at her Minnetonka office in mid-January 2008, nearly six months after the bridge collapse. The physical portion of my recovery had been going full steam ahead. I was walking fairly well despite some issues with balance. My left arm had healed and regained most of its rotation. The swelling in my cheeks and forehead continued to go down, which provided more symmetry and a more normal countenance. When I walked into a restaurant or other public place, folks were no longer staring at me. The only real repairs yet to be completed were the application of braces onto my teeth to get my jaw aligned so that I had a correct bite. Some cosmetic dental surgery would follow that. Then I would pretty much be done.

As the advancements in my physical recovery dwindled, the emotional damage done by the bridge began to poke through. I first noticed signs of frustration and irritability in late fall 2007. I tied my emotions to the fact that I couldn't yet accomplish some things physically, but figured that once I hurdled those obstacles, my spirits would be permanently lifted. For example, I thought I'd feel better inside once I was able to start eating whole foods again. However, when doctors gave me the okay to do so, the joy that I'd had in my life before the bridge collapse failed to reappear. I reasoned that it was because I couldn't yet do something else. "Once I'm walking again, I'll feel better inside," I thought. But when I started putting one foot in front of the other without the use of a walker, the ability to move forward emotionally continued to remain hidden. I kept reaching for the next thing, figuring it would pluck me from my sour disposition, but nothing did.

Sonja started noticing it, too. Over the Christmas holiday, we went up north to the Birkeland cabins along the shores of Lake Superior. The North Shore is a beautiful sight any time of the year, but especially during the early winter. The woodland is imprinted with the traffic patterns of hares, wolves, and moose. The crisp cracklings of tree boughs weighed down by virgin white snow echo across the sky under frozen stars. Chimney fires blanket picturesque log cabins with warmth. It sure beat the manufactured Christmases of urban America. Surrounded by such beauty, I shouldn't have had much reason to feel down. Not during the Christmas holiday, for sure. But there I was, plunked down on the couch in the cabin basement, staring blankly at whatever DirecTV had to offer. Sonja and the rest of her family remained upstairs, chatting, reminiscing, and sharing in the jolly of the season. I preferred to portray the lump of coal. It wasn't my intention to hide from the family, but for whatever reason, I felt the least irritated when I was away from the din of the celebration and the others. When the holiday gathering ended and Sonja and I drove south toward the Twin Cities, she called me out over my grumpy behavior. I took offense and pointed out all the ways I had participated in the weekend's activities. I argued that her perception of my behavior was merely her opinion, and that I felt I had struck a good balance between dividing my time between her family and myself. The discussion took up a good chunk of our three-and-a-half-hour drive home.

A few days later, as the calendar turned to 2008, Sonja and I traveled to Winnipeg, Canada, to celebrate my birthday and the New Year. While most wouldn't consider a trip to Winnipeg in winter to be a dream vacation, we were genuinely excited to drive the eight hours there. Our itinerary included a Manitoba Moose hockey game, a trip to the Manitoba history museum, and general sightseeing. I thought my mood during most of the trip was pretty upbeat. To my wife, I seemed generally quiet, not much interested in conversation, and distant. While our opinions on my disposition varied during the course of the trip, we could both agree that I turned downright ornery as we prepared to leave Winnipeg and head back home. It was early morning, and I had just stopped at a Horton's for a cup o'pick-me-up. We had pulled back onto the main road, when Sonja announced she wanted something to eat.

"We just left a place to eat, Sonja," I said in a condescending manner. "Why didn't you get a doughnut or something there?"

"I don't want a doughnut," she replied.

"Well, we're on the main road. I'm all set to get us out of town and back on the highway. Can you wait until we reach Grand Forks or something?"

"I can't wait that long. There's a Starbucks up ahead. Can you pull in the drive-through, please?"

"No. I'm headed out of town."

"Garrett, come on."

"What? You had an opportunity to get something. You're just being annoying now."

"Pull into Starbucks," Sonja pleaded. "Garrett!"

I pulled sharply into the Starbucks driveway, but instead of going through the drive-through lane, I pulled up to the store. "If you want something so badly, go in and get it," I told her.

"Why can't you use the drive-through?" she asked. "God, do you have to control everything?"

"It's your choice," I said. "Go in and get it, or wait two hours for Grand Forks." Sonja sighed, got out, and slammed the car door. I felt no remorse and hoped she learned her lesson, though I'm not really sure what lesson I had wanted her to learn. My fiancée returned to the car and sat in silence as I pulled back onto the highway. After a few minutes, the argument reignited. The air inside the car was chillier than the arctic temperature outside. We went back and forth about how each of us was right and the other was wrong. We scratched and clawed, and when it was finished, the good memories of our trip were left tattered. A few days later, Sonja approached me with an ultimatum: get help or risk breaking off the engagement. I relented and made the appointment to see Laura, whom Kristen, my qualified rehab consultant, had referred.

My first meeting with Laura included an evaluation. In order to help me, she had to diagnose my problem. Following a series of questions, she determined that I was battling with "adjustment disorder with depressed mood," a variant of post-traumatic stress disorder. To simplify, I was suffering from symptoms similar to PTSD, except I didn't have the anxiety and fear that often appear after undergoing trauma. Laura chalked that up to the fact that I could not remember anything from the accident immediately following the collapse.

According to WebMD, "a person with adjustment disorder develops emotional and/or behavioral symptoms as a reaction to a stressful event."

Symptoms generally begin within three months of the event and may cause problems with a person's ability to function. According to the National Center for PTSD, 8 percent of men and 20 percent of women who undergo trauma also experience PTSD. Thirty percent of these individuals deal with chronic symptoms of PTSD that can last a lifetime. Of all Americans, eight out of every one hundred will experience some form of PTSD in their lifetimes. Symptoms may include:

- Feeling of hopelessness
- Sadness
- Frequent crying
- Anxiety or worry
- Headaches or stomachaches
- Withdrawal or isolation from people and social activities
- Feeling tired or without energy
- Increase in the use of alcohol or other drugs
- Loss of interest and pleasure
- Poor concentration
- Irritability
- Anger

The diagnosis made sense to me. I was irritable. I was angry. I had difficulty concentrating at work, to the point that my supervisor sat me down and asked me why I was having trouble focusing. Headaches became more common. I was lethargic, and I felt hollow inside.

Now that the problem was diagnosed, we had to fix it. The cure? Psychotherapy. Laura and I had to hone in on the stressors and reprocess my thoughts and emotions. My brain took a major hit during the collapse, and it no longer processed thoughts as it had done previously. I was relying on the old way—an approach that didn't work anymore. That led to frustration.

I found out over the course of months and months that therapy consisted of peeling back layers like the skin of an onion. When the top layer was processed, it exposed a deeper layer that required more psychotherapy to resolve. This, in turn, revealed another layer, and so on. The first layer for me was trying to reconnect with the present world. I felt stuck as the world moved forward around me. I didn't feel like I was part of what was going on. I was a ghost.

I recall a moment in which I went to a local mall. I felt like I was in a blanket of fog as I walked through the corridors, passing people with destinations in mind and determination etched on their faces. They had things to get done. To me, their pace was fast and furious. They were blurs that made me dizzy. I stepped into a shop to purchase a greeting card. I made my selection and paid at the counter. Then I left. Halfway down the corridor, I realized that I had paid for the card but never picked it up off the counter when I left. I rushed down the hall and back to the store to retrieve my purchase. The young woman behind the counter handed me my card and laughed. Unfocused and in my own little world? Definitely.

Therapy is a journey of revelations. Therapists don't hand you an answer like hardware store employees hand you the right tool to fix the job. They help lead you to your own answer. A parent can tell a child how to ride a bicycle, but a boy or girl ultimately has to figure out how to do it alone. Every journey is unique to the individual. There is no cure for PTSD and its sister disorders, and recovery isn't a race. Some can get a handle on their disorder in a few months. Others take years.

My first major revelation happened at the fitness center. I was having difficulty fully committing myself to therapy. I felt that perhaps it was a lot of New Age hooey. I wanted a real solution—simple talk, I surmised, wasn't going to fix my problem.

I walked past a phalanx of exercise contraptions until I reached the elliptical machine. I hopped on, and as I began my revolutions, I looked across the aisle to my right. A repairman had dismantled one of the machines. A few dozen metal pieces lay strewn across the carpet. I guessed that the malfunction was likely nothing major, but for whatever reason, required a complete disassembly in order to fix the machine. That's when the light bulb went off: I was like that piece of equipment. In order to be made whole, I had to be stripped down and built back up! This revelation helped me understand that therapy was no quick-fix solution.

The delayering continued over the months, and the reprocessing was slow. I encountered false impressions of emotional recovery due to major life events. These temporary adrenaline rushes made me feel better; however, when the moments passed, I found myself back in the pit. These events included getting my braces removed, getting married, receiving compensation from the state of Minnesota, and searching for and purchasing a new home. Laura told me to beware of these, and even suggested postponing the wedding. I naively reassured her that I could handle both my emotional recovery and the wedding.

I am an introvert. I'd much prefer to be the observer than the participant. That makes talking about my feelings especially difficult. I could sense that Laura was frustrated by my reluctance to reach the in-depth conversations she felt were necessary to stimulate change. This did not shock me, as my wife has endured the same struggle. Sonja would have been better served going to dentistry school; getting me to tell her how I feel is like pulling teeth. I clench my emotions. They are very personal to me. I play my thoughts close to the vest. When I'm asked how I'm doing, I say "fine," even if I'm far from fine. It's learned behavior. I didn't have a problem with that; it was who I was.

Adjustment disorder amplified this trait. This was no more apparent than during the holiday season of 2008, a few months after Sonja and I had gotten married. We were back up at the North Shore property. It was early afternoon on New Year's Day. Sonja had been down at the lower cabin, near the Lake Superior shore, doing craft projects with her nieces. I was at the upper cabin, near the highway, and had decided to take my new snowshoes—a Christmas gift—out for a hike. I told Sonja's mom that I'd be out trekking through the snow, but I didn't pass the message on to Sonja. I hopped into the car and drove to nearby Temperance State Park. I strapped on the snowshoes and headed upriver, along the trail.

As I got farther and farther from the highway, I felt a real sense of peace come over me, something I hadn't experienced since the accident. The world had slowed to a stop. Nothing moved. I didn't see a single squirrel or crow. It was silent except for a light wind that turned my nose and cheeks a rosy red. For a long stretch of trail, I encountered nobody. I found a place slightly off the trail that overlooked the frozen Temperance River. Wearing snow pants, I plunked down on the white blanket between some evergreens and listened to the silence. It was like a door had opened, and God was standing there leaning against the frame and asking me how I was doing. I couldn't lie to him. I couldn't say "fine."

I sat in that snow pile for a half an hour, spilling my emotions down the riverbank. Tears flooded out of me and froze to my face. I told God that I couldn't do this anymore. I couldn't carry the weight of my emotions. I was exhausted, having spent more than a year trying to fix myself. "I quit," I told God. "I'm handing this off to you." I grabbed hold of a tree trunk and pulled myself up. I began my two-mile walk back to the park entrance. As I neared the trail's beginning, familiar faces popped up in front of me. It was Sonja's cousins, who just so happened to have stopped at the park for their own little hike. I took their photo and then headed back to the car.

It was midafternoon, and I wasn't quite ready to return to the cabin. I wanted to call, but there's no cell phone reception that far north of Duluth. I decided to head a few more miles up Highway 61 to Lutsen and stop in at the ski lodge for a bite to eat and to complete a form I had been asked to fill out by my attorney regarding my partial permanent disability and future wage loss.

I spent about ninety minutes at the lodge, munching on a sandwich and filling out several pages of a questionnaire, when I noticed through the window that the sun had begun to set. I paid for my meal and left, realizing that I was a good thirty-five miles north of the family cabins. It would be dark before I got back for dinner. When I pulled up to the upper cabin about forty-five minutes later, Sonja's mom stepped out and approached my car.

"Where have you been?" she asked. "Sonja and the others went out looking for you."

I gave her an odd look, as if I didn't believe her. "That's silly," I said. "I'm fine. Just lost track of time. Besides, it just got dark, and how would they even know where to look?"

We tried calling Sonja, her brother, and her father on their cell phones, but that proved fruitless. Not two minutes later, their pickup came rumbling down the driveway. Sonja jumped out of the truck and raced up to me. I was still standing by my car.

"Where in the hell were you?" she screamed. "Where in the fuck were you?" Sonja rarely cursed, so I knew this wasn't going to end well. "We were worried to death about you. We didn't know where you were—you could have fallen off a cliff or gotten lost or got stuck in the ditch!" With both arms extended, Sonja slammed me against the side of the car.

"I'm fine, Sonja." I tried calming her down. "I told your mom I was going hiking. Besides, I had a map. I'm smart enough not to go off the trails or put myself in a dangerous situation."

"You don't know these woods like you think you do. Besides, Mom thought you were hiking around the cabin."

"I've hiked around the cabin many times. I wanted to go somewhere new. I don't see what the big deal is. You completely overreacted." That was the wrong thing for me to say.

"Overreacted? You're lucky there are people here who care about you!" Sonja pushed me hard into the car a second time. "All you think about is yourself. It's always about you. We're supposed to revolve around you because you were hurt on the bridge. But what about us? What about me? Who was there every day that you were in the hospital, huh?"

"Yes, I know. You were there. I just needed to get away for a while."

"You need to really think about this, Garrett Ebling. You need to figure out whether or not you want to be in this relationship. This is about *us*, not just you." And with one final shove, Sonja stomped away from me and into the cabin.

I apologized to the family for making them worry. It truly was not my intention to prompt a search party. They said they understood, but I could tell they were hurt. Months later, Sonja would understand that my behavior wasn't a direct result of something she said or did. She learned not to personalize it. But that didn't make my behavior acceptable.

Unfortunately, episodes like that continued for another eighteen months. There were times when I felt more distant from my loved ones than ever before. I grappled daily with my frustration and irritability. There were times when the stressors' grip seemed tighter than it had ever been. Throughout recovery, the phrase "the new me" is often uttered. Part of the process is accepting the new me. But if how I acted in Winnipeg or at the cabin was an indication of the new me, I didn't like it. I didn't want it.

> *We cascaded into the crevices*
> *Tumbled into the darkness*
> *Our bodies bounced and rattled*
> *Off concrete rubble and ribbons of steel.*
> *Some landed wet, others dry,*
> *Gargling and spitting blood and water.*
> *Most were patched up like tape onto a bicycle tire,*
> *Set free to return to the roads and bridges that betrayed us.*
> *And like dogs who despise leashes,*

We pull the other way. Who wants to go there?
We stand unbudging and hollow.
The trembling gnaws from inside out—
It settles, then swirls, like garbage in the wind.
There is no savior. No finish line.
Instead we wander with aching feet, unsettled mind,
A countenance not unlike the walking dead.
We've become numb.
The rug was pulled from beneath.
We collapsed with no net below.
Where is our deliverer?

—Garrett Ebling, "Numb"

****

When the special masters of the 35W Bridge collapse compensation fund were called to divvy up the monies available for survivors and the families of those who had perished, they wanted a better understanding of what many of us were going through. This resulted in a meeting with an expert on post-traumatic stress disorder. I received a copy of the transcript so that I, too, might have a firmer understanding of why I was feeling and acting as I was.

My intent was to only read a few pages at a time, but I couldn't put it down. What I read fascinated me. I highlighted a few of the statements that matched what I felt, including:

- People (with PTSD) have a hard time engaging in their current lives.
- They have a hard time concentrating. They have a hard time taking in new information, and so it becomes very hard for traumatized people to continue to go on with their lives and to grow.

What seems to be the great tragedy is the loss of enjoyment of life and the numbing; the lack of ability to experience pleasure.

This expert detailed how the brain of a traumatized person did—or didn't—work. "The brain of traumatized people is much less capable of focusing attention to the here and now," the expert told the special master panel.

> The brain waves that you need in order to generate or focus a response to present experience is basically destroyed, so it is very hard for traumatized people to fully take in the present, and if you can't take in the present you cannot take in the pleasures generated by the present... It's about different parts of the brain not working together and not getting a synchrony, wrapping itself around current experiences.
>
> It kills one's life. It kills the pleasure of life...[They are] explosively angry, explosively unable to be with people, triggered violence, unable to control themselves...They would talk to you flat...[They did] not at all have any feelings for their kids. Their kids hated them because they were so distant and so uncaring about them... Gradually you see more and more numbing and being dead to the world and being a person who is barely alive over time.
>
> In order to overcome your trauma, sooner or later you need to go and revisit what happened and allow your brain to reprocess back. Then, while you are safe, activate the parts of your brain that got deactivated at the time of the trauma to have your brain complete the time sequence so you know that it happened a long time ago rather than it's happening right now...and that's really what treatment is all about—to help people to be here and not there.

His solution wasn't new to me; he reiterated what Laura had been telling me all along. The only way out of this was to talk my way out of it. But what shocked me most was his description of what PTSD did to those who never addressed it.

The expert told the story of a study done shortly after the end of World War II. Veterans were interviewed about their wartime experiences. Their accounts were grisly, detailed. They shared graphic scenes of injury and death, what it was like to have to kill a man, to fight for your life. Fifty years later, those who were still alive were interviewed a second time. They were asked the same questions. Those who had not suffered from PTSD told markedly different versions of what they'd experienced while fighting. Their accounts were romanticized. They focused on their relationships with other soldiers, how they fought as brothers, and what they learned from their wartime experiences. Those with PTSD, however, recounted their experience nearly word-for-word as they had done half a century earlier. They were stuck in that moment. They hadn't moved forward emotionally. They suffered from this emotional shell-shock all that time.

Not only does PTSD prevent you from emotionally moving forward from the trauma, it eats away at your lifespan.

"All literature shows that if people have PTSD, they die earlier, they age faster and it affects the whole aging process," the expert told the panel. "Your stress hormones are interdigitated with your immune system so your whole body starts really reacting differently to the environment than it did before."

I was amazed at what I was reading, and horrified to think that this could be me. Even though I had survived, was I going to let the bridge collapse shorten my life?

In his book *The Noticer*, Andy Andrews wrote:

"Whatever you focus upon, increases. When you focus on the things you need, you'll find those needs increasing. If you set your mind on loss, you're more likely to lose...But a grateful perspective brings happiness and abundance into a person's life."

Those words stuck in my craw when I first heard them. What had I been focusing on? My depression. Instances and situations that prompted my ire. Dissatisfaction with my relationships with others. My physical limitations. My loss of control. In short, I was focusing on the negatives. Andy Andrews was right: loss begets loss. The negative begets more negative. It's a slippery slope that sends you right back into the pit. As I looked back on the past several months, I realized that my focus had been considerably off. I hadn't been regularly attending church. I wasn't getting to the fitness center and exercising regularly. I had abandoned multivitamins and healthy eating. I was, metaphorically, cooking with a bad recipe.

I can't say that the author's words fixed me; in fact, things were soon to take a turn for the worse. But it was another revelation, like the tearing apart of the elliptical machine, that helped point me in the right direction.

****

On February 1, 2007, I gave a speech as part of a six-month remembrance service held at Roseville Lutheran Church in Roseville, Minnesota:

There is a Japanese proverb that goes, "Fall seven times, stand up eight." As bridge victims, survivors or whatever else you want to call us, we know all about falling. Fate, for whatever reason, put us on the I-35W Bridge that early evening of August 1—a mere six months ago today—and sent us flailing. We all fell—hard. And God decided to take some of us home. We continue to pray for them and their families. Our injuries ranged from a few scratches to life-threatening. There were several hospital stays, countless doctor visits, numerous counseling sessions. When the bills started coming in, we went out searching for help. Sometimes help found us. For those who survived, we are all back in our homes now. Thank God for that. These first six months found us lying down, dazed, struggling to make sense of something not one of us ever thought we'd see happen. Not here. Not to us. I have always tried to see the good in this—even as I sat in the bottom of the pit, looking up from the depths and knowing it would be a long, hard climb out. I'd let out a sigh and then with two broken feet I'd try to stand. At first it was on only one leg, with a walker.

Time marched on, and a hand-powered scooter replaced the walker.

And finally, weeks later, it became two feet. One day, a day as normal as the one that threw me into the pit, I stood again. That was more than that decrepit bridge could ever say. Now it is my time to climb. So here we are, standing. As survivors, each of us has our own load to carry, this much is true. And yet we are all in this together. Through this experience we have forged friendships much stronger than any gusset plate or steel beam. One thing is certain: not one of us deserved to have this happen to us. Even more certain, each of us has the capacity and will to become stronger because of it. Some of us seek retribution, others justice, still others simply the truth. I seek these things and more. I remember who I was before the bridge collapse. I've had six months to evaluate who I am, and God has given me a second opportunity to paint myself as who I ought to be: more loving, more committed, more aware, more like him. Now that's something worth standing for. People ask me regularly how I'm doing. Am I back to normal, physically and emotionally? No, not quite. If I were to really think about it, I suppose my answer would be, I'm "closer to fine."

9

"I'D BETTER GO," I said to myself with a sigh as I looked for the next interstate exit that would provide relief for my bladder. I had just left home twenty minutes earlier, and already I felt that uncomfortable pressure "down there." When I get anxious, I find I have the frequent urge to relieve myself, and today was one of those days. It was August 1, 2009, and I was headed south on Interstate 35W toward the Red Cross building in downtown Minneapolis, a stone's throw from the new 35W Bridge. The most direct way there from my house in Andover was to wind my way to I-35W south and shoot down into Minneapolis, and that would mean crossing over the new bridge, but I didn't want to do that.

I entered the suburb of Roseville and saw a sign for Perkins, a twenty-four-hour restaurant known for its home-style cooking. I pulled into the parking lot and walked briskly toward the building. I looked up and noticed the giant American flag—a Perkins trademark—fluttering at half-staff in the breeze of this unusually cool early August morning. Each year since 2007, the governor has ordered all state flags on August 1 be lowered in reverence for those affected

171

by the bridge collapse.

On my way out the door, I turned and looked over my right shoulder to view the flag again. It felt surreal to be staring at a U.S. flag at half-staff partly in my honor—and I was still alive to see it.

Two men of retirement age wcre standing next to a vehicle parked next to mine. One of them noticed me looking at the flag and said, "Do you know why the flag is at half-staff?" The other chimed in, "Who died?"

Their obtuse inquiry triggered a wave of anger and hurt. *Thirteen people died, idiot!* I screamed internally, but all that came out was a quiet "I'm pretty sure it's to remember the 35W Bridge victims."

"Oh," he said, rubbing his chin as if it were the ignition to his memory. "I guess that *was* today." They immediately went back to their conversation. I entered my car, shaking my head. How can something so intensely personal to me be completely dismissed by others just two years after the fact?

I sat there inside my car for a minute to calm myself down. The two seniors climbed into their own vehicles and pulled out ahead of me. I followed one of them back to the interstate. He was headed south, just as I was. As we both drove toward downtown, I couldn't stop thinking about these two individuals' comments. I was upset at myself for not telling them who I was, and why this was such a heavy, emotional day for me—and why it should be for them too. I should have lit into them a little, lashed out at them for forgetting, I thought. I also tried to think about it from their perspective. Why had they forgotten about something I think about every waking hour of every day? Had I apportioned too much importance to the day? If I hadn't been on the bridge when it collapsed, would the day be nothing more than a scan of a newspaper's anniversary article and a shrug of the shoulders?

I got so caught up in my self-discussion that I lost track of where I was. I had just about reached downtown, and found myself three lanes over from the last exit before coming up on the new 35W Bridge. While I had conquered other overpasses, spans, tunnels, and such, this was the one bridge that I simply did not want to cross. I feared doing so might unleash emotions or memories I wasn't prepared to handle.

"Crap!" I yelled. Without even checking my mirrors, I yanked the steering wheel to the right, glided across all lanes, and caught the off-ramp with but three feet to spare. I slammed on the brakes as I flew up to the stoplight at the end of the ramp. Ironically, my heart was now lodged further up my throat than it would have been had I crossed the bridge.

I turned onto a side street, crossed over I-35W, and then turned onto the road that crossed the Tenth Avenue Bridge, which runs alongside the new 35W Bridge. I glanced over my right shoulder and took a hard look at the 35W Bridge now beside me. In a few minutes, I'd be standing underneath it for the first time.

A few quick turns, and I arrived at the Red Cross building. Avoiding the bridge took a couple of extra minutes, but I was several minutes early anyway. I noticed a few collapse survivors standing in the parking lot; most of them I did not know well. I pulled into a spot and turned off my car. I wasn't ready to get out.

I was scared. I had done such a great job of stuffing my feelings down my throat that I hadn't given one thought to how and what I might feel in a few minutes, when I would walk down to the base of the bridge. Ignorance is bliss, someone once said, but now it had frozen me. I had become confined in my car mere yards from where I was trapped in my car two years ago to the day. Funny, huh?

I said a prayer. *God, I'm really unprepared for what I'm about to feel. It's been two years since the accident. Last year, I was in northern Minnesota getting married, standing on the shore and tossing a piece of the bridge into Lake Superior, hoping the tide would pull it and my despondency to its rocky bottom. And now, it's a year later. This emotional monster still resides in me. I want to drown him so badly. Lord, all I ask is that you speak to me. Let something good come from this visit today. In your name, amen.*

I took a deep breath and grabbed the door handle. I climbed out, clutching my hooded sweatshirt. *The first of August should never be this cool*, I thought to myself.

I walked toward the clump of people in the middle of the parking lot. A couple of them waved and shouted, "Hi, Garrett!" though I didn't know their names and they looked only vaguely familiar. The introvert in me gravitated toward those whom I already knew. I approached a man named Brent Olson and his wife, Chris. They were also represented by my law firm and had been very diligent in lobbying for the compensation bill, despite the fact that their automobile suffered more physical injury than they did on the bridge that day. I think it was Brent's fatherly persona that drew me to him from the beginning.

"Garrett! We're so glad you could make it," he said, giving me a shoulder hug.

"Good to see the both of you. I feel kind of strange. This is my first time visiting the bridge," I reminded them.

"Take as much time as you need," he replied. "It'll always be a day that holds special meaning for us."

After finally getting a chance to visit the bathroom, I headed with the group down to the new 35W Bridge. I walked ahead of a woman—another person I didn't recognize—who was upset about how the distribution of compensation funds had created a difficult situation for her and her family. Relatives and others had found out through a newspaper article how much money they had received. Now she and her family were being hit up for money. She was upset that the newspaper had published the amount awarded to her, the families of the deceased, and the other bridge survivors.

Whether we liked it or not, how much each of us received was open to disclosure, because the compensation process was detailed in a government document. Perhaps it didn't bother me because of my journalism background or my understanding of just how precious the idea of open government is. Or maybe I just didn't care what other people thought about the amount that I had received. What I did care about was that the general public didn't know or didn't understand that the amounts we received were much less than the amount of each person's total damages. I also felt that all the money in the world wouldn't give me back my old, normal self. I can't speak for others, but if I was on *Let's Make a Deal* and Monte Hall offered me a billion dollars or my old body back, I'd tell him to keep the money; I'll take my old self hidden behind the curtain.

I took my clunky, patched-up body down toward the bridge along the river's west bank, increasing my pace to distance myself from the discussion over money-grubbing relatives. I reached the base of the bridge and looked up. It towered above me as if it were a smooth, glassy Minneapolis skyscraper and I were the Mary Tyler Moore statue fixed along Nicollet Avenue. I couldn't get over the massive size of the span, how far above me it was. *I fell that far? Impossible*, I thought. Impossible that I lived through it. Impossible that I was standing here today.

Because of the steepness of the riverbank, the sidewalk wound back and forth down to the shoreline, as if its pedestrians were in line for the roller coaster at an amusement park. Come to think of it, my last ride on that bridge felt just like a trip on one of those coaster rides. I moved along, back and forth, until I reached the platform. It was a concrete landing, the same off-white color as the bridge, and it provided plenty of space to observe. Immediately to the left was the University of Minnesota St. Anthony Falls Laboratory.

The platform sat several feet above the water, enclosed by a railing. This proved to be a deterrent to one couple, who had brought a wreath of flowers they had planned to toss into the river to honor a loved one who had perished in the bridge collapse. The couple, along with a few others, walked back up the hill and approached the security gate at the entrance to the laboratory. A man came out to the gate and exchanged words with the group. Apparently, security procedures would not allow the family to enter the facility. After about a minute, the man took the wreath and walked out onto a catwalk that extended over the edge of the river. He paused so that the family could get their camera ready. Then, with an exaggerated motion, he heaved the wreath over the edge. The camera clicked. The wreath smacked the water and broke apart. It seemed to me that the significance of the moment was lost; policy had trumped a human need to grieve. These people didn't get to personally say good-bye to their loved one on August 1, 2007. It irked me that they were denied that opportunity once again.

When the unofficial ceremony ended, I turned my gaze to the other side of the river, to the north end of the bridge. I stared at the patch of river where my car had plummeted. The scene was a stark contrast to what it had been two years earlier. Then, the water was turbulent, riddled with twisted steel and concrete. Now it was calm, except for some babbling as it spanked rocks that protruded from the surface. Then, news and police helicopters chopped up the smoky air. Now, an occasional gull or hawk circled above us, gliding on the wind. Then, we were bloodied and broken, some screaming and others dying. Now, we were put back together and silent. I couldn't help but compare and contrast.

A hand touched my shoulder. It was Margaret McAbee. I hadn't seen her since my one and only visit to the Survivor Resources meeting she had led some twenty-two months earlier.

"How are you doing?" she asked.

"It's so peaceful here," I said, not answering her question and staring ahead at that same spot on the river. "I didn't know what to expect when I came down here, but it wasn't this."

"This is a very powerful place," she said softly, also looking out over the river.

"Being down here—this is my first time since that day, you know?" Margaret nodded. "I've been so angry at that bridge. At this place. I almost wish this new bridge wasn't built. It happened so fast. We're so quick to move forward and move on. And right now, I can't. But I'm feeling a certain sense of peace here. This feels like a memorial garden, a cemetery. I'm glad I came."

Margaret didn't respond. She and I just kept staring, and that was all right. To me, her silence was affirmation of what I was feeling.

"How did you get involved with Survivor Resources?" I asked.

"Several years ago, my husband was murdered," she replied. "I sought a resource to help me deal with my grief. Over time, I got more involved. I wanted to help others. I, along with others, helped start Survivor Resources in 1995. Then in 2006, my son was killed in a snowmobile accident. When the bridge collapsed a year later, we were called on to offer assistance. That's how the weekly group survivors meetings got started. The bridge collapse came along in a time of my life when I needed something to add some purpose to my life."

I nodded. It made sense to me now.

A comment from a man behind us broke up our conversation. "You see those young trees on the other side of the river there?" he said, pointing. "There's only twelve of them. I counted. They should've planted thirteen, one for each of us who died. Don't know why they didn't. Typical government screw-up."

I didn't know trees were planted in memory of those who died on the bridge. And we were so far away that I couldn't tell how anyone from this distance could know for sure that thirteen weren't planted. But I simply let it go. I wasn't here to grumble; I was here to grieve.

My gaze wandered up above the dozen or so saplings, to the embankment north of the railroad tracks that ran parallel to the river. It was on that embankment that Paula, her husband, Brad, and their daughters tumbled in their van like dice inside a cup. I focused on the spot where their vehicle likely came to rest. I had seen photos taken shortly after the collapse of Brad lying on the ground next to his van. I couldn't begin to imagine what that must have been like, being a husband and a father and being unable to help his family. What was it like to hear their screams, see their blood and tears, and feel handcuffed by his own physical injury and shock? A chill shot through my body. I wasn't sure if it was from that thought or the breeze that had picked up along the waterfront.

A female voice shook me from my internal conversation. "Can I talk with you for a minute?"

"Hi," I said. The woman's face was unfamiliar to me.

"I need to talk to you about him," she said as she turned and looked over her shoulder at her boyfriend, who stood about thirty feet from us. He was a fellow bridge survivor, whom I recognized.

"Um, sure," I replied. I wondered how I could be of assistance. I didn't really know anything about him.

"I don't know what to do. I feel like my relationship with him is hanging by the final thread."

I looked at her helplessly. "What do you mean?" I asked.

The middle-aged woman grabbed the conversation by the horns. "It's his moodiness. He's so moody. And he's got such a sensitive trigger finger. One minute, he seems to be fine, and the next, he just suddenly goes off. I feel like I can't get close to him."

"It sounds like he has PTSD," I said. "It's pretty common for people who endure trauma to have it. My therapist says I have a form of it. I know where you're coming from, and I'm sorry to hear what you're going through."

"That's not all," she continued. "He says, 'You don't understand. You weren't there,' and he's right. But I *have* been with him every step of the way. Where were his daughters when he needed them? I took care of him when he was injured. I came over and did the cooking, the cleaning. Everything. I've tried to endure it, thinking he'll get better. But it's not getting better."

I pursed my lips and nodded.

"I just don't know if I can stay with him. This is too hard. I've given everything for him and get little in return," she added. It was easy to see the frustration on her face.

"He needs to go see a therapist," I said. "It's the only way. He has to process his feelings. Stuffing them in won't help. Believe me, I know."

"He won't go. He says he can handle it."

I felt like I was a fly on the wall watching my own situation unfold a year and a half earlier. Her words were Sonja's words. He was me. I didn't want to upset her by telling her that fifteen months later, I was still battling those same demons. My best advice was to reiterate the importance of seeking a mental health counselor.

It was time to start heading up the hill. We had given ourselves an hour's worth of time to pay our respects. In thirty minutes, a filmmaker named Daniel Kenney was going to show an unfinished version of a documentary about the 35W Bridge called *One Day in August* at a theater across town. He invited bridge collapse survivors and their families to view the film and provide feedback. Most of us at the bridge planned to attend.

I made my ascent back up the winding sidewalk as Margaret and I engaged in small talk.

"You're more than welcome to stop by and visit the group," she said. "We're still meeting twice a month. I understand why you stopped going. I just want you to know the group isn't like that anymore."

"Thanks, Margaret," I replied.

Grieving is a process, not a moment. I learned that lesson the hard way over the past two years. I had thought that tossing debris into Lake Superior would somehow complete my grieving process. I thought the same about avoiding the bridge site altogether. There is no elixir or magic pill for getting over trauma. You paddle hard through it. And sometimes you have to paddle upstream.

****

I briskly walked into Romano's Macaroni Grill for a midday lunch away from the office. My lunch date? My former rehabilitation consultant, Kristen. I had e-mailed Kristen a couple of weeks prior to see if she'd be available for some catching up over a meal. I hadn't seen her in more than a year and a half. Our professional relationship had ended the moment I returned to work full time in May 2008. In that time, I had gotten married, had braces put on my teeth and later removed, and purchased a home.

Kristen waited for me under some shelter from the achingly cold, late-October rain, and we walked into the restaurant together. The host greeted us in Spanish as his way of being funny. I ignored his attempt at humor. "Table for two, please," I said to him, then suddenly realized that I could have easily replied in Spanish, having taken an introductory course a few years earlier.

Kristen spit out a rapid response in Spanish, and I looked at her with a "Where did that come from?" expression on my face.

"I'm taking Spanish lessons," she said. "And guitar lessons, too. You play guitar if I remember correctly, right?"

"Well, I don't know if I'd call myself a musician," I replied. "I only know a handful of chords. But if all you know is the G, C, and D chords, you can play a lot of songs."

We pored over the menu and decided that on such a cold, wet October day, some warm soup, pizza, and pasta would heat us up from the inside out.

"So, tell me," Kristen said, "What's been going on with you? You look great! Your facial swelling is gone, your scars have blended in nicely, and you've gotten your weight back."

I rolled my eyes. Gaining back my weight wasn't part of my plan, as I had been slightly pudgy when the accident occurred.

"Oh, boy. Well, as you know, Sonja and I got married one year after the bridge collapse," I reminded her.

"That's right. You've been married for over a year now. It's amazing how fast time flies," she remarked.

"Yeah, it sure has. Which reminds me, I brought a book of wedding photos that Sonja put together, like you asked."

"Wonderful," Kristen said, and I pulled two books from my satchel and handed them to her as we continued talking.

"And in May, we purchased a home, so we've been busy getting used to domestic life."

"Where are you living now?" she asked.

"Andover."

"Where's that?"

"Do you know where Coon Rapids is?" I asked. She nodded. "Well, it's just north of there." I often joke to friends that I live in the south metro—of Duluth.

"Say, that reminds me. Did you ever receive money from the state?" Kristen asked.

"Yes. I used that to put a down payment on the house. But there are still lawsuits pending. It likely won't be resolved for a while," I said.

"Are you still seeing Laura?" she asked, referring to my therapist.

"Yes, it'll be two years in January," I said.

"Do you feel she's helping you through your trauma?"

I paused for a bit while chewing on my lower lip. "Yeah, she is. If I'm frustrated at all, it's because if you'd told me at the beginning that I'd be in therapy for two years or more, I'd have called that a failure. But I've learned a lot so far."

"Like what?"

The waitress arrived and interrupted to take our orders.

"I'll take the soup and try the pizza," Kristen told the young woman in the white button-down shirt and apron.

"And for you, sir?" the waitress asked.

"I'll have the rigatoni," I said, double-checking the menu. I turned to Kristen. "What did you ask?"

"Your therapy. How is it going?"

"Oh, that's right. Well, it's a slow process. I'm discovering that some of the roots of what I'm feeling are found in moments and relationships before the bridge collapse."

"That makes sense," Kristen said. "I've seen it in many of my clients where a severe trauma can unlock things that had been suppressed in the mind. They no longer have the ability to lock these emotions away."

"That's what Laura told me," I said. "This emotional part—I feel like it's the one thing that's so hard for the outsider to understand. I mean, take my situation. Overall, I had a miraculous recovery. I got married. I got a check from the government, paid off my car, student and credit card loans, and purchased a new house. In most people's eyes, I should be the happiest person on the planet. But most of the time, I'm just the opposite. And the strangest part is that I'm an intelligent guy, I'm rational. I can see all this. Yet when the irritability and frustration set in, I'm paralyzed. I succumb to it and can't fight it. So I can see the outsider's get-over-it viewpoint. I tell myself to just get over it. But I can't turn it on and off like a switch. Early on, I thought I only had bones to heal. But I didn't realize I had my mind to heal as well, and it's not an easy thing to fix."

Kristen nodded. "People in my position, we hear our clients' stories, we're around them, but even though we're trained to help them deal with their injuries, I can't say we can completely understand what you and they have gone through," she said. "Say, have you ever thought of writing a blog?"

"Not really," I replied. I had blogged in the past, but it was about the National Hockey League. Only five people read it: three were my close friends, and two were coworkers.

"There's a guy who was on *Oprah*," she said, "and Oprah found him through his blog. He started a blog as a resource for widowers and, uh, what's the term for—men are widowers so women are…"

"Widows?" I said, and shrugged my shoulders.

"Yeah, whatever. Well he started this blog, and it got all these followers and became a great thing that helped a lot of people."

"That sounds like a great story."

"Yes, and I think you could do some good with it. You've got an interesting story to tell. I've had so many clients who were far less injured than you but for whatever reason, they can't find it in them to work to get better. I mean, you broke every bone in your face! And these people might have a back fracture and can't find motivation to improve. I think people would read your blog and maybe find it in themselves to take that next step."

"Well, that's definitely an idea." I did, indeed, find it plausible. I just wondered if I'd be able to pull in double-digit readership. It would be a first.

The food arrived, and we continued our chat. The conversation turned to Kristen's family, specifically the struggles of managing a melded family with teenage children from previous marriages—a topic on which I couldn't provide much input, but I think an attentive ear was all she needed. I asked if she had plans to do any downhill skiing this winter, as she is a well-known thrill seeker.

"Oh yeah, we always plan a winter ski trip. Montana, Colorado. My family loves it."

We wolfed down our food and absorbed its warmth. I grabbed the check.

"You don't have to do that," said Kristen.

"Oh, I have to," I said. "After all you did for my family and me? It's the least I can do." We headed for the door. Outside, the drizzle had evolved into a full-fledged, forty-three-degree downpour.

"Did I tell you I went skydiving last year?" Kristen asked as we prepared to part ways and dodge raindrops.

"No." It didn't surprise me. "What was it like when your feet left the plane floor?" I asked.

"Incredible. For the first few seconds, you're just spinning in free fall. It takes a few seconds to gather your bearings, but it's awesome," she said.

It's not the fall that kills you, it's the landing, I thought as I said farewell to Kristen and dashed to my vehicle. We both fell. Hers was exhilarating. Mine was terrifying. Her emotion lasted minutes, if not a handful of seconds. Mine eats at me to this day. And here we were, both back on solid ground, sharing our stories. It's all in the perspective, I guess.

****

When I spoke with Margaret from Survivor Resources on the second anniversary of the bridge collapse, I told her that I would return at some point to a 35W Bridge survivors' group meeting. I hadn't been to a meeting in nearly two years, having been put off by the negative emotional climate created by a few of the participants. Additionally, the group met in downtown St. Paul, a commute for me that led through both Minneapolis and St. Paul during the evening rush hour—hardly a pleasant driving experience. I had decided that my individual therapy sessions and the occasional survivor reunions at various attorney functions and anniversaries, as well as Facebook greetings, were more than suitable. However, in mid-November 2009, I made the time to travel from work in Edina over to St. Paul to see how the meetings had progressed.

In a way, I was surprised these meetings were still happening. Originally, I had assumed that the group therapy sessions were meant to be short-term, a temporary foothold for those beginning their ascent back into the world and their new sense of normalcy. In other arenas, support for survivors ended months, if not a year or more, earlier. This group continued, though.

I wondered how many of my peers from the collapse would be attending the evening session. Would I be the only one there? What could there be to discuss twenty-seven months after the accident, more than a year after the replacement bridge had opened? I pulled into the parking lot right at 6:30 p.m. The November sky had grown dark more than an hour earlier. The air was warmer and calmer than when Darin and I had arrived during my previous visit. I walked to the door and recognized four faces. Brent, Chris, and the

182

woman I had spoken to at the bridge site during the second anniversary and her companion greeted me with handshakes, hugs, and pats on the back. "Garrett! What a great surprise," Brent exclaimed as he held the door open. Brent, Chris, and the other couple were session regulars, I soon found out. Apparently, the handful of individuals who still met had become a tightly knit group. We made our way up a flight of stairs and down a couple of hallways until we arrived at Margaret's office. We grabbed some office chairs just as a few other familiar faces popped through the door. Coincidentally, of the more than 170 people on the bridge that day, I knew the names of each of the eight people gathered with me in an arc around Margaret's desk that night.

The intimacy of the group was evident from the get-go. Omar Abuabara, who was a regular call-in to the meeting from his home in Texas, was on the phone providing jabs at the others in the room for not coming to visit him, as two others in the room had just recently done. A practical jokester, Omar had actually been calling from his cell phone and was coming up the stairs of the precinct for a surprise visit. There was a collective gasp and celebratory cheer when he walked in.

As the outsider, I was the first to be asked about how I was doing. "Physically, I feel really good," I said. "My body is as healed as it can be. Yes, I still have soreness in my left ankle, and I still can't smell. My face can hurt sometimes, and I do seem to get headaches a little more than before the bridge, likely a result of the brain trauma. But emotionally, it's as hard now as it was when I felt my darkest right before starting therapy. It's like there are two me's: the kind, gentle, moving-forward me, and the angry, irritable, frustrated, stuck me. It's this never-ending battle inside my skull, and I'm just so damn tired of it. I'm weary."

"Are you going to therapy or taking any medication?" asked Margaret.

"My therapist suggested antidepressants, but I haven't gone there yet," I said. "I just started taking fish-oil pills, multivitamins. And I just started my gym membership up again last week, and I'm trying to exercise regularly. That seemed to help me before. But the arguing with my wife has become more frequent and intense. I feel apathy toward my marriage, and it's dangerous."

"You should try Cymbalta. It doesn't make you high, but takes the edge off," a woman from the other side of the arc suggested. Of all of us seated there, she was the one hurting the most physically. She had suffered a significant back injury that day on the bridge, and two years later, she still had terrible discomfort. In fact, she was about to return to the doctor and have a procedure to install a pain pump.

"If this doesn't work, I…I…I'm just going to give up," she said as tears welled up in her eyes. "I'm out of answers, and out of patience."

Another man spoke up. I'd gotten to know him as we both lobbied the legislature for compensation during the spring of 2008. I learned at this gathering that he lived but a mile from me, in neighboring Ham Lake. He was about twenty years older than me, with grown kids. Prior to the collapse, he worked in construction. Injuries from the bridge stopped that career short, and he had become a real estate agent. He also began flipping houses, but now hired out the work.

"I understand what you mean," he said as he turned toward me. "I get like you, too. My kids say I've changed and that 'Dad acts differently now.' My wife and I've been in counseling. We never used to fight—well, we had our arguments, but not like this." He paused, and the tears exploded from his eyes. "I'm sorry."

He didn't have to say he was sorry. We all knew how he felt. We felt it too.

The discussion turned to the proposed 35W Bridge memorial. A few months earlier, the city of Minneapolis had hired a fund-raiser and tasked her with finding over $1 million for the memorial. The idea for a memorial had been brought up immediately following the bridge collapse. Initially, there was much zeal for the project, but time and a recession had put a significant dent in any progress toward raising the needed funds. This fund-raiser, the city hoped, would be able to convince the metro's philanthropists to open their wallets and purses for the cause. I had met with this woman over a cup of coffee earlier in the fall. She wanted to know my bridge story and what I wanted to see in a memorial, if I wanted to see one built at all. Throughout the autumn, she had met with several others like me.

The consensus of the group that night was that a bridge memorial was a welcome thing *if* it emphasized not just the thirteen who perished, but also those like us who survived but are now left dealing with our physical and emotional junk for quite possibly the rest of our lives. We felt the original concept—a fountain with thirteen beams—failed to address the impact on the living. (In the end, the memorial design met the desires of most survivors and family members of those who had died. The mayor deserves credit for leading the memorial project and always keeping the thoughts and wishes of those directly involved in the collapse paramount.)

The meeting ended with plans to hold a holiday party at the home of one of the couples who regularly attended the group session. "Garrett, you're going to be there, right?" Brent asked. "And bring Sonja with you this time!" was his parting shot. As I said my good-byes and climbed into the car, I was caught off guard by what had just happened. My emotional issues, while unique to me, were not very unique at all. My feelings were not abnormal. Granted, they weren't healthy, but they were legitimate. I wasn't going through this alone. I still didn't know where this emotional journey was leading me, but wherever I ended up, I wouldn't be the only one there. There was comfort in that.

✻✻✼Υ✼✳✳✴✶✴✶✴✷✦✦✦

ERICA GWILLIM

The unofficial definition of faith is a well-known passage from the New Testament: being sure of what you hope for and certain of what you do not see. For Minneapolis resident Erica Gwillim, it was her faith that pulled her safely from the tangled web of bent beams and rubble of the 35W Bridge that fateful day.

In the summer of 2007, Erica was working as a home-based mental health therapist and supervisor for Nystrom and Associates, a company with a Christian background and several Minnesota clinics, including New Brighton, an inner-ring northern Minneapolis suburb. She adored her job there, with the challenges and discoveries that accompanied the position.

"I traveled around the Twin Cities to meet with my clients and their families in their homes," Erica said. Her clients were children and young adults between the ages of three and twenty-one. The mental health conditions she came across ran the gamut: attention deficit hyperactivity disorder, anxiety, Asperger's syndrome, autism, bipolar disorder, depression, oppositional defiant disorder, you name it. Erica also worked with the families of these children on parenting and family dynamics in order to enhance the treatments' chance of success. For a host of reasons, she worked often with low-income families.

"At the time, I was more of a supervisor than an actual therapist, but I routinely went out in the field to meet with clients," said Erica, a native of Sycamore, Illinois, who attended the University of Minnesota for her graduate degree in social work.

As for so many who were on the 35W Bridge when it collapsed, Erica's day began normally. Her commute led her north out of Minneapolis, where she lived near Hennepin County Medical Center with her uncle, aunt, and cousin. The trip to New Brighton almost always included a jaunt across the 35W Bridge deck. She had meetings that morning, then she planned to spend the afternoon accompanying her staff to the homes of a few clients in the northern and western suburbs.

Throughout the day, Erica looked forward to the evening, when she'd meet her cousins for dinner in Richfield, a suburb south of Minneapolis along I-35W, then head to her church's outdoor gathering, "Worship without Walls," with her boyfriend, Bryan.

By early afternoon, Erica sensed that the evening rush-hour commute was going to be slow. She was in Plymouth, heading north to Coon Rapids to see her last client of the day. She called her mother in Sycamore, as she did each weekday. "I don't know if I should go to this last appointment, Mom," Erica said. "I have so much paperwork to do. I should just go home. I'll be sitting in so much traffic." The client's needs would still be met even if Erica didn't attend this particular session in Coon Rapids.

"Finally, I was like, 'No, I really should go,'" the then-thirty-three-year-old decided. This visit held special meaning. It was the child's last session, a sort of graduation. "I ended up being glad I went. It's always rewarding to hear an adolescent talk about how he or she has improved," Erica said.

About to run out the door after the appointment, Erica was stopped by her staff member, who asked if she had time for a short discussion. Erica said she was reluctant, thinking, *Shoot! I'm already late for my dinner with my cousins, and I have to go to the bathroom, too!* But, characteristically, she took the time to answer a few questions before hitting the road.

Erica's route down to Richfield via Interstate 35W was roughly twenty miles. To take her mind off the heavy traffic, she called her coworker and close friend Marleen. They often chatted on the phone on workday evenings. They'd worked out a protocol for their frequently dropped calls: Erica would always be the one to call back. On this day, the phone kept cutting out, and each time Erica called back, she got Marleen's voice mail. As she crossed the 35W Bridge heading southbound, Erica gave up, deciding to leave a voice mail.

To this day, Erica doesn't recall seeing construction workers on the bridge. She doesn't remember bumper-to-bumper traffic. Her focus was on leaving a message for her friend. In a few short seconds, Marleen's voice mail would capture Erica's screams as her silver-colored 2002 Pontiac Grand Prix fell in a mixture of concrete and metal.

Erica eventually received a digital copy of that voice mail. In it, one can hear her voice waver, unnoticed by her, as the bridge begins to shake. As it collapses, Erica repeats, "Oh my gosh! Oh my gosh!" in a rising, haunting pitch. At impact, the phone cuts out.

I felt a back-and-forth motion," Erica recalled. "This all happened so quickly; it's kind of hard to piece it together. I remember seeing the back ends of the cars in front of me bounce. It was like a movie. Then the cars just dropped out of sight, and I saw the last one tip over the edge.

Then, almost right away, I felt myself dropping. I began to pray. *Lord, we're going down. I don't know how far, but we are going down. Please help us!* It felt like that lasted forever—that falling feeling. My stomach was in my throat and I felt like I was continually dropping.

Her life flashed before her eyes. In an instant, she saw her parents, her brothers, different family and friends, her church, and much more. "All these different snapshots in my brain. It was amazing how fast the brain can filter through all that information," Erica said. "I thought, *This is done. I'm gone— going to a better place*. It was a surreal experience for me."

Luckily for Erica, her car didn't flip. It didn't strike water. When the plummet ended, Erica reached for her cell phone immediately and called 911. She didn't feel any pain, but she was shaken up. When the emergency dispatcher answered, Erica suddenly realized she didn't know where she was. How would rescuers know where to arrive? She did recall seeing a sign for the Washington Avenue exit shortly before the bridge fell.

"I told the operator I was on the Washington Bridge." There was no such thing.

"Are you over the Mississippi River?" the female dispatcher asked.

"I'm glad she asked me that," Erica said. "Had she asked me what river I was over, I wouldn't have been able to tell her, even though I knew. I was in such shock."

Erica hung up the phone and took a minute to scan her surroundings. There was an SUV next to her car. The man inside of it got out and started walking around.

"I wasn't sure where we were. Could we fall further?" Erica wondered. "I saw this section of road just shooting up in front of me."

When the span fell, Erica's Grand Prix did not reach the river. It was on a section that landed between a rail line and the riverbank. The roadway in front of her launched upward like a ski jump. Vehicles on that part during the collapse slid backward. Behind her, the road surface buckled in the shape of an inverted V.

"It was so silent and really eerie," Erica remembered. "This major thing happened, and more should be going on. I rolled down my window and all this dust came in. I coughed a little and yelled to the man who was in the SUV, 'Is it okay for me to get out of my car?' He said, 'Oh yeah. We've landed. We've gone as far as we can go.'"

At this point, Erica really didn't know what to do—about anything. Logic seemed to have fallen from her mind, just as she had fallen with the bridge. "Should I turn my car off? I didn't know what to do."

She began making calls. She reached her cousin Gina, who was waiting with another cousin, Nicole, at the restaurant for Erica. Erica told Gina that the bridge had collapsed, but Gina and Nicole couldn't comprehend the enormity of the accident. Nicole believed Erica was exaggerating. Gina later recalled that Erica told them that she didn't know how she was going to get her car off the bridge, which now seems funny to them. Gina called her fiancé, Ted, who decided to try to get to the bridge site with a friend. He ended up being interviewed by a reporter and finding his face on the local news as well as CNN.

Erica got out of her car. "It wasn't long, and you just heard people crying from their cars. Some were screaming out for help. The guy in the SUV was running around checking on people," she recalled. Erica, on the other hand, stood by herself in a bewildered state. A woman named Danielle exited her car, also a Grand Prix, which was in front of Erica's. There was another man in the car next to the SUV who couldn't get out of his car. His back hurt, and he couldn't move his legs, Erica remembered. "So I stood there and talked to him, along with other people…It was really hard to comprehend all that had happened and take in the whole picture."

Then, seemingly from out of nowhere, two men rushed to the scene. They scaled a ten-foot-tall wall with an eight-foot wooden ladder to get to people on Erica's section of the bridge. The men said they wanted to get those who could walk out of there.

"I didn't know what to do at that point. Nobody was coming. On the other hand, do you leave the people who can't get out?" Erica felt she was in a no-win situation.

One of the men asked Erica if she had extra clothes or water. As fate would have it, Erica had packed several water bottles that she had frozen because she planned to be on the road that hot summer day. She had no extra clothes, but did have some blankets in her trunk. Unfortunately, the trunk had been damaged by debris and wouldn't open, so one of the men climbed into it through the backseat and retrieved them. Erica grabbed her work bag—it contained some important items that she knew she would need the next day—and walked through the rubble toward the wall.

"I was wearing a skirt that day. This guy is holding onto this rickety wooden ladder. I'm thinking, *I don't know if I can do this.* I tell the guy, 'You better watch out, because I might give you a show!' So he looks away and I was like, 'You *can't* look away because you can't help me if you look away!' He must have thought, *This chick is crazy!*"

Once she got over the wall, Erica placed her belongings by the riverside. Soon after, she spotted firefighters peeking down from above, from the point at which her section of bridge had detached. A few of them decided the quickest way down was to roll. Erica recalled one firefighter scaled the wall, surveyed the bridge, and then returned to the wall. While this was going on, more people from the community began showing up. The firefighter told each person what to do and where to go. "I was so impressed by that and amazed," she recalled. "At that point, he didn't know I was on the bridge, so he told me to grab equipment from the fire truck to bring to the collapse site." So she did.

Eventually, her help was no longer needed. Erica stood at the riverbank, talking to some survivors who were lying on the ground waiting for an ambulance. "That's when I saw the first body being pulled out of the river, mostly covered," she remembered. "I just lost it. *I can't be here. This is horrible.* So I tried to get busier to remove myself from the riverbank."

Erica tried once again to call her friend Marleen, for whom she had left the message when the bridge collapsed. This time, Marleen picked up. "I told her to turn on the news. She hadn't listened to her voice mail yet, at that point," Erica said.

"All I see is a school bus and a truck on fire," Marleen replied.

Erica didn't know what Marleen was talking about, and assumed this was happening at a different location. Erica wondered, *What else is happening in this city?*

She then turned around and looked beyond the river to the south side, or west bank, and saw the truck and the bus. "Oh, I guess you *are* on the right channel," she said, realizing that the collapse was far bigger than what was going on right around her. "It looked like a war zone," she said, "a complete war zone, complete destruction."

Erica briefly talked with her aunt—who had spoken with her cousins—on the phone. She hoped her aunt could get in touch with her parents in Illinois. The phone cut out.

By now, the service road leading down to the riverbank was lined with ambulances, fire trucks, and police cars. Erica connected with Danielle, who had been in the car in front of hers on the bridge. Law enforcement wanted everyone unconnected with the rescue and recovery effort to leave the site. The duo asked a police officer what they should do. He suggested they flag down an EMT.

They found one who told them, "If you can walk out of here, go find someone to take you to a hospital. If you don't, you'll be waiting hours for us to take you there."

Danielle and Erica walked up the winding, narrow service road. Danielle's back was hurting (she had broken three vertebrae), so Erica helped her carry her heavy bags. Erica half-jokingly wondered if Danielle was hauling weights around; it turned out Danielle had wedding invitations stuffed inside.

They approached the intersection of Sixth Avenue Southeast and Main Street. Hordes of onlookers were heading one block south to the Stone Arch Bridge to get a better glimpse of the wreckage. Erica's emotions took over.

"The amount of people was so overwhelming, and trying to get through them while figuring out what I was going to do was more than I could take," she said. "I was just bawling. People were stopping, asking if I needed help. I told them I was fine."

It was then that Erica decided a prayer was in order. *Lord, show me a patch of grass where I can sit down.* Right about then, Ted sent her a text message. "Give me street names, and we'll come get you." Gina had returned home, and she and Ted were coming to the rescue. Danielle, meanwhile, was on the phone with her sister.

Erica spied a little condominium building across the street with a little patch of grass near the entrance to the parking garage. "Danielle, that's where we're going," Erica said as she led the way.

Erica's father then called. "Where are you?" he asked. Erica's aunt had called her parents and let them know what had happened. Erica's bawling continued.

"Well, we're coming," her father, a former Assembly of God pastor, said adamantly. "We're packing the car and we're coming."

"No, it's okay. You don't have to," Erica said. Erica and her father eventually came to a compromise: her parents wouldn't leave their northern Illinois town until the next morning.

Ted and Gina arrived shortly thereafter and picked up Erica and Danielle. They drove until they found Danielle's sister, at which point Danielle left them. They then drove Erica to her home in downtown Minneapolis.

Ted's mom had come down from Anoka in the meantime. She was a nurse and wanted to evaluate Erica's condition. It was decided that Erica should be taken to Abbott Northwestern Hospital in Minneapolis as a precaution, where it would probably be less busy. Erica didn't mind, as she was starting to hurt everywhere. "Even my pinky toe hurt. I did not feel good at all," she said.

As they drove to the hospital, Erica received a call from her friend Phaedra. Phaedra had called Erica several times while she was at the bridge site, but Erica decided not to answer each time. After all, how could she possibly describe her situation to her friend?

This time she answered.

"Are you okay?" Phaedra asked. "What's going on? I saw the bridge collapse and I *knew* you were on it."

Phaedra's declaration took Erica off guard. There was no way Phaedra could have found out that Erica was on the bridge. Later, Erica discovered that other friends and family members, too, sensed that she had been in danger.

"It felt to me like, *Okay, God, you are in such control of this that you're even telling my friends*," Erica remarked.

Erica didn't spend long in the emergency room; her name was called right away. After taking her vitals, the nurse left. Erica was suddenly by herself for the first time since she'd fallen.

"I felt completely alone. I began to cry. *You can't do this to me!* I just felt so alone. It was a deep aloneness, like somebody with depression. Whenever a nurse came, I would plead that they bring somebody to come be with me."

As she had her X-rays taken, Erica would break down emotionally when the technician would leave the room—even though it was for only a couple of seconds. "Never do I want to feel that alone again."

The X-rays came back negative, but the doctor suggested she see her own physician in the near future. Erica was prescribed some pain pills, and she left the hospital at about 11 p.m.

Erica returned home and settled in for the night with Gina, Ted, and her boyfriend Bryan. They turned on the television and began watching the live coverage of the bridge collapse. "Part of me didn't want to watch it, but part of me was pulled to it. How could I not watch it? It was addictive," Erica recalled. Her friends eventually forced her to turn off the TV and go to bed.

The next morning, Erica made a conscious effort to avoid thinking about the previous day's events. She had forgotten her eyeglasses in the car, and she decided not to put in her contact lenses; that would remove the temptation to turn on the TV. She stayed in bed a little longer. She took a really long shower. She did "piddly" things.

Meanwhile, her support group was on its way. Her parents had left their home seventy miles west of Chicago and were headed to Minneapolis. A cousin was also on her way from a visit to in-laws in Wisconsin. Ted dropped by for lunch with frozen pizzas and Diet Coke.

Erica also recalled a conversation with her pastor that day. She, like so many other bridge survivors, was dealing with remorse. She told him, "I don't understand it. I'm ready to go [to heaven], and all I'm thinking about are the people who died. I think seeing the image of them pulling somebody out of the water really stuck with me. That could have been me. It *should* have been me." Erica was confident about where she was going, but she didn't know what those other people believed, "and I was concerned about that."

The pastor referred her to a chiropractor who had helped his wife after a car accident. The chiropractor in turn referred her to a colleague closer to her home. The next day, she drove to St. Paul to see him, and they came up with a plan. She got an MRI and soon learned that she had two herniated discs in her lower and middle back.

Erica had been proactive with her physical health. Now it was time to address her mental health needs. She called one of her former bosses and asked for a reference to see a specialist. The next Tuesday—six days following the collapse—she met with the therapist and was diagnosed with post-traumatic stress disorder.

"It was good to get it all out with somebody who didn't know me, who could be this neutral person who I could just spill it all to," she said. "They didn't have to feel like they had to fix me, they just had to listen. It was such a release. I knew I needed it."

For a long time, Erica had difficulty trusting any structure. "Even going to Target was hard for me, to go into a big building. How do I know this structure is safe? I had to go to Target with friends and didn't even think about going to the Mall of America," she said.

Going under bridges bothered her more than going over them. "I'd look up at the underside of the bridge and wonder how stable it was. And elevators? Yuck," she said. She also said she experienced loneliness, depression, and anxiety.

She still sees her therapist off and on three years after the bridge collapse.

"I figured that if I hide these feelings, they will come out eventually, and it will be ten times worse. So I have to feel anxious and I have to feel sad now, so that I won't later. I have to work through it."

Erica holds the distinction of being one of the first members of the

Survivor Resources bridge collapse group. She learned of it through a friend who watched the local news. It's been crucial to her:

> I think there is power in groups. Sharing our experiences helps us to know we are not alone, and I felt so alone those first few days. There are lots of times where I'm not sure if people in my life want to talk about the bridge. [The] group was a place where I could go and always talk about it because it was a part of all of our lives. Hearing others' stories helped me to heal, and I felt like I had to keep going, because if people were helping me to heal, hopefully I was helping somebody else to heal. It was a great opportunity to meet random people from all walks of life and have these different friendships that I otherwise would never have found.

****

Erica returned to work six weeks after the bridge collapsed. She started slowly, beginning with two-hour workdays and building herself back up to full time in January 2008.

Three years later, Erica still feels pain. "Mostly it's my lower back and sometimes my middle back. My neck can also tighten up," she said. "Every morning when I wake up, I'm extremely stiff."

Everyday chores can set off the pain: mowing the grass, vacuuming, washing dishes, sitting, bending, lifting. "I sit on kid chairs a lot for my job."

One of Erica's favorite hobbies is running:

> It does aggravate my back, but it's part of my life and who I am. I can't give it up because it's really helpful to me in other ways, like mental

health and feeling good generally. I have nobody telling me it's going to get better, but that it's status quo.

I can't stop my life from happening and doing the things I love to do. This bridge is not who I am. It doesn't determine my life, and I can move beyond it. I have to in order to take back my life. I won't let it dictate what I do.

Erica said she doesn't expect there to be a tidy conclusion to her recovery and this experience.

"This is a journey that each survivor has to be on," she said. "We carry it with us as we go along. And the emotion lessens. But I carry the memories and the friendships I've gathered along the way."

On September 9, 2010, Erica spoke at a press conference unveiling the design for the 35W Bridge Remembrance Garden. The gathering was held at the future site of the garden, adjacent to Gold Medal Park in downtown Minneapolis and upriver from the collapse site. The memorial will honor the thirteen individuals who died in the bridge collapse, as well as highlight the survivors and credit the first responders. On that day, Erica shared what the memorial means to her:

I remember the many days after the bridge collapse and begging people in my family to take me back to the bridge…On August 4, my parents drove me around downtown and the University of Minnesota trying to find the best spot to get a good look at the bridge, but there was not a place to get a good look at its rubble. I knew I had to get back there—it was almost like an obsession. I wanted to see it, to know that it was real, that my car was still sitting on the bridge deck, that the concrete and girders were all still in knots. I wanted to go there to remember, to try figure this thing out— but most importantly, I wanted to grieve.

It was difficult to get anywhere near the bridge during those first few days and weeks, but as roads and bridges began to open, I would be there as quick as I could to gaze at the wreckage and remember—and grieve.

As the bridge was slowly taken away from the river and its banks, I was devastated. I never wanted to forget that day, and I was so afraid I would, and that others would forget as well, and we would all go about our lives as if nothing had ever happened.

The 35W memorial garden…signifies to me that we have not forgotten that tragic day, where families lost loved ones, survivors suffered horrible trauma, responders served heroically, and the community embraced us all.

My hope for the garden is that the people who passed away that day will always be remembered, even if we never crossed paths with them in this life, that families and survivors will always have a place to go to grieve, that responders will have a visual reminder that they were and continue to be our heroes. And, ultimately, I hope the garden serves as a reminder to the community that even in our busy day-to-day lives, we stopped everything that day to care for each other. Each moment is precious…Now that the remains of the collapse are gone and a stronger bridge is in its place, this garden will be a place where I can remember—and grieve—and continue to grasp that every moment I have is a gift.

****

There are two pillars holding up Erica: faith and family. It was these two mainstays that helped her through her recovery.

"My faith is the only way that I made it through this, because I have hope in something bigger than what is going on in my life. I also feel like God, for some reason, put me on that bridge. I felt that from the get-go," she said matter-of-factly.

On the second anniversary of the bridge collapse, the family and friends who surrounded Erica on that tragic day gathered beneath the new 35W Bridge. Along with Erica, each shared his or her story—and the actions and emotions that painted the tapestry of Erica's experience.

"It felt to me like, *Wow. I am so blessed to have all these people who cared about me two years later come back and share*," she said.

Erica sees her position on that section of the collapsed bridge—cupped between the inverted V and the ski jump as a metaphor. "I felt that I was in the palm of God's hand," she said. "I was supposed to be there, and he protected me. It showed me that he has this all under control."

10

THE BRIDGE SHOOK MORE than its own foundations. It shook every facet of my life and tossed each of them into the air like the plastic pieces of the game *Perfection* when the timer runs out. All of a sudden, up was down. Things I trusted were now in doubt. I had terrible difficulty relying on and trusting people and things I hadn't hesitated grasping onto before. Every part of me was now under inspection: my abilities, my appearance, my relationships with others, even with my God.

This introspection extended into my career. Great Clips had provided well for me through the entire ordeal. It allowed the workers' compensation to advance without interruption, it looked out for my family while I was hospitalized, it even helped with some bills when I was not working during my recovery. But I never felt comfortable there after returning to full-time employment in May 2008. When I first started working there, I envisioned myself once again becoming a people manager, taking the lead on projects and making a mark within the company. When I returned to work following the accident, climbing the corporate ladder was the farthest thing from my mind. I felt as if I were starting over at the company, as with every other part of my life. The brain trauma made it difficult to focus, and I began struggling with parts of my job that were easy prior to the bridge collapse.

I began to look at the bigger picture. Was this trauma itself a door to earning an income in a different arena? Was I being called to something else? And if I was, what was that purpose?

I decided to start searching. I had the funds from the lawsuit settlement to provide Sonja and me with some money should I decide to veer down an alternative path. I began with a list of possible careers that didn't involve departmental staff meetings, supervisors, and hour-long commutes. I liked to write, so becoming an author interested me. I also enjoyed desktop publishing, so becoming a publications designer intrigued me. These seemed like good ideas, but they didn't appear promising as immediate, bill-paying professions. I batted around the possibility of using my experience with Great Clips and opening a franchise. Unsure of exactly what I wanted or needed, I turned to a colleague and friend for advice.

At Great Clips, I worked with a vendor who published a magazine for stylists for which I wrote and assembled content. It was a significant task, as the periodical was between twenty and twenty-eight pages long and was sent to more than 2,700 salons on a quarterly basis. Four times a year, I sent all of the content to Kelly, who, with some assistance, placed it on pages and sent it back to me in magazine form. For the longest time, I only knew Kelly on a professional level. Then, one day, we discovered each other on Facebook, and I became tuned in to her personality. Over time, the conversation turned more colloquial, and one day in late November 2009, I e-mailed her, hoping to find out how she had started her own business. "I'm looking at my calendar and wondering if you'd be up for a coffee chat? I'd be interested in talking with you about design stuff. I'm also trying to feel out what my next step is, in terms of my own career, maybe starting my own business. Not sure how long I can stare at the beige wedge created by the walls of my cubicle."

She replied, "Sure. I should warn you that the real reason for my success is a little out there. I rarely talk about it. Let's just say it's time to stop making fun of *The Secret*."

I chuckled when I read that, because I thought she was kidding. Turns out she wasn't.

We met at a Dunn Bros coffee shop off of Lake Street in south Minneapolis. Kelly, a single mother of two in her early forties, opted against a drink, while I ordered a cup of regular coffee. We began with small talk but soon turned to my journey to find myself.

"So, you're planning on leaving Great Clips?" asked Kelly.

"Like I said, I need to do something else. The bridge really gave me time to look deep within," I remarked. "I have an opportunity to do almost anything I want. I just have to figure out what that is, and do it smartly."

"Well, like I said, my path to success isn't traditional. It started more than twenty years ago," she said from across the table.

"Let's hear it." I pressed my hands against my paper cup. I always let fifteen minutes pass before I start drinking my coffee, afraid of burning my mouth.

"I manifest good things," Kelly said in a low voice, as if she were giving me the PIN to her ATM card.

I hoped my face didn't show it, but I was beginning to think Kelly might have been staring at her computer monitor too long. "You manifest good things?"

"Like I said, it started a long time ago," she continued, "when I went and heard a speaker. The idea was that our thoughts controlled our actions. Well, today there is science behind this. It used to be thought that light, or energy, was either in the form of waves or particles, but now it's theorized that our minds can control what form this energy takes."

Yes, she was definitely sitting too close to her computer way too often.

"So." I paused. "How does this make you a successful entrepreneur?"

"I've always found that when I think positively, positive things happen. It's the law of attraction. Like when strumming guitar strings—like vibrations move in harmony. Conversely, negative thoughts lead to negative actions," she said. "For two years, during the most difficult time of my life, I intentionally laid off the positive thinking, and it led to more problems. I then decided to be positive. I began writing goals—like things I wanted in the future, but I acted as if I had already achieved them."

I was confused, but this seemed similar to what the author Andy Andrews had had to say about focus.

"I didn't say I wanted to be rich, but whenever I needed money, it would happen to show up. I'd write down things like, 'I desire more free time.' I recall once when I had problems getting the girls to the bus stop on time," Kelly explained. "The bus came at 6:40 a.m., and the girls would wake up at 6 a.m. It was always a rush to get them to the bus on time. Sure, I could have gotten them up earlier, but I kept writing in my journal about how more time was important to us. Then, one day, the bus company called and said that, because of a route change, the bus would be arriving ten minutes later each day."

"And this was a manifestation?" I asked.

"I've always been able to do it," Kelly said. "I don't know. It just works. I don't get anxious. I don't swear when I'm stuck in traffic. I think to myself, *If I'm a little late, that isn't a bad thing. Maybe this traffic has kept me from being in an accident farther down the road.*"

I rubbed my chin. "I don't think this will work for me," I said.

"Why not?"

"Well, I'm very sarcastic and cynical. I think that creates a negative tinge to my perception of the world. It would be downright impossible for me to forgo negativity and emit only positivity. Add to that, I'm pretty controlling. When the bridge collapsed, I lost all control of my life. My whole recovery has been a mission to regain control, and it interferes with my relationships and my recovery," I admitted.

"I can't understand how people want to control things; it inevitably leaves you disappointed, because it's an impossible task," Kelly said. "And as far as being positive, you don't have to be Pollyanna. You just need to focus on your goals. This isn't about discovering the process. The process figures itself out. What do you want?"

Kelly stumped me. I guess I hadn't really thought about it. "I know what I don't want," I said. "I don't want to feel like I'm stuck in my life."

"Turn that around," she advised.

"I like to write, but that doesn't pay the bills, at least initially."

"Have you heard of *Thirty Days*?" Kelly asked. I shook my head. "It's a series of shows about people trying different things for thirty days, and they take each thing real seriously. On one show, a couple lived thirty days as if they only earned minimum wage, and the wife flipped out because her husband wanted to buy licorice."

"That's really interesting," I said. "That's something I'd like to do, wander into new experiences and write about them. I guess I want freedom. I want to be creative. I want to experience life in a way that leaves me fuller than before I started the experience."

"That's a start," Kelly said as I stared into my now empty coffee cup.

The conversation began to set with the late afternoon sun. We bid each other farewell, and I thanked Kelly for her insight, even though I hadn't fully processed it. I got home and turned on my computer. There was an e-mail from Kelly with a link to a Hulu video of *Thirty Days*. "I just saved you $13.49. I'll split it with you. You owe me $6.75," she wrote.

I replied, "With that avenue of thinking, no wonder you never worry about money. ;)"

Her response: "Law of Attraction + trickery = awesome!"

Awesome? Perhaps. Kelly's mantra seemed so simple I doubted its merit. Could happiness and success in work—and in life—be the cause, not the effect? And if so, why wasn't this practice as commonplace as belly-button lint? If it's too good to be true, then it probably is, right? Could a solution to my emotional hurricane be this easily found, when two years of therapy had yet to pull me from the stormy sea?

****

Jon Hovde grew up in small-town, rural northwest Minnesota. Jon, now in his early golden years, has led an accomplished life. He was a successful businessman, a leader of local groups and organizations, head of the state school boards association, and now a well-known motivational speaker. And, like me, his life became defined by a traumatic experience.

As a young man in 1968, Jon fought in Vietnam. In the process, he lost two limbs. It was a struggle for him to recover—not just physically, but emotionally as well. While I cannot speak for Jon—I've never met him—I'd guess that for him the emotional battle was much harder than the physical rehab. Jon shares his story in his book *Left for Dead: A Second Life after Vietnam*. The book was given to me by family friend Bruce Lambrecht, who asked me to mail it to another friend of his after I had finished reading it. Somehow, the request

203

to pass it on motivated me to at least thumb through its pages.

Two things from Jon's book struck me especially. According to him, every soldier was on high alert in Vietnam. Any second could be your last, and there was no safe haven, even while on a U.S. base. Also, Jon describes an episode after the war when his emotions got so out of whack that he jumped into his vehicle and left everything—his wife, kids, home—and wasn't going to stop driving until he reached the mountains and then the West Coast. PTSD had seized Jon, so he chose flight over fight.

The part that got me, however, was that this didn't happen one year after his return from Vietnam. It didn't happen five or ten years after. It cropped up thirty years later! Up until that point, Jon had handled the emotional side of his journey well. He hadn't stuffed away his feelings; rather, he spoke to students and civic groups, and he actively attempted to get in contact with old war colleagues or their families. If anyone had processed their feelings, I'd have thought it would be Jon. But that wasn't the case.

This frustrated me, as I had originally been told that my reprocessing would take six to twelve months. *That's manageable*, I had thought. But it was now two and a half years after the collapse, and its emotional grip was stronger than ever.

In December 2009, my marriage was crumbling furiously. It seemed that I tensed up around Sonja, which of course made her tense as well. Little things Sonja did set me off. If she left the garage door open, I'd get angry. "Somebody could have broken into our house or stolen tools from the garage!" I'd yell. If Sonja said she'd buy milk, then later ask me to buy it, I'd snarl, "You're always going back on your word, Sonja. Don't make promises if you can't keep them!" If Sonja left her purse at my sister's house, the hairs on the back of my neck would stand at attention. "Why can't you remember even the simplest things?" I'd mutter under my breath. "If you weren't so scatterbrained we'd be on time!" These daily incidents mired our house in an ugly stink.

I'd try to hide it around friend and families, but it wasn't possible, at least not entirely. Sonja—well-known for her abstract stream-of-consciousness narratives and malapropisms—would make others laugh while I seethed, and, inevitably, I'd shoot some curt comment in her direction. As other couples held each other or smiled, our glances at each other became infrequent and, eventually, purely accidental.

Disdain slowly replaced affection as my adjustment disorder evolved from every-so-often moods to a permanent emotional cloud. We had built walls, Sonja to protect herself from my outbursts, and me to keep the hurt I was spewing to a minimum as I continued to fight this branch of PTSD on my own. This disease was no longer just eating me out from the inside; it had infected my marriage as well.

Sonja and I had a big blowup just before Christmas in late 2009. We had originally made plans to visit my family in New Ulm on Christmas Eve and then drive north to her parents' cabin for a few days. However, the largest Christmas snowstorm in Minnesota history was preparing to hit, and I told Sonja we'd postpone the holiday plans to visit my relatives in New Ulm, and that she should head up to the cabin to be with her family. "What about you?" Sonja asked.

I told her that I would stay behind at home in Andover and shovel snow. "Besides, I need some time apart from us," I remarked. I then told her that I wasn't sure this marriage was going to work, that I felt like a different person since the bridge collapse, and that I felt we were no longer compatible. That's a lot for anyone to swallow just before Christmas, and I feel bad now about how I dropped that bomb.

Sonja left, but not before calling my mom and my therapist. When I received an invitation to talk over coffee from the husband of one of Sonja's friends, I put two and two together and realized that my wife was planning something just short of a full-scale intervention. Just like that time at the cabin, I felt as if an unwelcome rescue party had been organized for me.

To appease the masses, I made an appointment with my therapist for the next day. Sonja told me that if the therapist said it was okay, then she would leave for Lake Superior's North Shore and I could stay home alone for the holiday. The therapist found me to be no threat to myself and granted her approval for a weeklong separation.

I spent the next several days shoveling and contemplating. The break from the tension of the relationship felt like a breath of fresh air. Yes, I missed my wife, but there was a weight off my shoulders. In addition to shoveling the driveway clear of sixteen inches of snow, I tried my hand at repairing some drywall that had been damaged during our move, and I sanded and stained the banister where the dog had chewed it. I did some reading and writing as well.

And I checked in with my therapist. I told her I felt less stress on my own, and I feared it would return with Sonja. I wanted to work on the marriage, but it seemed impossible if that underlying current of hostility remained.

Sure enough, our arguing reignited not long after Sonja came back to unopened presents and still-full stockings. She urged me to get on medication. I, finding security in my stubbornness, initially refused. In the meantime, Sonja and I decided to set some boundaries at home so that I could find some peace of mind, work on my issues, and, in the process, save our marriage. I moved some clothes and toiletries to the lower-level bedroom and slept there.

As my therapist Laura had pointed out when analyzing my dream, I was in the basement emotionally, even as I was there physically. I was cloaked in fear, afraid that my form of PTSD—my feeling of being "stuck"—would never go away. Since the bridge collapse, I had felt unsafe, unable to trust, unable to smile or laugh, unable to be fully at ease. Nobody wants their marriage to fail. Now it was happening, and both Sonja and I felt helpless. I felt unable to fix myself, as if my adjustment disorder was a tractor beam that pulled my emotions wherever it wanted. I didn't control them.

I felt as though God had left the room. "I've gotten you this far, now you're on your own," I imagined him saying. I'm sure there were other world catastrophes he had to tend to. I wasn't mad at God per se, just annoyed that the hardest part of my recovery was happening two and a half years after the collapse, when the whole time, I had thought I had gotten through the worst part in the beginning. I had told people in speeches that the God who allowed the bridge to fall was the same God who reached down and pulled me from the debris. Now he didn't seem to be around. Maybe he thought that my recovery was over. I guess I felt deceived. My inability to trust extended to the deity, so much so that the New Age ideas of the law of Attraction and manifestation seemed plausible to this lifelong Christian.

This frustrated me, too, as I had always relied on my faith to see me through the gray areas of life. I had relied on God and felt unfulfilled. I had relied on myself and felt unfulfilled. I felt at a loss for solutions, other than to accept my emotional state as cancer patients might accept their terminal illness. There was no joy in Mudville, and I decided that this would just have to be okay.

But there was one alternative I hadn't tried. Taking antidepressants felt like throwing in the towel, and that hurt my pride. But when I peered over my shoulder and saw the path of destruction I was leaving, I finally made the call to my physician from HCMC, Dr. Herrera. After I answered a few questions, he agreed to mail a prescription to my home.

I remember holding the Celexa pills in the palm of my left hand. They seemed so small that I wondered how such tiny tablets could bring my depression under control. I took a break from my cynicism and downed them with a gulp of water.

Amazingly, the pills did their job, and I stopped taking them after six weeks, annoyed by some of the side effects. The triggers that led to anger either seemed not to materialize or I could stamp them out if they did. I felt a new level of clarity. When the weight of depression lifted after a few weeks, Sonja noted that I seemed to be more at ease. I smiled more. I wasn't as prone to making cutting, sarcastic remarks. I wasn't letting external forces get me down.

But as good as all those things were, Sonja and I still weren't bonding. It was mid-February 2009, and I was about to leave on a five-day trip to Jamaica with some very close friends, who happened to be single. Sonja wasn't happy about this; we had argued at Christmastime about whether or not I should go. I told her I needed to be with my friends and have some fun, that it was my gift to myself for all the crap I had gone through in the last two and a half years. Sonja reluctantly gave in. To her, my vacation with a group of bachelors was a minefield. And when she discovered that I had been communicating with an old flame from my college days, she decided that she'd had enough. Enough of always feeling like I wasn't pulling my share of the relationship. Enough of feeling like a roommate instead of a wife. Enough of waiting around for the old Garrett to come back around. Enough of feeling like I made others my top priority instead of her.

Sonja decided to speak to a divorce attorney while I was in Jamaica. She also asked to join me in therapy with Laura when I returned from the vacation. I felt I had no choice, and I really didn't object. We were both on the brink of giving up.

I was able to allow myself to enjoy my time in Montego Bay, Jamaica, but when I returned, the emotional baggage was waiting for me at the airport. I picked up that heavy load, swung it over my shoulder, and in a few days headed to Laura's office. Sonja met me there.

We stepped inside and sat side-by-side on the love seat. Sonja started.

"I went to the divorce lawyer last week," she said. "I walked in feeling strongly about divorce. We went over my rights as to what I'm entitled to, but…" Her voice trailed off. "For some reason, I feel we can still make this happen. I think we can give this another chance."

Laura looked over at me. I stared at the window. "Sonja, it's like we keep trying to squeeze a lemon, hoping to find juice, and nothing ever comes out no matter how hard we squeeze. Over and over. And when we fail, we say, 'Maybe we just need to squeeze harder!' But that isn't the answer. You want kids; I don't know anymore if I can handle that. You want us to worship together; I don't want to join an ELCA church. I can't even begin to work on us as a team until I can get myself figured out. And, honestly, I don't know if that will ever happen. I know your clock is ticking. I feel horrible making you wait around hoping for something that may never be. I'm tired of being unfair to you."

There was no more dancing around it. But it still burned my throat as I coughed up the words. "I think I want a divorce."

I'd never wanted a divorce. I'd seen its effects firsthand. My father had been divorced twice. My mother had been divorced twice. I had read the studies. I knew that the odds were stacked against me, but still—I wanted to overcome that. Be better than that. And yet here I was, asking for one. It made me sick to my gut, but on the other hand, I felt I was saving Sonja by pushing her away.

God bless us, but we had been fighting the current the whole way. There was no engagement euphoria. There was no sweetheart honeymoon. That joy that other couples take as a given had detoured us like an airliner diverting from its course to avoid a line of thunderstorms. Sonja and I had never had it easy. I never had the opportunity to bond with her. Our entire engagement period, I had to expend all of my energy on my physical recovery. Sonja, on the other hand, had bonded greatly with me. She became my caretaker. She grabbed all of the wedding-planning duties by the reins. She sat at the hospital every day waiting for her love to get better. But when I did get better physically, all of my attention then shifted to my emotional recovery. Sonja would have to wait yet again, and we ended up on two very different planes.

Before Sonja and I got married, Laura had asked me to consider postponing the wedding. I told her it wasn't an option. We were going to do this. I wasn't going to let my stubborn pride down. Granted, I had no idea at the time of the depths of emotional trauma that lay before me. To me, the wedding was a way of reclaiming my life path. There was significance to being married on the anniversary weekend of the bridge collapse. It was supposed to signify the bookend to the trauma. I didn't realize that, like the collapse itself, I had no control over the recovery timeline.

It's not that we didn't love or care for one another. We did. "I always thought that if two people really loved one another, that's all it would take," Sonja told me one time. "I thought God would push us through whatever it was. It was my answer, but now I don't know what the answer is."

****

March and April were difficult months. We remained in the house together, but continued to sleep in separate rooms. We found we were much more genial as roommates. It was refreshing, but it also made us question ourselves. If we were kind and loving now, could we also be that way in a renewed effort to save the marriage? Many times, we sat down and talked about what it would take to make a second chance work, but each time we laid down our requirements, we hit a stalemate. A stable marriage necessitated that I relinquish the control I craved. Sonja could not continue to live as a glorified roommate with separate checking accounts, separate e-mail accounts, and a husband who could not share his deepest inner self.

Like me, Sonja had several theories about why we didn't work. Above all, she thought that I couldn't separate her from "the Bridge." In attempting to overcome the trauma, I was, in effect, pushing her aside. Honestly, I don't know if that was true, but it could have been. In any case, I didn't want to believe it if it was true. It sounded cold. It sounded like defeat. It sounded like the bridge had taken one more thing away from me.

I found the divorce documents we'd need to file online, and Sonja and I gathered the data to fill them out. Our possessions became dollar amounts dropped into a ledger. Remarkably, we didn't argue over who would keep what. Sonja made her pitch for what she felt was fair monetary compensation, and I simply nodded my head. In the following days, we closed our joint checking account and visited our financial adviser, who split our assets as we'd requested.

209

The only thing left to do was file the paperwork with Anoka County. There were several opportunities to do so—I even took a day off from work to go with Sonja to the courthouse—but I could never pull the trigger. It didn't feel right. I didn't feel ready. And I didn't want to continue what seemed like a never-ending series of mistakes. Still, I felt that the new me and the marriage weren't compatible, and that divorce was the best thing, even though Sonja didn't want the marriage to end. I was completely conflicted.

I wished I had Kelly's ability to turn positive energy into results. I yearned to tackle my PTSD with a militaristic fervor like Jon Hovde. But I found those were their paths, not mine. All I wanted was the old Garrett back, just like Sonja wanted. I decided that such a thing was never going to happen.

"Maybe we can be the best divorced couple ever," Sonja said to me with tears in her eyes as she drove me in mid-April to Minneapolis–St. Paul International Airport, where I was to catch a flight to San Francisco for a weeklong social media seminar. I was crying, too—and I hoped she was right.

11

WHILE I WAS IN SAN FRANCISCO, my attorneys informed me that they had struck a deal with my workers' compensation insurer. For the previous six months, my share of the settlement with the road construction company had been held up. The insurer wanted that settlement in order to recoup the more than $300,000 it had paid toward my medical expenses. Through the efforts of my attorneys, a deal with the insurer was struck: I would get to keep the settlement in exchange for forfeiting a portion of any future settlements. (At the time, litigation continued against URS, a firm that had contracted with the state of Minnesota to inspect the 35W Bridge. That firm settled with bridge survivors and the families of the deceased in August 2010.)

This was good news, giving me some flexibility in my life plans—with or without Sonja. However, I was far from ecstatic, just as when I received my settlement check from the state in 2009. Don't get me wrong; extra money is a blessing. But it's a poor excuse for justice, even though society has equated the two. It can't erase the physical pain, terrible memories, and emotional trauma I continued to endure. It didn't fix me. It only shined a spotlight upon my struggles that were already all too apparent.

Sonja was happy to hear that the settlement had come through, and she hoped that it would give me some relief. In an amazing display of grace, she told me that she would not fight for any of it, if and when we divorced. I was glad to hear that, but puzzled about her motive. Perhaps she was just as ready to walk away and be done?

In May, Sonja scurried to finish seemingly endless tasks before heading up to the Boundary Waters region of extreme northern Minnesota for her summer job as the chaplain at Wilderness Canoe Base, a Lutheran camp for high schoolers. A short time earlier, Sonja had been invited to take the position by the camp director, a good friend of hers. She agreed, but later discovered that he had resigned upon taking a ministerial position at a church northwest of the Twin Cities. She wasn't happy about being up there alone, but she decided to make the best of it. By spending some time away from the house, she was allowing us an informal separation. When she returned in mid-August, we could proceed with the divorce if we both felt that was the direction we needed to go.

One of her precamp chores was to find a temporary home for our Tibetan Terrier, Chauncey, because I didn't feel I could cope with him on my own. If Chauncey were a fictional character, he'd be Lennie Small from *Of Mice and Men*—a soft, simple individual who means well, but if you leave him alone, you'll wish you hadn't. Thankfully, my sister agreed to take Chauncey on, and in rapid succession, Sonja and Chauncey—the two main sources of my consternation—were out of my immediate life.

I was expecting to feel relief, a giant exhalation of angst and frustration. The arguments were through, because there was no one to argue with. I wouldn't be tied down by the dog, so I could go wherever and whenever I pleased. There was nothing holding me back. I could freely move forward with my life—or so I thought.

Not four days later, Rhonda called. "I don't think I can keep Chauncey for the summer," she said.

"Why not?" I was more than a little annoyed. Rhonda had originally purchased Chauncey when he was a pup, and he had spent several months at her house before Sonja and I took him in.

"Well, he keeps getting loose and running away. And he won't stop whining."

"Whining? Why would he be whining? He's got two other dogs to hang out with and six kids!"

But I relented, and two days later, Chauncey was back in Andover—back to digging holes in the backyard and crapping on the carpeted stairs inside. He was ecstatic to be back, and couldn't seem to contain his grin or his floppy, pink tongue. And for some reason, I really didn't mind cleaning up after him all that much. Just call me George Milton.

While caring for my slobbering, four-legged furball felt right, my job was feeling more and more wrong. In the several months since my conversation with Kelly at the coffee shop, it became increasingly clear to me that I was a poor fit for my senior communications specialist position at Great Clips. I felt I was overqualified for the job when it came to writing feel-good articles about franchisces or putting together content for our stylist magazine. And I was underqualified when it came to communications planning and working within the political system of a corporation. The two parts of my job that I did enjoy—the design work and managing our online reputation through social media—either had been or were about to be farmed out to freelancers or vendors. I had difficulty feeling like a valued member of a team, even though I knew my colleagues meant well. I would be easy to replace, and I knew that. With my settlement finalized, I finally decided to take the leap of faith I'd been contemplating for more than a year. I called Sonja, who was in the midst of staff training up at the Boundary Waters, to get her opinion on whether or not I should quit my job. After all, if I did quit, there would be no health insurance, so it would affect her. Without hesitation, she told me to put in my notice. The next day, I did exactly that.

Everyone I spoke to in the office over the next two weeks asked what I'd be doing next.

"Did you take a job with another company?"

"Nope."

"Are you going back to school?"

"Nada."

"Well, there's no way the military would take you!"

"You're right about that," I said "Let's just call it temporary retirement."

And that's how I approached my upcoming free time. I wasn't going to worry about what I would do next. My primary focus would be on getting emotionally healthy, getting unstuck. I'd be able to pay the bills for a while, if I was careful with my money.

On my last day at Great Clips, my department peers huddled next to a block of cubicles for my unofficial sendoff. Everyone signed a farewell card, similar to the congratulations-on-your-engagement card I'd received on that fateful day nearly three years earlier. There were no buffalo wings, but we did munch on ice cream sandwiches. I received a Minnesota Twins gift card, some books on eating healthy, and two-and-a-half-year-old decorated cupcakes—a white elephant gift I had started in 2008.

I put my few remaining personal effects into a box, including a yellowed newspaper clipping of an Associated Press article that ran in the *Rochester Post-Bulletin* on December 27, 2007, about my bridge recovery, with a photo of me peering down at the collapse site from the Tenth Avenue Bridge and a headline that read, "Survivor Slowly Rebuilds His Life." *Ha!* I thought. *If only they knew how slow it was!* I handed over my corporate American Express card and entry key, and said good-bye. If my slate hadn't been cleared off before, it was now. No wife. No job. I needed a hobby.

About the same time I resigned at Great Clips, I enrolled in a beginners' motorcycle safety course. I had only ever ridden a motorcycle one time. I was probably about thirteen years old. I was at my great-uncle's farm, and I watched my cousin pull his motorcycle out from a shed, fire it up, and zip around the pig barn, chicken coop, and gravel road. I was mesmerized, and I asked him if I could try it.

He gave me minimal operating directions, while it sat there sputtering and coughing up exhaust. I grabbed the handlebars to steady the bike while I climbed aboard. However, as I did so, I accidentally twisted the throttle. The bike shot forward as if from a cannon. I, for some reason, hung onto the handlebars. After I finally let go and tumbled to the ground, the motorcycle crashed into the side of the grain shed with a loud thud. My cousin laughed as I spat gravel from my mouth and inspected my scrapes. I hadn't touched a motorcycle since that day.

So I signed up for the course with some trepidation. I couldn't explain why, but the thought of cruising down rural back roads on a rumbling steel horse appealed to me. The four-day course ran concurrently with my final days at Great Clips. The class was terrific. The teachers were thorough, drilling us on taking a corner, braking suddenly, driving over obstacles, and swerving. We all passed the final exam and got our license endorsements.

Two days later, I found my bike, a 2008 Kawasaki 900 Classic. It looked shiny, black, and mean—Darth Vader on wheels. I took it for a test drive, and fell in love. That evening, it was in my garage.

It would be a few days before I could drive it, as I waited for the drivers' insurance and sunnier skies to kick in. One of the perks of living in Andover is that it sits on the northern fringe of the metro, straddling rural Minnesota with its curvy, two-lane roads, open fields, and pocket-sized lakes. Within a few days, I was feeling quite comfortable on the country highways and city streets.

The bike gave me something I hadn't felt since the bridge collapse: a feeling of complete control. The handlebars became reins, the cycle a bucking bronco beneath me just begging to be tamed. I felt like Austin Powers, reunited with his mojo—and it felt so good. I was dictating my course. I was moving forward.

****

My new cruiser came equipped with a passenger seat. Like the unused pillow lying next to me on the queen-sized bed, it reminded me that something wasn't right. I had seen divorce in my own childhood home. I had seen friends go through it, and now I was going through it. But something was off. *I should be angrier*, I thought. *I should never want to see Sonja again.* But I didn't feel that way at all. Sure, we argued and bickered all the time. We frustrated each other. But was it at a level that required divorce? How much of our trouble could be attributed to incompatibility, and how much of it was due to my adjustment disorder? Or maybe there was a third reason. Or a fourth? The last thing I wanted to do was "Ready! Fire! Aim!"

It was at this point that I determined that I really needed to do all I could to get myself emotionally well. It was the only way I would know if divorce was the right answer for me. I had to get serious about therapy and turning my life around, regardless of what Sonja would decide when she returned on August 15. And if divorce wasn't the answer, I had to fix me before I could even consider doing my part to fix us.

I called Laura. I'd stopped going since our last session several weeks earlier, when I'd told Sonja I wanted the marriage to end. In that time, I had felt better. Sure, the marriage was tattered and lying in ruins, but the pressure was no longer there—and there was the motorcycle, my midweek softball league, and partial season tickets to Minnesota Twins games to distract me. But now it was time to really work.

Laura and I began meeting weekly once again in the middle of May 2010. However, this time I promised myself that I would remain fully engaged for the duration. It was time to delve into areas of my past that I had kept at arm's length. It was time to deal with issues prior to the bridge collapse, issues I had never put to bed, which the collapse had dragged to the forefront of my mind. Laura had an inkling that there were traumatic incidents in my past that had created irrational beliefs. She thought that I'd coped with them, but when I suffered my severe brain trauma on August 1, 2007, my normal coping mechanisms started to fail. In short, we needed to go back in time and process out some bad feelings, feelings I had been able to stuff into boxes I stored on the top shelf in the back closet. In particular, she wanted to focus on things in my past that made me feel trapped, just as I had felt trapped when I was in my car when the bridge fell.

First up: my estranged relationship with my father.

My relationship with my dad, though difficult, was hardly unusual in modern America. My mom left my father when he began having an affair with the beer bottle. Prior to that moment, our family home was a roofed container of anger, yelling, disappointment, and breakdown. When Rhonda, who was just a toddler, and I went to bed, the fireworks would begin. Loud, filthy words oozed in from the living room and underneath our bedroom door. I remember covering Rhonda's ears with my tiny hands to protect her. For me, it was too late.

A judge gave Dad visitation rights every other weekend. When I went to see him, we didn't attend baseball games. Dad didn't teach me how to change the oil in a car. I didn't learn from him how to knot a tie. All I really learned was how to shoot a gun. I didn't enjoy it much, but it was perhaps the only thing that he taught me, and I clung to it in order to feel like a son. He took me on a few deer hunts, though for most of the day I was alone in the woods, as we each manned our hunting spots waiting for that big buck or doe. I recall getting up before dawn to head out to the hunting land, but first Dad had to remove the license plates from his car and reattach them to his pickup. I guess I learned how to trick cops into thinking you were driving a registered vehicle, too.

Over the years, every other weekend became every other month, then a couple of times a year. When I went to college, Dad and I didn't communicate. He always had my phone number; he just never called. I had moved on, understanding that not all men make good fathers. I just got stuck with one of those, though I never could figure out why I wasn't good enough. I got really good grades in school. I was well behaved. But it just didn't matter to him.

"Was there one moment with your father that you'd consider traumatic, where you felt trapped?" Laura asked.

I thought for a second. "Yes."

"Well, let's talk about that then, shall we?" she suggested.

"It was Christmas Day. I was home from college, so I must have been twenty-one years old. I was at my mom's house in New Ulm. It was in the afternoon. There was a knock on the door, and Mom went to answer it. It was my dad. He'd driven two and a half hours from Rochester, and he had gifts in tow. He hadn't told anybody he was coming. I hadn't spoken to him in a year."

Laura interrupted. "How did that make you feel?"

"I was angry. Christmas was supposed to be a time of joy and family. I didn't consider him part of my family. Thinking about my relationship with my father made me sick to my stomach. Here he was, standing in my home, sucking the joy of Christmas from all of us. I remember thinking, *Who does he think he is?*"

"Then what happened?" asked Laura.

"He handed me a gift-wrapped box. I opened it, and it was a flannel hooded jacket from Fleet Farm. I sort of thought it was funny. *He doesn't even know me. How does he know what I'd want for a gift?* I was surprised that it was even the right size. Then he handed me a greeting card. I opened it. Inside he'd written, 'Merry Christmas. Love, Dad.'"

"How did you feel about that?" asked Laura.

"Normally, I'm very passive. Normally, I'd just say thanks, give a fake hug, and let the incident pass. But the word 'love' made me boil over. I yelled at him, 'Who do you think you are? How can you say you love me? How have you ever shown that you love me? You know nothing about me! You've never cared! Do you think you can just show up, say you love me, and everything is okay?' I stormed to my room. Dad left. A few minutes later, my mom came in and tried to comfort me."

Laura asked me how that felt.

"Mom has always been there for me. Has always sacrificed. She was the opposite of him. Regardless, I felt everything there had suddenly become toxic. I had to leave. I quickly packed up my things, hopped into my car, and headed back to Madison. I cried for thirty minutes straight in the car."

****

The next week, Laura suggested I delve into another incident in which I felt trapped. This time I chose the topic: Sonja.

Sonja struggles with transitions. Major life changes inevitably cause her anxiety to shoot up a few notches. Many times, she can regulate it with medicine, but there are times when her body chemistry cannot adjust, and her anxiety becomes severe. The spring of 2009 was one of those times. Toward the end of winter, her father had suffered a heart attack while shoveling snow in the driveway of his Columbia Heights home. Sonja was inside the home at the time. Luckily, two Comcast workers were at the home installing cable at that moment, and one of them happened upon him lying in the driveway not breathing, and began performing CPR. Sonja's father was taken to the hospital by ambulance and had heart surgery. The operation was a success, and he recovered.

Her father's near death shook Sonja's foundation. On top of that, she and I had made the difficult choice of putting her beloved old cockapoo, Peanut, down. In addition, her temporary position as a youth director at a church in St. Louis Park was coming to an end, and she worried about what she would do next. Sonja and I were also about to move into a new home, and were stressed with all the packing and organizing. She was dealing with all of that, on top of putting up with me and my adjustment disorder. It was enough to make anybody snap.

Two days before we closed on our home in Andover, Sonja reached her breaking point. Her anxiety medication wasn't working. She couldn't control her emotions, and it was affecting her physiologically. The panic attacks became regular and uncontrollable. She met with her therapist, who advised her to seek some additional help. Her therapist called me at Great Clips and asked me to take Sonja to the emergency room. I drove up to New Brighton to pick her up, and we headed to the University of Minnesota Medical Center in Minneapolis. We sat in the waiting room. I held her hand. I think I was more scared than she was.

After an initial evaluation, we were led to a room where specialists could check Sonja over and determine what to do next. We sat in there and waited. I remember holding her and telling her it would be okay. The doctors could fix this; they just needed to get the medicine right. It was here that I first realized that Sonja might not be coming home.

After what seemed like an eternity and visits with two doctors, the decision was made: Sonja would voluntarily enroll in the inpatient program until doctors could stabilize her emotions both through medicine and by teaching her some coping strategies for any future panic attacks.

We took an elevator to a special wing. Two thick doors locked by security codes prevented anyone from coming or going without permission and an escort. It felt as if we were entering a prison ward. Inside, it was bustling with activity—nurses on phones, patients in gowns, visitors. A nurse issued Sonja a gown and a long list of rules. She couldn't wear her regular clothing while there. She couldn't carry sharp objects, even though she was no threat to herself or others. No rope or string. Her days would be filled with learning coping strategies for her anxiety, art projects, and getting to know her peers.

"How did this make you feel?" Laura asked me.

"I was furious at first," I replied. "Sonja didn't belong there. I met some of the other patients. They were certifiably crazy. My wife wasn't crazy. Her chemistry was off. But she had to follow rules like a prisoner. She didn't do anything wrong. Plus, I could only see her for one hour a day. And I had to share that hour with everybody else who wanted to see her. I got zero alone time with my wife, and they didn't care. That first evening, I had to drive home and get her some toiletries and books she wanted. I cried the whole way back to the apartment."

Sonja was in the hospital for about five days. The doctors found the right cocktail of medications. She learned some new self-relaxation techniques that really proved useful. She also reconnected with drawing, a passion that she had left on the windowsill for many years. Unfortunately, her hospital stay prevented her from attending the closing of our home. Instead of Sonja, I carried an Ikea chair across the threshold of our new residence.

"You must have had a lot to talk about when she got home," Laura said matter-of-factly.

I paused and bit my bottom lip, scrunching my eyebrows together. "I can't recall us ever talking about it after we got home," I said.

"How could that be?" Laura asked. "I mean, that was a very traumatic experience, wasn't it?"

"Well, yeah, I suppose it was," I said. "But we had this new house to get in order. Things needed to be done." I paused a second time. "The train derailed. My job was to get the train back on the tracks and moving forward."

"What do you mean?" Laura inquired.

"That's how I've always operated," I remarked. "Whenever there's trauma, that's what I've done. That's what my family has always done. When my parents divorced, I had to become the man of the house, even though I was five years old. My sister and I were latchkey kids. My job was to take care of her. When my grandparents' attic flooded, I felt compelled to do everything it took to clean up the mess. When the bridge collapsed, I fought tooth and nail to get better physically as fast as I could. You don't think; you just do."

"So how do you process all of the emotion?" Laura asked me.

I paused a third time. "I don't think I ever did."

"Where does it go? It has to go somewhere," Laura stated.

"It gets stuffed away. That or pushed aside. If it's in the way, I can't move forward. I have to discount emotion in order to move forward."

This time Laura paused. "Did you hear what you just said?"

I repeated the sentence under my breath, slowly. "I—have—to—discount—emotion—in—order—to—move—forward." I felt as if I had just been hit with a fifty-pound sack of potatoes. This was the illogical belief in my world. I suddenly realized that this had been my modus operandi for decades. Want to move forward? Push emotion aside. Block it out. Step away from it, or even better, run from it. I had run from my dad. I had run from my life when I moved out East after college. Now I was running from my marriage. Push emotion aside, move forward.

I couldn't help but think of my new motorcycle. I'd learned in my beginners' class that there are two ways to move a motorcycle forward. The first is the most common: turn the throttle. The other, less-used method is to engage and release the clutch lever. This comes in handy when moving the motorcycle slowly, especially in U-turns. The only problem with this method is that you don't move forward very far. You lurch, and you quickly grab the clutch lever. Back and forth repeatedly. The only thing you really get out of it is a sore left hand.

Perhaps I was leaning on the clutch method too much in life. I thought I was moving forward, but in reality, I was merely lurching, because I wanted to feel safe, travel slowly. However, anybody with a motorcycle will tell you that you are more likely to tip over when traveling slowly than when moving at a higher speed. You are much more stable when applying the throttle.

Maybe it was time to stop discounting emotion. Maybe it was time to twist the throttle.

I left my therapy session in Minnetonka and headed home. However, I had one more errand before landing in Andover.

****

Mark, the head pastor at the local church Sonja and I had been attending, invited me to join him at the local Caribou Coffee. His church also happened to be one of two congregations where Sonja was a finalist for a youth director position.

Sonja and I had started attending this church together that spring. Ever since we had married, we'd had immense difficulty finding a place to worship. I grew up in the Wisconsin Evangelical Lutheran Synod, a more conservative branch of Lutheranism. She was a member of the more liberal Evangelical Lutheran Church in America (ELCA). As an example, the ELCA had debated the issue of homosexual ministers. They decided to leave it up to individual congregations to decide whether or not to call a gay or lesbian noncelibate pastor. The Wisconsin Synod preaches homosexuality was a sin, and would never allow a minister who openly sins to lead a congregation.

Our doctrinal differences extended to Holy Communion as well. The ELCA allows all who affirm Jesus Christ as their savior to come to the altar to receive communion; the Wisconsin Synod only allows those who profess the doctrine espoused by the Wisconsin Synod. As a result, we had never taken Communion together.

When Sonja became a serious candidate for the director position, she implored me to attend church with her, even though we had already begun to move forward with divorce. Externally, she wanted to look like a solid candidate. We attended services together a couple of times. After that, Sonja attended on her own until she left for her job in the Boundary Waters.

Two weeks before my meeting with Pastor Mark, I decided to attend the church's Saturday-evening worship. There were about a dozen of us there. I don't know why I went that night, but I really felt the need to be close to God. After the sermon, Pastor Mark called the entire congregation to the altar for a group prayer, since there weren't many of us there. After prayer, Pastor Mark launched into the introduction for Holy Communion. I was about to return to my pew, but I suddenly began to question that. *Why am I so averse to taking Communion?* I wondered. Was my decision really doctrinally based, or was I simply too stubborn to open my mind? I knew why I was taking Communion: to accept the forgiveness of sins and honor my Savior. Wasn't that enough? I decided right there to remain standing at the altar.

The next weekend, Sonja came home temporarily from camp in northern Minnesota, as she had another interview with the church. It was right about this time that I felt something begin to turn within me. I was excited about Sonja's return. I cleaned the house from top to bottom, vacuuming, mopping the hardwood floors, dusting, doing laundry, cleaning windows—you name it. I spruced up the home with vases of fresh flowers. I bought Sonja a greeting card and filled it with long-distance calling cards so she could contact friends and family while in the Boundary Waters.

My efforts didn't go unnoticed by Sonja, but she was more than wary. I had established a pattern of doing kind things to win favor, only to slip back into my grouchy ways. She wasn't buying it, and could I blame her? We attended church that following Sunday. She seemed a bit confused that I wanted to come along, but readily allowed it. Sitting beside her in church brought forth a spring of emotion for me. I always embraced the times when we could share our faith together, even if I didn't verbally acknowledge it. More than once, my eyes teared up as we sat there singing songs of praise and hearing God's message. Then it came time for Communion.

Sonja sat to my right. When the usher called us forward for the Lord's Supper, Sonja stood up first. I stood up after her and followed her down the aisle. She turned and gave me a stunned look, as if to say, "You *do* realize you're in the line for Holy Communion, right?" I smiled and touched her shoulder. We reached Pastor Mark, who gave Sonja a piece of bread, and she moved on. He gave me a portion, and then, unexpectedly, gave me a giant hug. He placed his lips near my left ear. "God is healing you, Garrett." I began to cry. When I returned to the pew, tears streaming down my face, Sonja mentioned that she'd seen Pastor Mark hug me. After church, she asked me why I had attended Communion. I can't recall what I said, but I think it was something to the effect of, "It was time."

So it was at this point that I walked into Caribou Coffee to meet with this man of God, who obviously knew something about me. If anything, I wanted to know what he knew and how he knew it.

Pastor Mark was already there when I walked in, wearing a wildly colored and patterned dress shirt. He looked tired.

"Hi, Pastor," I said. "How are you?"

"Hello Garrett," he replied. His voice was soft. Because my voice doesn't carry well either, we both had difficulty understanding one another amid the din of the coffee shop. "We have vacation bible school this week. I've been over there all day."

"Wow, that must be exhausting," I said.

"I'm in charge of the audio/visuals, and I spent a lot of time just trying to remember how to use the software," he said.

Pastor Mark is a thin fellow with a thick, gray-and-white coif, and has been leading the congregation for more than a dozen years. He is a dramatic sort who uses facial expressions and gestures to his advantage, which makes him interesting to chat with. I began our conversation by giving him a brief synopsis of my life—my time at school in Madison, my move out to the East Coast to begin my journalism career, and my return to Minnesota. And, of course, the bridge.

Eventually, Pastor Mark got to the reason for our meeting. "I had no set agenda for inviting you out to coffee," he said. "I just wanted to get to know you a little."

"You know," I said to him, leaning in, "when you gave Sonja and me

223

Communion last week, that was the first time we'd ever taken it jointly."

"Really?" he asked. I then went into my theological upbringing and its differences from Sonja's. I also explained my change of heart and why I had taken Communion the week before. Pastor Mark then asked me how I was doing in terms of my relationship with God.

"I was never really angry at God about the collapse," I said, "but I did get increasingly frustrated. I became upset that he had taken so much away. I was bitter because I thought things would get easier—that the hardest part should have been the physical recovery. But it didn't get better with time. The emotional trauma has been infinitely worse than the physical despite the surgeries, the lasting pain, the scars. God has allowed so much to be taken away: my joy, my hope. And now he's taking away my marriage! When does it end? Does it end?"

"You know," Pastor Mark revealed, "I've been in therapy too. I imagined my journey, like yours, to be through a long, dark tunnel. I could barely see. I had to feel my way. And God talked to me. He said, 'Mark, there is no choice. I am going to put you through this journey. And you are going to have to do the walking yourself. You are going to have to do the work. I'll be with you every step. But I won't be carrying you. But if you need me, just say the word, and I will come to your aid.' People look at their situations and see it as the end-all. But you know what? We only see the slice. God sees the whole loaf."

That was an interesting way of looking at it. It wasn't new theology to me by any means, but it was a much-needed reminder.

"I knew when I saw you in church that God was stirring inside of you," Pastor Mark said. "I don't know what he has planned, but I'm sure it's something significant."

Pastor Mark yawned and rubbed his eyes as we wrapped up our conversation. "I have to get back to church. A group of us is weeding."

I was glad he didn't invite me along.

****

AMY LINDHOLM

"I hate myself for being alive sometimes. If I could, I would give my life for them to be back."

Amy Lindholm can't shake that notion. Working as a medical assistant, her job is to improve the health of those she treats. Her reward is in seeing recovery and renewal. When that fails to happen, the thirty-five-year-old feels she has let the sufferer down. Her devotion to others lies deep within.

When the I-35W Bridge collapsed on August 1, 2007, it stretched that innate part of Amy to its very limit. Amy worked at Edina Sports Health and Wellness at Fairview Southdale Hospital. She was in charge of the lab.

"It was just a normal workday, except that I was working later than usual," Amy recalled. "A coworker had to leave early for an appointment, so I covered for her. On a normal day, I would have left at 3:30 p.m. That day, I left about 5:20 p.m."

That summer, Amy was living in an apartment in Mounds View, a northern suburb of the Minneapolis–St. Paul metropolitan area, with her three-year-old daughter, Sophia. Sophia's half sister, Maria, would also stay with them from time to time. Like many single parents, Amy relied on the help of others periodically for daycare, and on August 1, Sophia's paternal grandparents had taken her; the plan was for Sophia to stay at their home in Forest Lake overnight. Amy looked forward to an evening alone at home to unwind.

When Amy left work that evening, she took her normal route: east on Highway 62 to Crosstown and then north on I-35W. Crossing the bridge was a twice-daily occurrence. As she headed north through downtown Minneapolis in her silver-colored Saturn L200, she tried to weave through the heavy rush-hour traffic. The attempt was futile, however, and Amy conceded and remained in the left lane as she got onto the bridge deck. During this time, Amy was on her cell phone discussing the kids, Sophia and Maria, with their father, Jeremy Hendren.

Her car was above the river when the collapse began.

"It was weird. All of a sudden, the bridge shook," Amy recalled. "It was like lightning hit the ground, and then I heard a big boom."

Amy's section of bridge dropped straight down into the river in one long chunk. "I kept hitting my brake, because I felt like I was moving. Then all of a sudden, it just went dark," she said. "I don't know if my mind shut down, but everybody was gone." When she landed, the bridge section became a sloping, jagged, uneven island of debris. Her car, which landed upright, slanted downward as if parked on a hill. The section in front of the car buckled and rose up; rebar protruded out from the concrete, like spears pointed at her windshield.

Amy's Saturn was rear-ended during the fall. Later, Jeremy said that Amy was screaming during those few seconds when her world crumbled around her. She picked the cell phone up from the car floor. She was still connected to the call.

"Hello?" Amy asked.

Jeremy replied, "What just happened?"

"Well, I'm in the river."

"Okay. What river?"

"The bridge is in the river," Amy said, leaving it at that. "I have to let you go because I need to help somebody."

Amy got out of her car and surveyed the chaos. Several feet behind her was a blond woman trapped in her car, yelling for help.

"I can't open my door," the woman said as she pushed on her passenger-side door. Amy succeeded in opening the door, and asked the woman if she was okay.

"Yes, I'm fine," the woman replied, though it was apparent she was stunned.

Amy returned to her vehicle and focused on what lay ahead of her. The island of concrete, rebar, and metal beams descended into the dark brown river. The tops of vehicles poked out of the water like bobbers attached to a fishing line.

Amy asked those who had emerged from their vehicles, "Are there people in the cars in the water?" Nobody had a definite answer. "Well," Amy said, "someone has to go check."

The medical assistant, wearing her tan-and-blue scrubs, eyed one vehicle in particular, which was later found to have been driven by Sherry Engebretsen, who died in the collapse. She hopped onto a car's roof, trying to leapfrog to her destination. When she did so, the car began to shake. Amy felt it was unstable and could tip at any moment. She had to make a difficult decision: move forward or go back. Her own safety in question, Amy forced herself to turn back.

"I felt selfish, because I'm in the medical field and I like to help people."

At that point, she realized that there were others who needed first aid in the southbound lanes, people she knew she could get to. She crossed the median to the other side. There she found two teenagers, a handful of construction workers, and Lindsay Petterson—seven people in all.

"I asked everybody if they were okay," Amy recalled. "Lindsay's like, 'Yeah, I'm fine.'

'Do you hurt anywhere?'

'Yes, my back kind of hurts.'

'Well, don't move, because you probably broke something.'"

Amy next moved to the construction workers, a group that included a state inspector. One of the construction workers had debris in his eyes. The inspector had fractured his back and elbow.

"I remember looking at his elbow and seeing his bone and joints. I started picking out rocks," she said.

Amy also noticed a young woman standing alone on a small, tilted slab in the river. She must have swum there. Amy asked her if she was okay, and if she wanted Amy to come get her. The young woman froze and asked to be left alone.

By now, breathing was getting difficult for everyone. The air was thick with concrete dust. "You're just breathing it in. Your lungs feel thick," Amy said. She added that it smelled as if it had just rained, though the day was sunny, hot, and dry. Everything smelled damp. To this day, when Amy passes a construction site, the smell gets to her.

Along that island of debris, survivors paced, looking dazed. "How long are we going to be here? What are we supposed to be doing? Are we just supposed to stay here? Swim to shore?"

With no rescuers in sight, Amy felt compelled to take charge. She instructed folks to stay out of the water, reassuring them that somebody would come to get them. "I remember asking, 'Did anybody call 911?' But the cell phones weren't working. Well, I hope somebody called 911."

It took roughly two hours for Amy and the others to be removed from the site. First responders worked from the edges of the bridge toward the center. There was also fear that the collapse might not be over, or that the Taystee truck (the only vehicle on the bridge that caught fire) might explode and destabilize the rubble.

During the lengthy rescue, Amy asked if anybody had towels and water in their vehicles. Amazingly, everything that she asked for could be found. "I was able to clean wounds and the construction worker's eyes. I remember one of the construction workers said, 'My daughter is going to be born soon. I have to get there.' I told him, 'No matter what happens, you will be there. I will get you there no matter what.'"

She also recalled joking with the teenagers, trying to make them feel okay. In the meantime, she pushed her own pain aside. "Adrenaline really works," she said.

When help finally did arrive, the responders showed up wearing hazmat-like yellow suits. They first went to the semisubmerged vehicles to check for survivors. Amy remembers them pulling a body from one of the cars. "They started doing CPR. They came to our side after that," she said.

With the attention turned to the stranded, Amy informed the first responders of their needs. "I need back boards. I need neck braces," she told them. The response was not kind.

"We're taking over, so don't worry about it," they said.

"Yes, but I'm telling you what we need. You're going to move these people, and they're going to be more injured," Amy pleaded.

"We're going to take care of it, ma'am. Just go off and do your thing," the responder stated.

This isn't my thing, I just happen to be here, she thought. *It's not like I climbed on board and said, 'Hey, I want to help you people.'*

A boat eventually arrived. The survivors on the northbound side of the island were taken to shore first. The boat returned for Amy and the others on the southbound lane; however, they had to climb over the median to reach the boat. Amy recalled a gap between the lanes of about a foot and a half—looking down, she could see the almost-black water.

"All I kept thinking was *I don't want to smell like the river*," she said.

The rescue boat deposited them on the east bank of the Mississippi—the north side of the bridge. Amy wondered, *What are we supposed to do now?* Her purse, which held her driver's license, credit and debit cards, and a lot more, was inside her stranded car. All she had was her cell phone—and the lines were jammed with calls. She asked if she could go back to the collapse site. "My purse has my life," she begged.

"I'll take down your name and number," a first responder told her. It took more than a month and a half to get her personal effects back. Amy later discussed her opinion of the first responders. "I understand. It's their job. But it is also my job to make sure that people are okay too. I just wanted to hear that we're here for you. But it was strictly business."

After giving her name and number, Amy began to go into shock. "I can tell because I'm shaking, and my back is starting to hurt a lot," she said. They told her that she needed to go home, but how? Amy didn't have a ride. Her cell phone was useless.

With only one option, Amy started to walk. She walked up the hill and over to the adjacent Tenth Avenue Bridge. "Mom! Dad! Where are you? Come get me!" Amy screamed out. "I remembered telling Jeremy to call my parents in Minneapolis. I needed somebody to come here. People were probably wondering, *What is this nutcase doing?*"

A few people stopped to ask her questions. Amy said she had been on the bridge, and asked for some food. "No one wanted to help me, so I walked back over the Tenth Avenue Bridge and walked around the University of Minnesota campus looking for somebody to give me a ride home." She plopped herself down next to Annie's Parlour on the corner of University Avenue and Fourteenth Avenue SE in Dinkytown, waiting for anybody to come along. "I figured somebody would come get me sometime, somewhere," she said.

Approximately ten minutes passed before a vehicle caught her eye. Jeremy's parents had just happened to pass by. They had been driving around the University of Minnesota campus and had hoped to run into somebody who would tell them where to find victims.

Once inside the vehicle, Amy started rambling "like I wasn't there." Her neck hurt. Her head hurt. Her back hurt. Jeremy's parents took her to Unity Hospital in the northern suburb of Fridley. In the ER waiting room, she caught the live TV news coverage of the collapse, learning what had happened as she went through her own ordeal. Jeremy's mom called Amy's mother and let her know they were at the hospital, and her mother arrived soon thereafter.

X-rays revealed a couple of herniated discs. Amy was told to go home. No prescriptions were written. Amy went with her mother to spend the night at her parents' home. She ended up staying there for a couple of weeks. She had to wait for a new set of apartment keys. She applied for a duplicate license. "I just went in and did everything over. I basically had to start my life over again," she said.

Amy felt compelled to return to work as soon as possible. That Friday—two days after the bridge collapse—Amy was back at the medical center trying to make patients' lives better. It wasn't without difficulty, though. With all the standing and walking, her left leg went numb; she couldn't feel her foot. To this day, she still deals with numbness that can cause her to stumble.

Her back pain also continued. Finally, in June 2008, Amy underwent surgery to help relieve the discomfort. Surgeons implanted five bolts to bolster the two herniated discs. A shattered disc was also replaced with one from a cadaver.

"I think the hardest part is, I haven't been able to carry my daughter," said Amy. "I can't lift her up; it's too much pain. I'm 25 percent disabled because of the collapse. I'm only thirty-five years old. I feel like I'm eighty."

Bones heal more easily than the heart, and the emotional component of the trauma took its toll on Amy. "For a while, I didn't feel anything. The only time I would cry about it was because of my kid. I couldn't be there for her. I couldn't carry her. I just felt numb. I had the same nightmare over and over for about two months. It was a totally different collapse—different bridge, different place. I was always on it. Once in a while, I would drive off it, most of the time not," Amy recalled.

The effects of the trauma continue. "I haven't had a good night's sleep for the last three years," she said. She still has nightmares occasionally.

Sudden movements, like a vibration or a shaking sensation, can trigger her post-traumatic stress disorder. She also gets anxious when she finds herself confined. In one work meeting, Amy recalled, "I panicked and almost had to leave because there were a bunch of people in the room, and I can't handle that anymore. I don't know how I became like that. If there isn't an obvious way out—I panic."

Amy started meeting with the Survivor Resources group shortly after its inception and continued going each Wednesday for about a year. She found some emotional relief there. "I thought it was very helpful, because you didn't feel alone. You felt like a family," she said. "Ever since the accident, we all became one big family. Only certain people know what you really went through on the bridge that day. I call us the 'bridge family.'"

After her back surgery in summer 2008, Amy lost her job—and her health insurance. Prior to that, she had been going to a mental health counselor to help her through the PTSD. Amy said that the therapy helped in "trying to get me to relive everything and to focus better." She currently works part time, and though not having insurance coverage for therapy keeps her from attending sessions regularly, she knows she needs them to help her get emotionally well.

In 2009, Amy attempted to improve her emotional health on her own. She had stopped attending the Survivor Resources meetings. "I really just tried my best to block out the bridge," she said. That summer, she even crossed the new 35W Bridge for the first time. She figured that one day she would have to cross it, so why not on her own terms? Because Sophia's father and grandparents lived north of the river, the bridge was—and remains—the easiest route. She thought that by crossing the span, she would reclaim some piece of her that the bridge had taken, but that wasn't to be.

"It's a totally different bridge to me," she said. "It's bigger and wider. If I could picture where I was when I fell, I might feel like a conqueror, but that isn't the case."

When she crosses the bridge, she does so with a lead foot, and she makes sure to focus on something other than the river below.

The third anniversary of the bridge collapse became a trigger event for Amy. It was the first time she had "celebrated" the date. That morning, she viewed a documentary of the bridge collapse at a theater in south Minneapolis. She stepped onto the shoreline at the collapse site. She attended a meeting led by the mayor of Minneapolis updating a group of survivors and victims' families on the plans for the I-35W Bridge memorial.

Before August 1, 2010, Amy had been able to block the emotional trauma of the bridge collapse from her mind—but no longer. "It all came crashing back." The emotions she had stamped down for months began to burst through the dam:

> I think about the bridge collapse a couple
> of times a day. I think of the people I couldn't save.
> That's the part that really haunts me, because I
> went into the health field to help save people, and
> I couldn't do it. You hear, "You gotta get over it.

Move on. It's been three years." When it happens to you, tell me when to get over it. But you can't. Unless you fall 117 feet without wanting to, you won't know what it's like.

Running into the family members of those I couldn't save made me feel guilty. I felt so bad. I was afraid they would yell at me because I couldn't help their loved one. I'm here and they're not. I could have done something. With adrenaline, I could have found a way.

The bridge collapse has changed Amy. She feels the experience has made her less shy and more aggressive, not necessarily a bad thing. Her memory has suffered. As a nurse, she relies on her ability to recall readings, measurements, and other data. She can get distracted more easily. "I need to write things down to remember," she said.

Most trauma victims say they desperately seek closure, but that isn't necessarily the case for Amy, because she's still haunted by her inability help others that day:

In one way, I don't want closure. I don't want to forget, and I worry that if I find closure, I will forget. I mean, I want closure, but I want it in the way where I still will have the same remorse for all those people and the same feeling I have for everybody who was on the bridge...I'm always going to have to deal with it. It will always be a part of my life. It comes down to how I'm going to deal with it.

Though she can't change the past, Amy feels she can influence the future. She adamantly supported the construction of a bridge memorial, because of what it will mean to those who were on the bridge and those who weren't.

I don't want people to forget what happened that day and how many lives were changed. Everybody who was on the bridge—their lives are never going to be the same. They are living a new life. We need a place to go and be at peace. It will be a place where people can remember and reflect, a healing place, and somewhere where survivors can get together. And the thirteen who passed away, we can be there with them—and apologize.

12

AS THE SUMMER PROGRESSED, I continued to feel healthier. I had engaged the clutch and rolled the throttle—and I was moving. While many events, conversations, and realizations contributed to this, there was one ah-ha! moment that really helped. I kept returning to the conversation I'd had with God the day I snowshoed in Temperance State Park in December 2008, the one in which I'd decided to let go of the reins and put it all in God's hands. At the time, I'd thought that was the correct thing to do—after all, that's what I'd been taught in parochial school and during Sunday sermons. "Give it up to God," my pastors and teachers would preach. So that's what I did. But time passed, and God seemed to be silent. I had felt my worst long after I had given my problems, fears, and anxieties up to him. Had my Creator not heard my prayer that silent afternoon, as I sat in a bank of freshly fallen snow beside that frozen river?

I picked apart that conversation, looking for any reason why my prayer might not have been answered. Suddenly, it made sense: I had asked for the wrong thing. I'd begged God to take my problems on so that I could walk away from them. I wanted God to take the reins, but that wasn't what my Heavenly

Father desired for me. He knew I wouldn't learn the right things if he did that. He wanted me to ask for something else.

So, one afternoon on an ordinary day in mid-June 2010, I did exactly that.

God, I was foolish for what I asked you out in that forest. I wanted an easy way out, a fast solution. I wanted somebody else to fix my problem. I thought I had to perform enough hard work just to get healthy physically, and that it was unfair to be asked to do anything more to improve my emotional health. So, I asked you to take the reins. But what I really should have asked of you was to place your hands over mine and guide me, rather than allow me to walk away and demand you do the work. I apologize for that and ask you to accompany me as I continue this journey. Help me when I need it, but allow me and demand of me the work I need to do to become a healthier person, a stronger friend, a respectful husband. In your name, amen.

This simple shift in focus turned out to be what I needed. I felt hope. I felt reassured. I felt like I was actually breathing again, feeling again. I also realized that there was a lot of work to do. This time, however, I felt committed to seeing it through. It would take a lot of submitting, compromising, and giving up control, and I was afraid, for these were not easy things to do; however, I knew that if I could do so, there would be blessing and reward—and I might just learn something about my marriage and myself in the process.

As July began, I understood that at the tender age of thirty-five, I couldn't stay unemployed forever. With my newly found financial stability, I decided to start my own business and be my own boss. I had witnessed the merits of franchising firsthand at Great Clips. Now, I felt, it was time to find a franchise of my own that could become a solid investment.

When Sonja and I had driven to Colorado in September 2009, we had stopped at a casual restaurant in Boulder called Which Wich. We really enjoyed the experience there—it was different than Subway, Quiznos, and Potbelly—and we walked away with content tummies. At the time, we didn't think further about Which Wich, except to be disappointed that the Twin Cities lacked one. I decided that should perhaps change. I e-mailed a franchise application to Which Wich headquarters in Dallas. They sent me some information, and I then had a phone conversation with the man in charge of franchise development. He got me in touch with a couple of franchisees, and I pursued the opportunity further. By early July, I was ready to make the trek down to the Lone Star State to check out the company's corporate office.

I planned to drive from the Twin Cities to Dallas, a distance of 981 miles. My friends and family thought I was nuts, but I wanted to make a minivacation out of it. With Sonja at the Boundary Waters and my dog at my mother's house in New Ulm, I headed south alone to Texas the morning after Independence Day.

I get my love for the highway from my grandfather. He was notorious for finding the long way from point A to point B. There wasn't a back road too remote. It's no coincidence that my grandpa taught me how to drive a manual transmission on some deserted gravel path up the side of a river bluff in southeastern Minnesota. I felt we were in the middle of nowhere; he knew exactly where we were.

On my trip to Dallas, I took the old man's lead and headed off the main road, Interstate 35, in favor of two-lane highways in rural Kansas. I bounded across rolling, green hills dotted with cattle. I stopped for gas in little towns where patrons wore cowboy hats and trucks sported bumper stickers cheering on the Jayhawks. I spent the night, coincidentally, in Independence, and as I entered the city limits, I gazed as tardy fireworks streaked across the sky.

I set out early the next morning, hoping to make Dallas by dinnertime. About five miles north of Okmulgee, Oklahoma, my cell phone rang. It was Sonja.

"I'm pregnant," she said.

The phone call seemed brief, or maybe I was in shock, but I don't recall much of what was said. Once I reached Okmulgee, I pulled into the parking lot of the local Dairy Queen and stepped inside. I needed a few minutes to digest Sonja's news.

My breathing was heavy and labored. Wow. I mean, wow! I knew that Sonja was "late," but it had happened many times before, and nothing ever came of it. We'd even wondered if something might be reproductively wrong with one of us. Of course, our marriage had been so rocky for so long that having a kid would have been the worst thing for us. We were far from out of the woods at this point, but if we ever needed any extra motivation, this was it.

Sonja and I spoke daily after that. She needed reassurance that I was happy about the pregnancy. I'd been very ambivalent in the past about kids, and I'd told Sonja I'd be happy either with or without children.

Now, I was excited by the news, but I was also scared to death; I felt

I had no idea how to raise a child. My father was all but absent during my younger life. My mom was great, but was always working to keep our heads above water, and my sister and I became good at being left to our own devices. My grandparents were a solid couple, but I had never seen them parent a child. I had few role models, except for perhaps the Bradys, Cosbys, and Keatons of the TV world. This would be one area where I needed God's extra attention.

I'll admit, it became very difficult to think about Which Wich with a baby on my mind, but I continued with the trip, visited Which Wich headquarters and a few sandwich shops, and left feeling positive about the business and where it was headed. Suddenly, I had a lot on my plate.

The next week, Sonja returned to the Twin Cities, and the two of us went to the neighborhood clinic to get an official ruling from a doctor. Sonja's results confirmed her self-test. She told her parents; I filled my mother in. There was guarded joy, but it was joy nonetheless. Now we needed a plan.

If this marriage was going to work, we had to change things. Oh, we had tried strengthening our marriage in the past: date nights, nightly devotions, gatherings with friends. But they always fizzled when the next big gust of discord blew through our home. If we were going to be successful with this renewed effort, it would take accountability, we decided.

Sonja asked me to come up with a constitution of marriage, of sorts. I searched my brain and the World Wide Web and came up with what I thought was a workable plan. It consisted of three major realms: physical, spiritual, and emotional. We needed to stay active, be it swimming in the community pool, hitting the exercise machines at the YMCA, or going for a bike ride. Spiritually, we needed to commit to delving into our Bible and devotion books. We asked a pastor if he'd be willing to meet with us quarterly and hold us to our attempt to strengthen our relationship with God. Emotionally, we agreed to meet with a psychologist monthly to check in on our relationship and offer advice. Date night would no longer be compromised. We'd ask our friends in relationships to help hold us accountable and plan group dinners, board-game nights, and the like. We needed to find a hobby we could enjoy together. And at the top of Sonja's list was taking another honeymoon vacation before the baby arrived. We put it on the calendar.

In August, the third anniversary of the bridge collapse arrived. I felt much calmer this time around, not as edgy as I had been the year prior. I attended a second screening of *One Day in August* that morning in Minneapolis. Over the past year, new interviews had been added, and that seemed to give more depth to the original version. I met some of my bridge peers at the showing, and I answered a few questions from local media, though I would rather have just continued talking to my compadres. That evening, I returned to the underbelly of the new 35W Bridge, this time with my mother. We met Margaret from Survivor Resources, as well as about a dozen bridge survivors and their spouses. A construction worker was also along the riverbank, recalling when this calm location was anything but peaceful. While we stood there, a yacht pulled into the lock and dam filled with a wedding party and guests. "Stayin' Alive" by the Bee Gees boomed from the boat's speakers. Revelers raised their champagne glasses and waved as they passed by. Two people were celebrating the best day of their lives, August 1, under that bridge, as we quietly reminisced about our worst.

I left home the next morning at dawn. Mom had promised to stick around for a few more days to watch our dog, Chauncey, giving me the time to make a long-overdue visit to Sonja up at her camp at the end of the Gunflint Trail. I was really looking forward to seeing her and spending our second wedding anniversary together, this time without the anger and resentment that had tormented our first two years of marriage.

I had never been to the edge of the Boundary Waters canoe area, so as I drove along the meandering two-lane Gunflint Trail, I kept my head on a swivel. Each curve unveiled a new panorama of Minnesota wilderness: a grove of white birch punching through scruffy pine, a glint of sun dancing across the ice-blue waters of a lake, broken tree trunks scattered across a striking green marsh. As the trail continued, signs of civilization—houses and gas stations—faded in the rear-view mirror. I began to feel alone and vulnerable, wondering what I'd do if my car happened to break down. As I reached the final few miles, the landscape changed drastically. In May 2007, the Ham Lake Fire erupted along the western end of the Gunflint Trail. The blaze consumed more than thirty-six thousand acres in northern Minnesota and more than seventy-five thousand acres total. It was the largest forest fire in that region in more than a century, and three years later, the damage was still apparent. The lushness was gone; trees were burned matchsticks. It looked as though the area had been blasted with bombs. Yet the underbrush showed signs of rebirth. I couldn't help but liken the scene to my own recovery and what I hoped would be my second chance with Sonja.

I reached Wilderness Canoe Base in the afternoon. I parked my car and met a camp employee at the dock. I climbed aboard the pontoon with my suitcase, and we motored across the channel of Seagull Lake. As we approached the landing, I saw a familiar figure waving from Fishhook Island; my heart skipped a beat.

Sonja stood at the shore and grabbed my bag as I clumsily stepped off the boat and onto the dock. My balance isn't the steadiest, especially on a pontoon. We embraced tightly and greeted each other with a kiss.

My wife led me up the hillside path to her cabin. Along the way, we passed the mess hall, an outfitters building, a nature center, some outhouses, and other cabins. We reached her cabin in less than five minutes, and as I stood by the door, I did a 360-degree turn and took in the scenery from horizon to horizon. It was breathtaking.

That evening, we had dinner in the mess hall with roughly a dozen camp employees and a group of campers who had arrived earlier that day. Typically, campers spent the first night on the island. Before they were sent out, they would attend a vespers worship service led by Sonja. Then they would head out in canoes for several days with a guide from the camp. At certain points along the way, they would study scripture, with the hope that, amid the recreation, they would renew their faith in God.

After dinner, Sonja led the evening worship service. I accompanied her as we crossed a suspension bridge that connected the island camp to another island where a shelter had been constructed for worship services. When the campers convened, we opened with a couple of songs accompanied by a guitar and viola, and then Sonja shared a message about Jesus being the bread of life. I was really proud of her as she spoke; she has a unique way of connecting with teens, which a lot of people—including me—would struggle with.

When vespers ended, Sonja and I decided to take advantage of the unusually warm evening and go swimming. We strolled to the dock as Sonja told me about her camp experiences: the morning sickness, the mosquito bites, bonding with certain camp employees, her eagerness to return home. I commiserated with her, but I felt that the inescapable beauty of the place was something I could easily enjoy for quite some time.

We reached the dock, and suddenly I felt reluctant to jump in. I prefer swimming pools to lakes, where the bottom isn't mucky and your legs don't get tangled in weeds.

"Don't be a scaredy-cat," Sonja teased. "This lake is different."

I eventually got over my fear and jumped off the dock. Splash! The water was cold but invigorating. And there were no mud or weeds. The lake bottom was filled with large, smooth stones.

"Finally, a lake I can enjoy!" I exclaimed as I splashed around. We took our time, enjoying each other's company and embracing as we treaded water. The sun set and the sky turned from pink to orange to dark blue. We reluctantly pulled ourselves up the ladder and scurried back to Sonja's cabin. We dried off and crawled into our pajamas. Bedtime comes early on a remote island with no TV or Internet, and it wasn't long before we fell asleep.

I woke up shortly after midnight. Needing to pee, I climbed out of bed and stepped out the cabin door. I looked up, and the island was surrounded by millions of stars. I hadn't seen that many stars since I had been to Sonja's family cabin along Lake Superior. The sky was so bright that there was no need for a flashlight. As I stepped back into the cabin, awed by what I had just witnessed, I turned around in the doorway to get one last look. A shooting star zipped above me. I recalled a quote from one of the bridge survivors in the *One Day in August* documentary: "God is good all the time; all the time, God is good."

The next day, Sonja and I ate breakfast in the mess hall with everyone. As the campers began their multiday journey, we spent the morning in a canoe as well, and found a quiet place to swim near some minor rapids. As lunch neared, we returned to the island and packed our things so we could celebrate our anniversary at Lutsen Resort north of Sonja's family cabin, where our wedding reception was held.

Our time in Lutsen was just as enjoyable. We ate dinner in the lodge where we had feasted on our wedding cake. We walked on the Lake Superior shore and talked about the future. How were we going to make it? Was our plan for a successful marriage going to work? What was life with a newborn going to be like?"

The next day, we ate breakfast at a roadside bakery and then went on a short hike at Temperance State Park—the same trail where I'd had my talk with God two winters before. We met a talkative young boy who was there with his parents, who were also celebrating their anniversary. When our hike was finished, I had to begin my journey back to the Twin Cities.

As we parted ways, we embraced tightly and kissed one another with all the fervor that accompanied the greeting at the pontoon dock. Yes, we had more questions than answers, but part of me wondered if that wasn't merely a definition of life. With the PTSD-like symptoms eased, the questions now seemed manageable.

At one point during the summer of 2010, I heard a song on the web site Pandora that seemed to sum up what we needed to keep our fragile marriage alive. It's amazing how songs can dance their way into your life in the very moment you most need them. This one was called "Flowerparts" by Bob Schneider. In it, Bob shares a list—from a male perspective—on how to keep your love growing, including "Don't forget the 'I love you's'—oh, and 'I forgive you's' too."

When I battled adjustment disorder, I couldn't find those things. The tragedy was supposed to strengthen our marriage, I thought. At least that's what people kept saying. No, Bob had it right. Only after reprocessing and revelation, after accepting my new self, could I even begin to realize once again the "flowerparts" of my relationship with Sonja. The emotional numbing had made it impossible for me to locate them.

It was the summer of my discontent
It was the fall of a lifetime
It was the winter of my penitence
Waiting on the springtime
Well, it was all sackcloth and ashes
For a couple of years
I took my licks and my hundred lashes
I cried a bucket of tears
That distant shore's forever out of reach
Before you know it you're washed up on the beach.
Welcome back,
It was a pretty dark day (and now the sun is shining)
Welcome back,
I guess I'm on my way.
I was bent but I was not broken
I was sinking but I did not drown
I was reeling but I was still hoping
I could be lost and found
Well, I was temporarily disconnected
In a state of disrepair
Disoriented and dejected,
I had to climb out of there.
That distant shore's forever out of reach
Before you know it you're washed up on the beach.
Welcome back,
It was a pretty dark day (and now the sun is shining)
Welcome back,
I guess I'm on my way.
Through the labyrinth and down
Till you land on solid ground.

—Eliza Gilkyson, "Welcome Back"

13

I LOOKED OVER AT MY BEST friend Darin, who was seated in the passenger seat. His face had turned ashen. He was biting his lower lip and his watery eyes stared straight ahead. We were nowhere near the new 35W Bridge. Rather, we were about two miles south of the small town of Milaca, an hour north of the Twin Cities. I hadn't told Darin what we were doing as we drove north on Highway 169; it was a surprise for his birthday, which had fallen four days earlier, on October 3, 2010. But he figured out what I was up to when we passed a road sign that read something like "Skydiving Ahead–Milaca Airport!"

"I'm not jumping out of [expletive] anything!" was all he could say when I asked him if he had figured out that afternoon's activity. I immediately felt bad; I didn't want Darin to be angry with me.

"Hey, you don't have to do anything you aren't comfortable with," I said, feeling as if I was coaxing a kitten down from a tree. "I just thought this would be fun and new. After all, a couple of weeks ago you said you'd try anything once."

"Discussions involving alcohol don't count."

"Well, you weren't drunk when you said it," I said. "Just be open to the skydiving instructor, but in the end it's up to you." Then I went for the low blow. "Either way, I'm doing it," I said. Yes, I had pulled out the "man card."

Why was I so willing to jump out of a small aircraft at ten thousand feet, tethered to a stranger, wearing a parachute I could only assume functioned properly? I didn't know why, but I had a sudden itch for an adrenaline rush. As with my motorcycle, part of the fun was accepting the risk. The lyrics of that Tim McGraw song, "Live Like You're Dying," had prompted tears when I'd laid in my hospital bed in step-down ICU. I was ready for the next step—and I guess that step was nearly two miles above the Earth's surface.

I parked the car in front of a white fence that divided the gravel parking lot from a row of hangars. We stepped out of the car and into the bright sun. Minnesota was basking in the warmth of Indian summer, and had just finished a stretch of sunny, eighty-degree days. Today it was seventy degrees, with nary a cloud nor breeze.

We walked down the gravel road to a large shed. As we entered, a blond woman in her forties wearing a gray "Skydive Minnesota!" T-shirt welcomed us. The sales counter was covered in decals and a bumper sticker that stated, "Skydivers. Good to the last drop."

"Hi! I'm the one who reserved the jump. My name is Garrett, and this is Darin. He's the one with the birthday I told you about."

"Wonderful!" said the woman. "You're gonna love this, and you picked a great day."

We were required to fill out paperwork, the likes of which I hadn't seen since I closed on my house. I noticed that the words "death and permanent injury" seemed to pepper each waiver we signed. I expected Darin to hightail it out of there, but he actually completed the form. I guessed that maybe he just wasn't reading it, and was merely signing his life away.

Darin and I handed in our forms, and we next watched an instructional DVD that looked like it was taped in the early 1990s. The narrator had a long beard and a short message: skydiving was very dangerous, and we shouldn't do it if we felt unprepared. Darin sat there with a worried look on his face. I couldn't stop laughing as I watched the man in the grainy video. The fact that a man who looked like Rip Van Winkle was warning us about the dangers of skydiving was so odd that I almost considered this whole operation a hoax.

Our instructor, Mike, approached us when the video ended. "Who's going first?" he asked.

"I'll go," I said, not even looking over at Darin. I'd dragged him here, and I couldn't ask him to go first on top of it all. Mike, sporting a buzz cut, a black T-shirt, black pants, and shades, asked us to kneel down on a mat on the floor with our feet tucked under our butts. He then told us to lie on our stomachs with our arms stretched. These would be the two positions we would need to perform—the first inside the airplane, the second while out in the wild blue yonder.

"Okay, are you ready?" Mike wanted to know. I asked him if he could go over the steps once more.

"Oh, we'll run through them a couple of times before we jump," he said. It was at this point that I started getting nervous. Up until then, I hadn't really pondered what we were about to do. Now I was anxious about jumping out of a plane ten thousand feet in the air, and Mike's instructions weren't sticking to the inside of my skull. What if I got the directions mixed up or missed a step? Would it spell my doom?

Darin left to get his camera from the car, and I handed him the contents of my jeans pockets: my wallet, keys, and iPhone. The last thing I wanted was for any or all of these items to be scattered across a five-mile radius of east-central Minnesota.

Darin returned, at which I was half-surprised, and the three of us, plus the driver, hopped aboard a golf cart and headed toward the Cessna. When we reached the plane, Mike called me over to the door behind the wing. "I want us to practice stepping out of the plane," he said. As he instructed, I climbed through the open door and sat on my knees next to the pilot's chair, facing forward. I noticed immediately that there wasn't much room inside, just enough for the pilot and maybe three other people. Mike then asked me to dangle my right leg outside the plane, then put my heel on a small platform, not much bigger than the lid of a shoe box, that protruded from the plane. I then needed to slide my left knee to the edge of the aircraft. I would now be in position to barrel roll out of the plane with the instructor. We then briefly practiced the body positioning needed at the precise moment we jumped. That maybe took, oh, all of two minutes. I don't know why, but I'd thought the entire preparation process would take a couple hours. Meanwhile, Darin made sure to snap some photos.

If I didn't survive, at least my picture on the obituary page of the newspaper would be current.

"Okay, let's do this, huh?" Mike asked, but he wasn't really asking. I climbed into the plane, wondering just what the hell I was doing to myself. Mike grabbed the parachute and came aboard last. When the door to the airplane shut and the engine revved, there was no turning back.

As the pilot, Mike, and I headed down the runway, I distracted myself by asking Mike how he'd gotten involved in skydiving. He told me that he took his first tandem skydive about three years ago, and it was love at first jump. He trained to jump solo and then later became an instructor. He now had more than eight hundred skydives under his belt.

We were off. For the beginning of the flight, Mike had me sit on my knees with my back to the plane's nose, facing him. This worried me for a couple of reasons. First, sitting with my weight on my surgically repaired ankle hurt. I wasn't sure how long I could keep it up. Second, my back was brushing against the instrument panel. With all the knobs and switches, I could have easily activated or deactivated something. The twenty-something pilot didn't seem bothered in the least. We ascended gradually. The clear skies afforded marvelous views of the fall foliage below.

"Do you think we're pretty high?" Mike asked. "We're actually only at one thousand feet. We still have nine thousand feet to go." I gulped hard.

I knew we were quite high when we could see all of Mille Lacs Lake, because on the ground you can't see the other side when you stand on the shore. My pulse kept getting quicker. As we approached eight thousand feet, the airplane made a U-turn. We began heading back toward the airport.

Mike asked me to turn around so I was facing forward. He slid right behind me. With four clicks, he attached my harness to his and handed me a pair of goggles to wear snuggly over my eyeglasses.

At two miles high, Mike opened the door. The cold blast of air caught me off guard. Just as we practiced, Mike stuck his right foot out onto the platform. I slowly did the same. There was a brief instant of relief, actually, in freeing my ankle from that weight. Then came a pause, as Mike waited until we were directly above the airport. It seemed like an eternity, one leg dangling outside and another inside the Cessna, as I stared ahead at the underside of the wing. It seemed like a balancing act between life and death. Then—in an instant—Mike and I tumbled out of the plane. The free fall had begun.

A couple of seconds passed, and Mike tapped my right shoulder, the sign for me to extend my arms as I had done on the mat in the hangar. The rush of air below me was intense. All I could hear was wind, as if a tornado were passing by. I looked ahead, but not down, and marveled at the curvature of the Earth. From above me, Mike lowered his arms and gave me a thumbs up. Then the strangest thing happened: I started to laugh uncontrollably, in the middle of an incredibly surreal experience. I was falling at 120 miles per hour, and loving it.

After about forty-five seconds and 7,500 feet, Mike gave me another tap. I brought my arms in and grabbed my harness straps. Five seconds later, I was yanked upward, and then—we started floating. The parachute had activated.

The deafening rush of air stopped. And as if we were standing next to one another on a sidewalk, Mike began speaking. "What did you think of that?"

"Honestly, words cannot describe," I told him. "Well, the only one that comes to mind is 'exhilarating.'"

"Pretty awesome, isn't it?" I didn't have to answer that question.

Mike then pointed downward. "There's the airport below us. See?" The words "Milaca Airport" were spelled out in large letters on the ground for those with a bird's-eye view. "It's time for you to drive," Mike said as he handed me the two toggles to the parachute. "Just pull down on one side or the other, and we'll change direction."

I pulled down on the right toggle, and we veered to the right. I then did the same thing with the left toggle. "This is awesome!" I yelled.

"Let me show you a trick," Mike said. He pulled hard on the right toggle, and we began spinning rapidly. I quickly got dizzy as he switched and did the same with the other toggle.

Another minute passed. "It's time to head in," Mike said. My heart, which had been in my throat when we jumped, now sank a bit. We floated like a feather, as the airport and the land that surrounded it sprang up. Cars and trucks on the highway were no longer specks. Mike told me to lift my legs as we approached the field adjacent to the runway. We landed—me on my backside, Mike on his feet—as the parachute crumpled behind us. Darin and the young woman who drove the golf cart met us. When I stood up, Mike congratulated me with a high five and a handshake.

Darin approached.

"Dude," I said. "I'm not trying to talk this up, but that was awesome! I can't even explain it. The climb, the jump, the free fall, the glide—there's nothing like it." I kept talking very fast. It was probably the adrenaline. Seeing me unscathed, Darin was now prepared to jump—at least, as prepared as one could be.

We returned to the hangar. I stepped out of the harness, and Darin stepped into it after one last trip to the portable toilet. Now I was jealous. I wanted another go-around. Shortly thereafter, the plane was up in the air with Darin and Mike in it.

The golf-cart driver and I returned to the field and waited for Darin and Mike to land. While we waited, I reflected on what had just happened and why I was so eager to do it. Without warning, the reason hit me, so obvious that I was surprised I hadn't been conscious of it. I realized this was about reclamation, just as everything I had done in the past three years had been about grasping what the bridge had taken from me. This was about reclaiming the fall.

I lost all control when I fell during the bridge collapse. I felt swallowed up, and there was nothing I could do about that. What I had just accomplished, however, was falling on my own terms. I wasn't in control, but I could accept that. Perhaps now I could learn to accept other things outside my control, the bridge collapse included.

I kept my eyes skyward, shielding them from the bright sun, and soon a speck appeared. Darin and Mike danced in the air, just as I had done, spinning and twisting. They landed without incident; I snapped off some shots with Darin's camera. Just like me, Darin could barely put into words what he had just done. And like me, he'd adored every minute of his experience.

The four of us headed back to the hangar. Mike signed certificates and handed us each a copy. Darin said his was immediately going up on a wall, or no one would believe he'd done it.

We headed home exhausted but still intoxicated by what had just happened. I played "Free Falling" by Tom Petty on my iPod over the car's stereo speakers, and we sang along. For one day, at least, we lived life to the fullest.

About three weeks after skydiving, I recalled a conversation with my former qualified rehabilitation consultant, Kristen. Perhaps it was the weather that jogged my memory, as a late-October storm pushed through with soaking rain, gusty wind, and diving temps, the same weather that day I met Kristen at

Macaroni Grill.

"Did I tell you I went skydiving last year?" Kristen had said. "For the first few seconds, you're just spinning in free fall. It takes a few seconds to gather your bearings, but it's awesome."

Perhaps Kristen's words had subconsciously pushed me out of that tiny plane. I yearned to feel "incredible" and "exhilarated." Somewhere up in the troposphere, I found them, and they snatched me up like an opening parachute.

****

In the aftermath of trauma, I held up a mirror to myself. I examined each piece of me meticulously, compared and contrasted. I recalled how I was before the bridge collapse. Then I looked at how I am now. How am I different? How am I the same? What is salvageable? What is condemned? What roads led me to that bridge? Where do I want this road leading from the bridge to take me?

In one respect, we bridge survivors received a blank canvas, a do-over. Yet we must start over with compromised minds or bodies, or both. We have no choice but to begin again, just as we had no choice but to be on that bridge when it folded. We can view this as an opportunity, a ladder to something greater. Or we can perceive it as a long chute tumbling us back to the game's start. I've seen it as both, depending on my emotional state.

It has been an exhausting journey, one I'd have hidden from if I'd had a choice. For a long time, I yearned for my old self to return, and I became despondent when I realized that was impossible. I stubbornly grasped for moments I thought would cure me: physical recovery milestones, the termination of relationships I felt burdened with. I even once thought that tossing a piece of the bridge into Lake Superior would break the evil spell!

As I blundered through therapy, accidentally stumbling against false beliefs I had accumulated for years, I slowly realized that the old me wasn't so great. There's an even better one out there that I can become. A bridge collapse can't squash that. So I'm on a new journey, one I embrace with open arms. I have a loving wife, a newborn son, a rascal of a pet pooch, great friends, understanding family, and a sandwich shop. And on top of that, I have a new, better me to mold into the best it can be. To me, that's not the burden of tragedy, but the beautiful call of opportunity.

There has been, and likely always will be, speculation about the exact cause of the 35W Bridge collapse. Was it because the gusset plates were half the thickness originally intended? Was there too much weight from the construction equipment sitting on the bridge deck when it gave way? Did somebody look the other way when the malfunctioning roller bearings were discovered? It likely was all of those things, but I can especially understand the concept of the "frozen" roller bearings. They aptly described me for a long time. I, too, was frozen. The stresses of my physical and emotional recovery, in addition to my new marriage, were great. The PTSD-like symptoms didn't allow me to expand or contract. The forces mounted. Eventually, I buckled. But unlike the bridge, I wasn't merely a pile of rubble. I could be repaired. And that's what happened, and continues to happen.

Back in October 2007, I visited the surgeon who had performed my two facial reconstructions for a check-up. It was the first time I had really gotten a chance to talk to him. My face was still fairly swollen, but the surgery was far enough in the rear-view mirror for the doctors to judge its success. The surgeon poked and prodded what seemed like every square inch of my face. Here and there, I would grimace when he hit a sore spot.

"All in all, you're a miracle," the surgeon remarked as he took a step back. That wasn't the first or last time I had heard those words.

"I really had little to do with that," I said. "That's all you and my Maker."

The doctor leaned in, took off his glasses, and stared me in the eyes. "I don't think you understand. Here at HCMC, we track every patient who comes in with facial trauma and needs surgery. We measure the severity of trauma on a scale of zero to ten. The average score is about a 2.4. Conservatively, I'd have scored yours a thirteen. That's unheard of. Anybody we see with a number that high is already dead." He slipped his eyeglasses back onto his nose. "You're a miracle."

Whenever I feel down, I try to remember that short discussion. If I am a miracle, then there must be a reason why I'm here, a purpose, if you will. If I was needed elsewhere, God would have taken me. That only leads to another question: if I'm needed here, who or what needs me, and how am I supposed to help? I guess that's what this second chance is about.

Life is definitely different now. While I've returned to moving forward, the numbing effects of trauma haven't completely gone away. I haven't smelled anything in nearly four years. My sense of taste has diminished greatly. My left ankle gives me fits, and on bad days, I limp painfully. My face often feels sore, and my lips go numb. And while my affect has improved, the fullness of emotions still evades me. I can feel happiness, but not exuberance. I still yearn to feel pure joy again more regularly—and as the skydiving experience showed me, no doubt I will.

To this day, I have yet to cross the St. Anthony Falls Bridge, better known as the new 35W Bridge. From an engineering perspective, it is the most technologically modern bridge in Minnesota, if not the United States. Sensors were even built into it to track any abnormalities. If there was any bridge you'd want to cross, this would be it. As of now, however, I decline to make that trek. Thirteen other people had that option erased when the collapse happened. It is my one, easy way to honor their memory.

Other bridge collapse survivors can drive across it today with little problem. I know of one survivor who made a point of being among the first to cross the new bridge when it opened in September 2008. She had to finish the trip she started. I understand. We each have our own journey.

I might drive across that bridge someday. I'm not ruling it out. And if I do cross it, I won't feel as though I am dishonoring those who perished on the old bridge that day. I'll drive across it *for* them. That just won't happen today.

****

As I was writing this memoir, I realized my experience certainly hasn't reached its finish line. Honestly, I don't know if I'll ever truly be done with what happened to me that hot, sunny evening of August 1, 2007, and that's okay. Occasionally, I revisit items that remind me of what happened: newspaper clippings; a chunk of bridge debris that sits on my desk; trinkets accumulated during my stay in the hospital; and my CaringBridge web site (something I had at one time checked daily). Recently I stumbled upon a passage I had written in late November 2007, as I began walking again. Those few sentences strike me in a way today that helps me focus on my path:

We, as humans, do a lot of questioning. "Why is life going so wrong? What did I do to deserve this?" In some instances, we might even have every right to ask such questions. But instead of questioning life, what would happen if we turned the tables and allowed life to question us?

Each of us encounters situations that leave us staring at life's challenges and difficulties. And many times these situations occur when we feel we are least ready to tackle them. We're tossed into a pool of trauma, adversity, stress, exhaustion, and pain. This is when we tend to pull out the blame card. Our response to life questioning us is to throw it right back by questioning life.

Instead, I suggest we seize the challenge. When I fell with the bridge on August 1, I was least prepared for what lay ahead. The path was filled with pain, stress, and depression. I didn't look forward to surgeries and the ensuing therapies. And I never really felt I had a choice. So it was with grim determination that I pushed forward. I mean, if I was going to get better, I wanted to get better as fast as I could. That instinct to push myself played a big part in having to spend only six days at Knapp Rehab.

We all have challenges, our own mountains to climb. Some of them will be voluntary. Others will show up unexpectedly, and we'll have to set everything else aside to deal with them. Either way, when life questions you—be prepared to give an answer.

Some of the first words I heard from my mother when I finally regained consciousness for good, eighteen days after the bridge collapse, were "everything is fixable." In other words, I could be repaired—not made whole or returned to my former state. It took a couple of years for me to accept that. I like to think that God wasn't content with the old me, even if I was. Perhaps the new me can do what the previous could not. I anticipate understanding what that entails.

Yes, life has taken a tragic turn, and I don't know who I would have become had I not been on that bridge when it collapsed. But I have a feeling this version, though broken and battered, will continue to get better.

AFTERWORD

I HAD THE IDEA OF WRITING A MEMOIR long before the 35W Bridge collapse. I had always wanted to write about my life and had kept notebooks of odd and fascinating experiences in the hope of compiling them into something slightly strange and hopefully humorous. The only hitch was that I had yet to collect enough anecdotes. Then, I just so happened to end up on the bridge when it collapsed. Even before my jaw was unwired, family and friends began bugging me about writing about this experience. I hemmed. I hawed. At the time, I was so exhausted by the physical recovery that writing about this horrible, draining episode didn't seem like much fun at all. It was two years before I was ready to sit down and start putting pen to paper—or, more accurately, fingers to keyboard.

I wrote this book in spurts. My conversations with those who were part of my journey happened long before I began writing them; my aim was to be as true to those as I possibly could. There were times when writing was easy. There were others when my adjustment disorder and my crumbling marriage pulled me away from adding pages. The writing process, as a whole, seemed to resemble my recovery. Where was the finish line? How will things look at the end? It seemed odd to be writing about my experience, when the experience was still happening.

I realized fairly early on that I needed to include other survivors' stories as well. I felt my experience was compelling, but what if my narrative was so peculiar that it didn't accurately reflect what most survivors felt? I desired a fuller, rounder picture of what I and so many others had gone through during the past three years. So I sought other 35W Bridge survivors to interview.

That process was eye-opening. I realized two things: I shared a lot of the same emotions and beliefs that these other survivors did, but even though we all went through the same event, we each had our own unique experience. We are all on our own path, and those different paths determine how far along we are in recovery. Those who weren't in our shoes may say, "Get over it." But "it" is so different for everybody. One person may have to step over a molehill. Another must climb a mountain.

I wrote this memoir for a few reasons. First, I felt that, even with all the information out there about the 35W Bridge collapse—the investigations, the politics, the engineering debates—there remained a void. The stories of the survivors were largely confined to sound bites and brief newspaper articles. A fuller story of the survivors needed to be shared. Second, I have a horrible memory. I can't tell you what I had for dinner two nights ago. I feared that if I didn't get my thoughts and experiences down on paper, they would be lost for good. As an introvert who panics at the thought of conversation, writing was a comfortable way of processing all those small experiences that make up my recovery. Third, I wanted to create something that will still be around when I am no longer. My children, grandchildren, and great-grandchildren can someday read this and know exactly what I went through. There will be something left of me other than a few blurry pictures.

****

The evening following my son's birth, March 2, 2011, I revisited CaringBridge, and wrote:

It's with great joy and enthusiasm that I introduce you to Cooper John Resoft Ebling, who came into this world—albeit grudgingly—at 10:06 p.m. Wednesday evening at St. Joseph's Hospital in St. Paul after thirty-four hours of labor. The big butterball weighed in at 9 lb. 7 oz., and measured 21.5 inches. Both mama and baby are doing well, although each spiked a fever at delivery, so lil' Coop had to be taken to the special-care nursery and hooked up to an IV with antibiotics as a precautionary measure. Unfortunately it means that he remains out of the public eye for forty-eight hours. On Friday afternoon we will pull him from his hole and hope he doesn't see his shadow! :)

I held him tonight alone for about ninety minutes and told him about Jesus, Santa Claus, and suicide squeezes (we'll be at plenty of Twins games together this summer, no doubt!). I am a very proud papa who promised him I would always love him, no matter what, and that I'd never put him in a position where he would doubt that. As I sat in the nursery and rocked him to sleep, I couldn't help but think about the bridge and my recovery. Every surgery. Every therapy session. Every pain. Every watery tear. Every step.

It. Was. Worth. It.

I love you, Coop! Thank you, Sonja, for this most awesome gift, and thank you, God, for Sonja.

Love,
Daddy

****

Writing this memoir has helped me process my emotions. I realized that my fears and challenges are both unique and shared. Whether I like it or not, I am forever one of "the bridge people." And despite the ongoing struggles and challenges I face physically and emotionally, I'm quite comfortable with that.

AUTHOR BIOGRAPHY

A NATIVE MINNESOTAN, Garrett Ebling earned a degree in newsprint journalism from the University of Wisconsin–Madison. He worked as a managing editor and senior communications specialist before becoming an entrepreneur. Following the bridge collapse, he was an active advocate of the victims' compensation bill. He lives with his wife, Sonja, and son, Cooper, in Andover, Minnesota.